Aa, Bb, Cc, Dd, Ee, Ff

Learning Activities and Teaching Ideas for the Special Child in the Regular Classroom

Peggy Glazzard, Ed.D

Dept. of Special Education,
Kansas University Medical Center

Illustrated by Jan Reese and Sylvia Robinson

Prentice-Hall, Inc. Englewood Cliffs, New Jersey 07632

Library of Congress Cataloging in Publication Data

GLAZZARD, PEGGY.
    Learning activities and teaching ideas for the special
child in the regular classroom.

    Includes index.
    1. Handicapped children—Education.   2. Mainstreaming
in education.   I. Title.
LC4015.G57   371.9   81-21113
ISBN   0-13-527093-6   AACR2

editorial/production supervision
    and interior design: barbara kelly
cover art: jean reese
cover design: ray lundgren/tony ferrara studio
manufacturing buyer: ed leone

Printed in the United States of America

10   9   8   7   6   5   4   3   2   1

ISBN 0-13-527093-6

Prentice-Hall International, Inc., *London*
Prentice-Hall of Australia Pty. Limited, *Sydney*
Prentice-Hall of Canada, Ltd., *Toronto*
Prentice-Hall of India Private Limited, *New Delhi*
Prentice-Hall of Japan, Inc., *Tokyo*
Prentice-Hall of Southeast Asia Pte. Ltd., *Singapore*
Whitehall Books Limited, *Wellington, New Zealand*

This book is dedicated to those youngsters who, for a variety of reasons, may have a handicap that prevents them from achieving academic success at the same rate as their peers. It is also dedicated to those classroom teachers who want to help all students achieve at an optimum rate to reach their potential.

Contents

Math: Readiness/Number Concepts/Skill Practice   73

Preface

The ideas in Chapter III were originally developed to accompany educational diagnostic reports with recommendations for better programming for students referred to a university interdisciplinary clinic between 1977-1981. Seventy-five percent of the referred students (aged 5-17) were attending regular classes but experiencing difficulty achieving academic success. Many of the youngsters exhibited behavior problems but the common referral problem from school personnel, parents and/or medical personnel was said to be that these students did not complete their assignments and would not work independently unless the teacher was standing next to them! Over the years many graduate students and teachers have asked for copies of the teaching ideas. These have now been rewritten and organized into a reference book intended primarily for regular teachers who have special students in their classrooms. The source book is also useful for special education teachers and future teachers in training as the teaching ideas have been developed based on particular students' actual needs. Some of the ideas were developed by the author for the "Special Touches" column in *Early Years* teacher magazine.

acknowledgments

Special education Master's and doctoral-level students who have participated in the interdisciplinary clinical practicum headed by the author have graduated with degrees in the following areas of emphasis: Hearing Impaired, Learning Disabled, Orthopedically Handicapped, Multiply Handicapped, Emotionally Disturbed and Mentally Retarded. The former students are:

Pat Alexander	Mary Goldammer	Ron Mimick
Melanie Alsup	Penni Holt	Steve Moore
Betty Arnoldy	Jean Horton	Jean Morton
Imelda Ayongao	Nadine Hunter	Ann Musser
Alison Banikowski	Leslie Immken	Ed Pieper
Katya Beer	Twila Jaben	Stan Pointras
Sr. Donna Jean Bodnar	Charles Jenkins	Jan Reinhardtsen
Robbie Campbell	Ruth Keeling	Lennie Reisberg
Steve Carlson	Jackie Lewis	Vickie Roberts
Joan Casson	Becky Luzar	Sylvia Robinson
Natalie Combs	Lee Ann Mallonee	Ruth Siebels
Judy Cone	Carmen Mayer	Janet Selders
Suzanne Donnolo	Jay McCarty	Ralph Seligman
Teresa Eurom	Loretta McGreevy	Jeanne Shidler
Patti Gnau	Tess Mehring	Suzette Slocomb

Sr. Mary Ellen Smith   Peggy Sullivan   Flo White
Betty Snapp   Dick Swenson   Gail Williams
Paulette Strong   Mary Von Seggern   Marge Witter

Other contributors to this collection of practical teaching ideas include: Dr. Barbara Burkhouse, Marywood College, Scranton, Pennsylvania; Dr. Pat Gallagher, University of Kansas; Ginger Porter, kindergarten teacher, Olathe, Kansas; Sharon Donovan, 3rd grade teacher, Blue Valley School District, Stanley, Kansas; and Mary Lou Sandquist, 3rd grade teacher, Shawnee Mission, Kansas.

A very special thanks to those who helped put this manuscript together:

Danielle Wesley—my patient secretary who typed the manuscript,
Kirsten McBride, M.A.—who painstakingly edited the lengthy manuscript,
Joan Casson—a graduate student who helped check on publication details and permission forms, and
Jean Reece, M.S.Ed., and Sylvia Robinson, M.S.Ed., who illustrated the manuscript.

Aa,Bb,Cc,Dd,Ee,Ff,Gg,Hh,Ii,

1

Integration Strategies for Handicapped and Nonhandicapped Students

The integration of handicapped and nonhandicapped students in the regular classroom can be a rewarding experience for all concerned. To facilitate the mainstreaming process, two elements are crucial in addition to any necessary curricular adaptations: empathy and understanding of handicapping conditions and peer acceptance. Although peer acceptance is important to all students, a handicap may compound the problem of being accepted. Educators have a responsibility to help alleviate misunderstandings and to promote acceptance of handicapped students.

A classroom teacher can better organize a specific mainstreaming plan if strategies are planned to encompass the following three main areas:[1] understanding exceptionality through simulated activities; preparing nonhandicapped students in regular classes for acceptance of the exceptional student; and preparing the exceptional student for participation in the regular class. This introductory chapter will briefly describe some activities for each of the three areas. Teachers and students will be able to contribute additional ideas once they understand the rationale behind the activities.

A. Understanding Exceptionality—Simulated Activities

The purpose of this section is to assist regular class students in understanding the difficulties of being handicapped by involving them in activities simulating a variety of handicapping conditions. The frustrating feeling of not being able to do what is normally taken for granted results in many new topics for discussion as well as increased awareness of what it might be like to have a handicap. Hopefully, the students will have a better understanding of the similarities and differences among people, handicapped and nonhandicapped, after experiencing the following simulation activities.

---

[1] P. Glazzard and M. Regan, "Integration Ideas for Elementary/Intermediate Classroom Teachers with Exceptional Children" (unpublished manuscript, University of Kansas, 1980).

visually impaired

1. Using a thick straight pin, punch a hole in blank index cards for each student. Ask the students to copy all chalkboard work by looking only through the tiny hole. This activity is very tiring and simulates "tunnel vision."

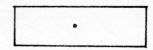

2. Have each student bring a blindfold to wear for part of the day including lunch. It may cause less havoc if only part of the students perform this activity at one time for three successive days. It is very important to hold a class discussion at the end of the activity to talk about the problems the students had and what strategies they used to alleviate the problems, and how they learned to adapt to their environment. The students may want to try wearing blindfolds at home while getting dressed or eating meals.

orthopedically handicapped

1. Get 3-foot sections of half-inch dowel rods from a local lumber yard. Ten rods are enough; they can be exchanged among the students when the activities have been completed. Have each student place the dowel rod behind his/her back and loop both arms over, around, and under the rod. This severely restricts arm movements. Ask each student to perform some daily activities using the restricted arm movements, for example, combing hair, eating a meal, tying shoes, tying hair ribbons, putting on earrings, brushing teeth, or writing an assignment. Hold a class discussion to talk about how each one felt during the activities.

2. Borrow a wheelchair from special education classes or rent one from an equipment rental dealer. Map out a route in your school that would be rather difficult and frustrating for a student to follow. Ask each student to complete the assignment. The teacher may want each student to spend at least one-half day in the wheelchair to gain a better understanding of what it would be like to be confined in this manner. One example of an assignment might be: "Take a note to the principal's office before going out for recess. Go into the restroom, stop and get a drink, and then come back to the classroom. Eat lunch in the cafeteria while in the wheelchair. You may need to ask a buddy to help carry your food tray. Come back to the classroom and continue your daily assignments." (Note: This activity is time consuming; two wheelchairs shorten the time required for the entire class to participate. It is not effective to stay in the wheelchair for only a short time.)

hearing impaired

1. Ask students to wear earplugs or cotton stuffed in their ears for three hours. Students are not supposed to tell their friends that they have partially blocked their hearing. It is particularly helpful if they eat in a restaurant or go shopping during the three-hour time span. Students will find out that other people tend to become irritated if they cannot understand everything that is said. This is especially true with waiters and waitresses in a noisy restaurant or clerks in busy stores. Hold a class discussion at the conclusion of the activity.

2. Ask each student to watch one entire thirty-minute television show with the sound turned off. Ask them if they understood what was happening. Were they tired from having to concentrate so intently using only visual cues?

mentally retarded

1. Pass out one sheet of blank paper to each student. Each student needs a pencil and a box of crayons for this activity. Ask the students to follow rapidly a series of oral directions that cannot be repeated. The following is an example: "Write your first name in the lower left-hand corner and your last name in the upper right-hand corner. Write your age on the middle of the bottom edge. Divide your age in half and write that in the upper left-hand corner. Draw eight circles across the middle of the page. Color the second and fifth circles yellow. Make an X with a line under it in the third circle. Make red and blue polka dots in the fourth and seventh circles. Black out the remaining circles and put your pencil down!" Exchange papers and ask students to grade somebody else's paper. Repeat the directions more slowly. Count off five points for each direction missed. Subtract the sum of the missed points from 100 and write that score on each paper. Hand back all papers to the original owners. Hold a class discussion and ask how the students felt, whether they had difficulty and whether they had the feeling that other students were going much faster than they.

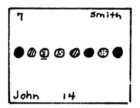

2. Obtain a complicated dittoed math or science worksheet from a class two or three grades above yours. Hand out copies of the worksheet and tell the students that they must complete the worksheet within fifteen minutes. Do not tell them where you obtained the worksheet or that you know that it is too difficult for them. They are supposed to become frustrated and discouraged as they try to work the difficult paper. At the end of fifteen minutes say "Time's up!" and collect the papers. Hold a class discussion and ask how the students felt when expected to work above their skill level. Tell them where you obtained the worksheet and what you were trying to accomplish. (Note: Both of these activities might be used to simulate emotionally disturbed handicaps as well.)

learning disabled

1. Hand out a math worksheet covered with addition or subtraction problems. Ask the students to use their nondominant hand to write the answers. Allow only a brief time limit and say "Go." Continue talking while the students are working on their papers. This is very frustrating to students especially because it is a timed test. The activity simulates poor muscle control or poor writing skills.

2. Make up a complicated reading worksheet placing carbon or ditto master paper (right side up) under your paper. When you have finished writing the lesson turn over your copy; the carbon paper will have reproduced the entire lesson reversed on the back of the master copy. Photocopy, or run dittoed copies of, the backward lesson. Hand out one copy to each student, give directions as you normally would, and do not answer the students if they complain that the words look "funny" or that they cannot read the paper. Tell them to get busy as you will collect the papers within ten minutes. This activity simulates word or letter reversals, which some learning disabled youngsters experience.

B. Preparing Nonhandicapped Students in Regular Classes for Acceptance of Exceptional Students

The purpose of this section is to suggest activities designed to provide personal involvement with handicapped students in a realistic environment as well as to provide a basis for developing positive attitudes about the handicapped. At times differences between students cause suspicion and lead to negative attitudes. Many nonhandicapped students have had little exposure to handicapped individuals and have never learned the facts about handicapping conditions. The following activities suggest ways in which students can explore likenesses and differences, discuss their feelings, ask questions, and develop realistic expectations.

1. Invite a special educator or a parent familiar with the handicapping condition of the student to be mainstreamed to give a talk to the class using pictures, charts, literature, and so on. Hold a question-and-answer session and encourage the students to express their feelings, fears, and previous knowledge. The guest speaker should be realistic in discussing limitations but also optimistic when talking about ways in which the students might be of help to the new student without making the new student dependent. The goal is to help the handicapped student be as independent as possible while becoming a regular member of the class.

2. Plan a library table exhibit and ask the students to find materials about a particular handicapping condition. Library books, newspaper reports, and magazine articles may be displayed for everyone to see. In intermediate classes appoint a committee responsible for calling or writing to a local agency (for example, Association for Retarded Children, Easter Seal Society, or Epilepsy Foundation) to obtain more information. All students should contribute something to the display. Students from another classroom could be invited to visit the display and ask questions of the students who have researched the topics.

3. Intermediate students could plan a field trip to a local agency for the handicapped. Assign committees to plan transportation, to obtain background information, to call the agency and ask if somebody from the agency could give the students a tour of the facility and answer any questions they might have. Another committee might be responsible for sending thank-you letters and organizing a follow-up discussion of the field trip later in the regular classroom. Handicapped preschools, schools for the blind, schools for the deaf, sheltered workshops, and special education self-contained classrooms are examples of local agencies.

4. If the exceptional student has not yet joined the class, ask the student to write a letter or send a scrapbook to the class to tell them about family, friends, hobbies, and pets. The student should include a photograph so that the regular class students become familiar with the new student before arrival.

C. Preparing the Handicapped Student for Participation in the Regular Class

This section presents activities designed to help the handicapped student adjust to the demands of the regular class. When planning the mainstreaming of a handicapped student, the curriculum and who will be responsible for teaching it often become the major concerns to the exclusion of the social and emotional aspects of both the regular class students and the handicapped student. Many handicapped students and their parents are anxious and uncertain about the student's acceptance into the regular class. Specific attention must be given to this aspect if the mainstreaming experience is to be successful.

1. Ask each of the regular class students to write a letter of welcome to the handicapped student if that student has not yet joined the class. The letters may describe each student's likes, dislikes, pets, and family members, and should contain a photograph or drawing of each student. Such information is intended to make the new student feel more familiar with other students in the regular class.

2. Invite the student and the student's parents to visit the school and the classroom after class hours to meet the teacher, the school nurse, the principal, and any other staff members who will be working with the new student. A tour of the building will help familiarize the handicapped student and parents with the physical facilities, noting in particular the location of restrooms, lunchroom, gym, recess doors, and principal's and nurse's offices. The teacher may need to draw a simple map of the building to give to the student at this time.

3. The teacher and a small committee of regular class members might visit the handicapped student at home before the student joins the class. This way the new student knows some of the students before actually joining the class and avoids the fear of not knowing anyone on the first day of class.

4. To prevent later confusion for the handicapped student, the teacher should carefully explain school rules and present a daily schedule of activities before the new student joins the class. Specific times for lunch, recess, music, physical education, reading, math, social studies, science, art, and so on can be written on a simple timesheet.

5. If present at the beginning of the school year, the handicapped student may be out of the class for special help at certain times during the school day (for example, speech, learning center, remedial reading, or counseling). Some class discussions may be held at this time. If not sufficient, activities describing each student are helpful in presenting the special student as a person who happens to have a handicap, rather than as a "handicapped person."

Aa,Bb,Cc,Dd,Ee,Ff,Gg,Hh,Ii,

2

Classroom
Adaptations
for Mainstreaming

Mainstreaming into a regular class is not always a successful experience for handicapped students. Often, with some simple physical or academic adaptations, exceptional students can function without difficulty in the regular class. It is generally agreed that no student will make academic progress unless the schoolwork is at the student's current skill level. Assuming that educators accept this concept, other adaptations may be necessary for handicapped students trying to succeed in regular classes. Adaptations are categorized in this chapter according to particular handicaps, but it must be emphasized that the ideas may also be used with nonhandicapped students who are distractible, disorganized, exhibit poor motor control, or fail to complete assignments on time. Many of the ideas can also be generalized to other types of handicapping conditions, that is, a hearing impaired student may not need the suggestions listed under "Hearing Impaired," but could use the writing adaptations suggested for the orthopedically handicapped. It is assumed that the teacher will use common sense in application of the information.

Hearing Impaired

Because a hearing impairment is not a visible handicap, it is important that the classroom teacher is reminded of its presence and is aware of necessary simple adaptations.

1. It is essential for hearing impaired students to see the lips of the speaker. When talking to the class, write on an overhead projector instead of turning your back to use the chalkboard, or write on the chalkboard and then turn around to repeat what was written to the class.

2. Do not talk to the class with your back to the window. The outside light creates a shadow across the lips.

 3. Do not cover your lips with the book when reading aloud to the students, or with a microphone when speaking to a large group.

4. Use visual instructions whenever possible to augment what is said. Place reminders on the bulletin board for class helpers, field trips, science vocabulary words, and so on.

5. Place the hearing impaired student close to the front of the room, away from a playground window or heating and air conditioning units. The extra noises can be distracting and confining. Teachers who like to talk as they wander around the classroom must be aware that the hearing impaired students only hear them part of the time.

Emotionally Disturbed

Many students who exhibit severe emotional problems attend self-contained classrooms but may be mainstreamed for some subjects. The special teachers usually have made careful plans before integrating these students into regular classes.

 1. Structure is the key word in working with this group of students. Do not change a daily schedule abruptly or move furniture without preparing the special student for the change.

2. Use a timer to remind the student how much time left to complete an assignment.

3. Provide immediate feedback to a student verbally or by checking and returning papers as quickly as possible. Parents or teacher aides are potential sources of help for the classroom teacher.

4. Daily schedules written down and attached to a notebook, desk, or clipboard hanging at the side of the student's desk are helpful reminders of what the student is to do and when.

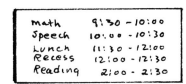

5. Keep a current seating chart of the classroom for use by substitute teachers. Any major change can be upsetting to highly emotional students.

Orthopedically Handicapped

The following ideas are also effective for students with poor or weak muscle control.

1. An orthopedically handicapped student may use a shoulder bag to carry books and supplies from class to class to leave arms free to handle crutches.

2. Appoint a buddy to bring teacher handouts to the student's desk.

3. Attach one end of a string to a pencil and the other end to the desk with a thumbtack or masking tape so that the student can easily retrieve a dropped pencil.

4. Use a chair equipped with wheels for students who otherwise need crutches. This allows the student to travel between reading groups, to the chalkboard, and so on and saves a great deal of time and student energy.

5. Allow students to answer test questions orally or have them record answers for later evaluation. Students with poor muscle control in their hands find it laborious to write their answers, as they need to exert much more energy than the nonhandicapped student for writing.

6. Make a copy of your lecture notes for the handicapped student who writes slowly or with difficulty. It is also easy for a classmate to use a sheet of carbon paper to duplicate a set of notes that can be supplied to the handicapped student.

Visually Impaired

Each visually impaired student will have unique needs, thus the teacher needs to understand fully the particular deficits of the student being mainstreamed.

1. Use a heavy black marking pen on dittoed worksheets to make them easier to read.

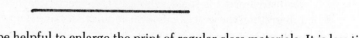

John can _____ fast.
ran, run, fun

2. Use the black marking pen to delineate lines on writing paper.

3. A magnifying glass may be helpful to enlarge the print of regular class materials. It is less tiring for the handicapped student to use such an aid.

4. Record reading material or other lengthy assignments for the visually impaired student. Parents, aids, or student volunteers are potential sources of help.

5. Write chalkboard directions on a separate piece of paper for the student with poor vision. Keep copying work to a minimum for the visually impaired student.

Educable Mentally Retarded

Although many of the educable mentally retarded students are in self-contained classrooms, they are often mainstreamed for more nonacademic classes. In cases where such mainstreaming includes academic subjects, the following suggestions may be helpful.

1. Shorten long assignments into smaller units. For example, if twenty addition problems on one page are too much, require the student to work only ten problems.

2. Use concrete materials such as blocks, counters, or pegs when working with math concepts.

3. Give shorter directions. Visual cues paired with oral directions are helpful for some students.

4. Assign a student from the regular class as a "buddy" to the handicapped student while attending class until the handicapped student is comfortable with the regular class routine. Choose a different "buddy" each day. This helps the new student to get to know all of the students.

5. The social behavior of an educable mentally retarded student may not always be appropriate. You must observe whether the student's behavior on the playground and in the school deviates from the accepted standard. You may need to take the student aside, explain what is wrong, and demonstrate the proper behavior through role playing.

Learning Disabled

Most learning disabled students are mainstreamed at least part of each day while also receiving special help in resource rooms or from itinerant teachers. These students may have difficulty working in the regular classroom.

1. Short oral directions are more effective with youngsters who have difficulty in processing long chains of oral commands. For example, "Take out your pencil." (Pause). "Take out your math book." (Pause.) "Turn to page 56."

2. Keep the student's desk organized. Learning disabled students need to be able to retrieve notebook paper, pencil, and textbooks very quickly to keep up with classroom assignments. Some youngsters may spend more than five minutes looking for a pencil only to discover that the teacher has already finished giving instructions. A weekly desk-cleaning session with teacher supervision may be necessary.

3. Allowing learning disabled students with poor auditory processing to use a tape recorder lets them replay your directions. This saves a great deal of time in the long run. If the student cannot read well, information may be recorded and listened to by the student.

4. A paper clock indicating the time a student is expected in a resource room may be taped to the student's desk as a reminder.

5. Cut long worksheets into smaller segments and give one segment at a time to the learning disabled student. When the strip is completed, the student hands it in and receives a second strip of paper. This procedure is followed until the entire worksheet is completed. By cutting down the stimuli, the assignment becomes more palatable and less discouraging to the special student who has the skills to complete the assignment but often does not do so because of short attention span.

All the adaptations described in this chapter are a means of individualizing instruction to meet the needs of particular students. Many of the activities are appropriate for use with any student who is experiencing difficulty in school. "Once educators become convinced that all class members do not have to cover the same material, in the same way, and within the same time frame, it will be easier to plan curriculum for mainstreaming handicapped students."[1]

---

[1] P. Glazzard, "Adaptations for Mainstreaming," *Teaching Exceptional Children*, 13, no. 1 (1980), 26–29.

Aa,Bb,Cc,Dd,Ee,Ff,Gg,Hh,Ii,

3

Learning Activities
and
Teaching Ideas

The following ideas are designed for regular classroom teachers, elementary grades kindergarten through sixth, who have handicapped students mainstreamed into their classrooms. The activities that can be easily implemented by teachers, parents, or teacher aides are useful for teachers whose students demonstrate a wide range of skills and educational needs. Each teaching idea is complete by itself and follows a general format for greater consistency. The ideas are presented in simple terms accompanied by visual representations in order to serve as quick reference sources. All materials have been field tested by parents and teachers over a period of years. The teaching ideas have been grouped together in the following six categories: reading, math, writing, phonics/spelling, language, and behavior management. Ideas are arranged sequentially by grade level ranges, thus readiness activities are at the beginning of each section whereas activities appropriate for intermediate grade levels can be found at the end of each section. Many ideas are appropriate for multiple grade levels; recommended grade levels are designated in the upper right-hand corner of each written description. Each of the six areas contains diverse activities. The reader is urged to study the table of contents before choosing the appropriate learning activity for remediating or teaching specific skills. This book presents options and alternative teaching strategies for use with students who are experiencing difficulty in academic achievement.

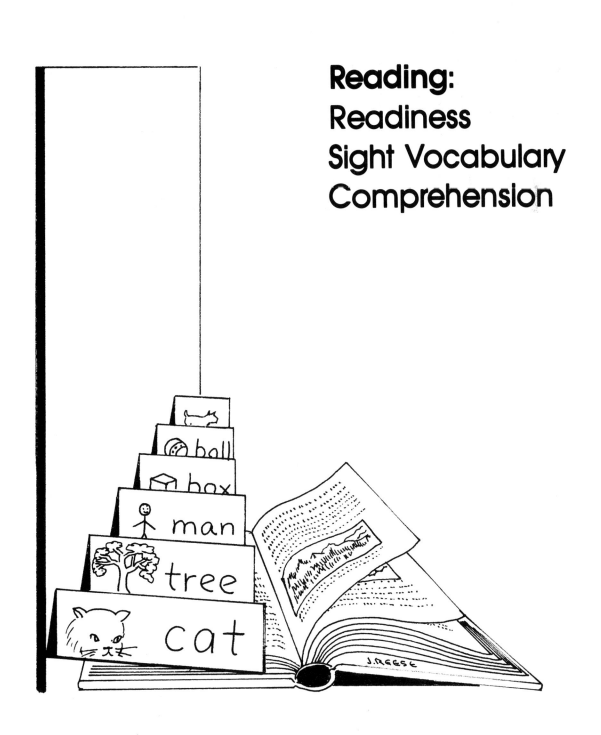

Reading:
Readiness
Sight Vocabulary
Comprehension

Descriptors: Similarities   **Grade Levels:**   K–1
                        Differences
                        Classifying
                        One-to-One Correspondence

Rationale: Readiness for reading requires that a student be able to match objects and letters. When these skills are taught in a game format, it is more fun for both the student and the teacher.

Objective: To teach a student to match objects or letters and to classify objects as a prerequisite for reading.

Materials: Small shoebox filled with small objects (bobby pin, paper clip, ring, small toys, buttons, rubber band, comb, pencil, clothespin, penny)
Large piece of tagboard
Marking pencil
Clear contact paper (large enough to cover tagboard)

Procedure:

Game 1. Matching and Classifying

Skills in matching similarities and differences can be learned by observing the shapes of objects and matching them to a corresponding picture.

Draw outline (around objects) on the tagboard and cover with contact paper. Have the child remove the objects from the shoebox, naming each object as it is taken out. The child will then find the appropriate outline on the tagboard answer sheet. You can follow up this activity by asking the child to remove the items as they are named one by one to the child.

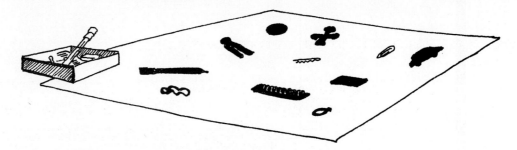

Materials: Buttons varying in size, shape, texture, and color
Matching set of buttons with at least 6 to 8 buttons per set
Apple separator

Game 2. Sorting and Classifying

Procedure: The child can learn skills in sorting and classifying according to size, color, and shape by sorting according to the similarities and differences observed.

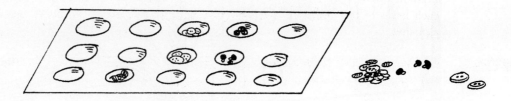

The child sorts the buttons according to the differences and similarities observed. Encourage the child to talk about the buttons, mentioning the colors, whether one button is larger or smaller than another button, how many holes the buttons have, and so on.

Game 3. Matching Letters

Materials: ½-pint milk cartons (top removed)
Marking pencils
8 to 10 tagboard strips for each letter (cut so that they stand up over carton lid)
Colored construction paper (to cover milk carton)

Procedure: Skills in matching similarities and differences can be learned by having the child sort out letter cards into small boxes labeled with matching letters.

    Label each milk carton with a letter on the front. The child sorts out the tagboard letters that have been cut into strips and marked with a letter at the top. When sorting out the letters the child places them in the corresponding letter boxes. The child should be encouraged to say each letter as it is placed into the proper box.

**Additional
Suggestions:**   This exercise can be adapted to a vast number of learning discrimination experiences for the child. At a more basic level it can be used for sorting out color strips and matching them in their appropriate box. It could also be used for digraphs or word families like cat, bat, rat, mat, pat or run, sun, fun, bun.

**Sound
Discrimination:** Use pictures beginning with a consonant letter sound.

Pre-Dictionary Skills

Descriptors: Following Directions
Visual Discrimination

Grade Levels: K–2

Rationale: Students are often asked to use dictionaries to look up words before they are ready for such a task. Prerequisite skills for such an activity are: recognition of upper- and lowercase letters, ability to name each letter of the alphabet, and ability to name a word that begins with one of the letters of the alphabet.

Objective: This teaching idea is designed to assist primary students who are having difficulty recognizing the sequence of the alphabet letters.

Materials: 5″ × 7″ file cards
Wide, dark-colored felt tip marker
Chalkboard tray
Primary dictionaries and/or picture dictionaries

Procedure: 1. Using 5″ × 7″ file cards, write one letter of the alphabet on each card with a wide, dark-colored felt tip marker. Make a set of both upper- and lowercase letters.

2. Take one-half of the set, either upper- or lowercase, and line up the cards in sequence on the chalkboard tray. The cards represent visual, sequential cues.

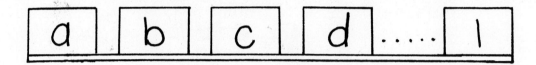

3. Separate the first half (A to L) from the second half of the alphabet by removing the remaining cards.
4. Ask a student to name a word that begins with one of the letters in the chalkboard tray. Or to provide for more success, you may start by naming a letter from one of the extremes of the alphabet, such as *a* or *l*.
5. Tell the student to open the dictionary to the part of the book where the student thinks the word can be found. Check to see if the word is there. Children may suggest words not found in this dictionary. If so, ask them to tell what *a* or *l* words they see on a particular page, or what *a* or *l* words might be there. Draw attention to the location within the dictionary, for example, the front of the book.
6. After students have experienced success locating words at the extremes, *a* and *l*, ask them to look for words beginning with *f* and *g*, and so on, and to find these words in their dictionaries. To avoid students suggesting words not contained in their dictionaries, you may suggest the words. Remind the students to look at the alphabet cards to help them find where to look in their dictionaries.

Additional
Suggestions: 1. *Alphabet Game*

    a. Tell a student to look away or close his/her eyes while you remove one card from the chalkboard tray.
    b. Ask the student to look at the row of letters and tell you which one is missing.

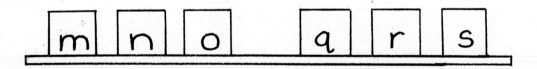

    c. If s/he has difficulty determining which letter is missing, tell him/her to start one or two letters *before* the missing one and say their names. Or you may give the names of the two or three previous letters as cues. It might be necessary for some students to begin with the first letter *a* and say each letter name in sequence.
    d. When a student guesses (or you identify) the missing card, replace it.
    e. After a student has become proficient at naming one missing card, remove two cards. At first remove letters that are adjacent. Later, remove two from opposite ends of the alphabet. Gradually increase the complexity of the task.

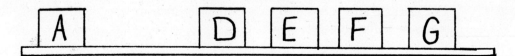

    f. Give the student a chance to play "teacher." The student removes a card or two while you close your eyes and then guess which one(s) are missing.

2. A variation of the alphabet game is to arrange the letters in incorrect sequence and ask the child to rearrrange them correctly.

3. Using five sequential letters (for example, A to E or H to L), write five words each beginning with one of the five letters. Mix them up and ask the student to arrange them in alphabetical order. Later increase the number of the letters, (for example, M to T) putting all eight letters on the chalkboard, but use only five words that must be placed in alphabetical order.

language experience approach

Descriptors: Reading Comprehension
Sight Vocabulary

Grade Levels: K–2
Special Education
Resource Room

Rationale: To help beginning readers it is important to show them that reading is no more than talk written down. The language experience approach can help build better reading skills. Use of the approach is recommended to supplement developmental reading programs.

Objective: To record a student's verbal description on a chart that can be used to teach word decoding.

Materials: 2′ × 3′ and 8½″ × 11″ newsprint
Black marking pen
3½″ × 5″ Blank index cards
Pencil
Metal recipe file box
Ditto master
Duplicating paper

Procedure: FIRST DAY.

1. The students dictate a short story as a group project. The story must be about a shared group experience such as a field trip, an animal, a guest, or a book read in the classroom by the teacher.
2. The teacher records the students' two- or three-sentence story on a 2′ × 3′ piece of newsprint mounted on an easel. The pupils' exact wording is recorded. (Note: There is some difference of opinion among professionals on this matter. Many educators feel that poor grammar should not be accepted and that the students should be encouraged to use proper grammar. Therefore, the choice is left to the teacher's discretion.) The teacher writes down each word and says it aloud. At the completion of each story the teacher reads it back to the group.
3. The story is then numbered.
4. The teacher selects one student to design an illustration for the story chart.
5. The students read the story in unison with the teacher as s/he points to each word as it is said.
6. Each pupil draws an illustration for the story on 8½″ × 11″ newsprint. The number of the story is placed on the drawing. This gives the students a pictorial representation of the story that can later be kept in a booklet with their personal copies. If desired, all the students' pictures may be placed on a bulletin board beside the story for a short time.

SECOND DAY.

1. The class is divided into three groups.
2. The teacher starts each group session by reading the story chart to the class, pointing to each word as it is read. The group then rereads the story together in unison with the teacher as s/he points to each word.
3. One of the group members is invited to stand beside the teacher to "read" the story with the teacher.

4. Other students in the group may volunteer to read the story aloud with the teacher. As each student reads, the teacher tries to determine whether the student is ready to learn individual words.
5. When a student is able to recognize a word in isolation, it is put on a word card for the student's word bank collection (see the description following the conclusion of the three-day sequence).

THIRD DAY.

1. The story is copied on a ditto master and duplicated by the teacher so that each group member has a copy for future reference. The copy should be placed in a booklet with the student's illustration of the story.
2. The teacher works with each child individually in private reading sessions. Each word that a pupil can read is underlined by the teacher on the pupil's own copy. This emphasizes the words the student knows.
   (Note: Each week the children dictate two or three group stories, following the same procedure.)

WORD BANK

A word bank provides the student with a personal listing of known vocabulary words while giving the teacher an indication of each student's current sight word vocabulary.

1. The words a pupil remembers for two consecutive days are placed on index cards 3½" × 5". The pupils read the words on each card aloud to the teacher before they return to their desks. They do not take any word to their desks they are unable to read.
2. After the pupils return to their desks, they number the card on the back corresponding to the number of the story from which it was originally read. This enables the students to return to reread the story if a word is forgotten.
3. All cards are kept in a recipe file "bank" at each student's desk.
4. Once a week, the teacher, aide, or parents may review all the words in the bank with the student. The pupil can also expand writing and spelling skills by inventing new stories using the words from the bank.

Additional Suggestions:

1. Invite other students to visit the classroom and use the large story charts as a program for the visitors.
2. The teacher may record the stories on numbered cassette tapes and place them on a table along with a tape recorder and earphones. Students may use free time to listen to the stories through earphones while they read the corresponding large charts or the individual story booklets.

color words

Descriptors: Word Recognition   **Grade Levels:**   K–2
Independent Worksheets

Rationale: Many youngsters who cannot read can quickly learn color words, thus allowing them to work independently on individual worksheets using reading comprehension. It is important to teach one color word until the student completely masters it before introducing a second word.

Objective: To teach a student to recognize a written color word without a color cue.

Assumptions: The student can point to the correct color when given an oral stimulus, and can orally identify the color when it is visually presented.

Materials: 3" × 6" tagboard cards
Ditto master and duplicating paper or blank paper
Black marking pen
Primary coloring book
Crayons

Procedure:

1. Present a flashcard with a red balloon and the color word *red* beside it. Write the word *red* in black letters on the reverse side of the card.

2. Point to the balloon and ask the student to name the color.
3. Point to the word and say, "This word is *red*."
4. Ask the student to repeat the word.
5. Turn over the card exposing the word *red* without any visual cues. Ask the student, "What is this word?" If the student's answer is incorrect, repeat steps 1 through 3.

Additional Practice:

1. Write the word *red* on six cards. Write other color words on additional cards, but do not tell the student the new words. They are to be used as distractors for the following game. Spread out all the cards word side up on the table or floor. Ask the student to "fish" out only the cards that have the word *red* on them. Tell the student that you are trying to fool him/her by adding some extra words but repeat that you only want the word cards that say *red*.

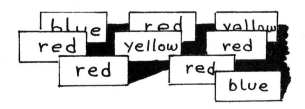

2. Construct a simple balloon worksheet. Write the word *red* in most of them, but add several distractor words. If the student asks what those words are, do not confuse the student by telling him/her at this time. Just say, "This is not red." Ask the student to color only the balloons that contain the word *red* stating, "I'm going to try and catch you. I have some balloons that do not say *red*. I want you to color only the words that contain the word *red*."

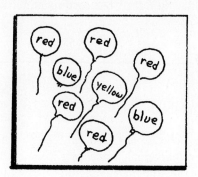

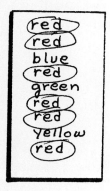

3. Write a list of color words with most of them being *red*. Ask the student to circle only the words that say *red*. You will need to demonstrate the procedure on a short practice paper to ensure that the student understands the directions. Many young students can do this independently. Some students may find it easier to underline the words than to circle them. If the student has poor motor control ask the student to point to the word, which the teacher then circles.
4. Use a commercial primary coloring book for preschoolers as the drawings are very simple and free of distractions. Write the color word *red* on various parts of the picture and use distractor words on other parts, but ask the student to color only the parts that state the color *red*.

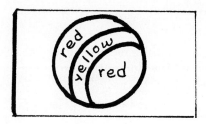

Practice only the color word *red* using these suggestions until the student has consistently mastered the word and can correctly identify it on successive trials. Some students will learn quickly whereas others may need several days. It is important to review the mastered word(s) continuously to ensure long-term memory.

Continue introducing additional color words (one at a time) in this manner, allowing a great deal of practice over each newly acquired skill.

Additional Suggestions: As more color words are mastered, the student may be asked to color each section of the drawing in the color stated.

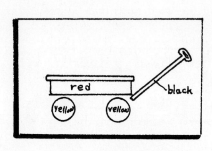

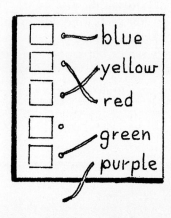

LACING BOARD

Color or paste solid-color squares on a large piece of tagboard. On the opposite side print the color names in a scrambled order. Punch holes beside the color blocks and the names. Shoelaces or thick string is threaded through the holes on one side and knotted to hold them securely. The student connects the color block with the correct color name by lacing the shoelace or string through the corresponding hole. Feedback is provided to the student when the task is completed by reinforcing correct responses and helping the student make any necessary correction.

COLOR PIN WHEEL

Divide a tagboard or cardboard pizza board into eight sections. Write one word in each section. Have the students paint spring-clamp clothespins with tempera paint to represent each of the colors written on the circle. Have the students match the colored clothespin to the matching color word on the circle. The teacher, aide, or peer who can correctly identify the color words can monitor the students and reinforce when correct.

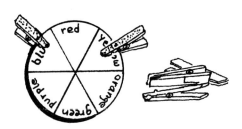

_____ **punctuation practice** _____

Descriptors: Reading
Language Arts

Grade Levels: 1–2
Learning Disabled
Educable Mentally Retarded

Rationale: Many students have difficulty using and reading punctuation correctly. This activity is designed to stress the rules of the period and the question mark at a very basic level.

Objective: The student will be able to add the correct punctuation marks (period or question mark) at the end of sentences provided on individual worksheets.

Materials: Ditto masters
Ditto paper
Pencil

Procedure:
1. Using teacher-constructed worksheets, discuss the use of periods with the class. Demonstrate how the voice falls at the end of a sentence when there is a period.
2. Orally read the worksheets with the students.
3. Allow the students individual time to complete the worksheet.
4. Provide immediate feedback in the beginning so that students are not allowed to practice a wrong response.
5. Provide similar worksheets for several days to be certain that the students have mastered these punctuation skills.

Worksheet #1

⟦·⟧

This is a period.
When we see this ⟦·⟧ it means to stop.
Read this story. Put your finger on the ⟦·⟧ and stop.

The car is blue.
It goes fast.
It is new.

Worksheet #2

Put a ⟦·⟧ at the end of each sentence.
Read them to your teacher. Remember ⟦·⟧ means stop.

Tim has some candy
He gave some to Sally
Sally fell down
She lost the candy

6. Use the same procedure with question marks. Remind the students that when a question is asked, the voice goes up at the end of the sentence.

Worksheet #3

⟦?⟧

This is a question mark. We use this mark when someone asks a question. Read these sentences. Put your finger on the ⟦?⟧ and stop.

Where did you go?
Is it big?
How fast can it go?
Did you see the ball?

Worksheet #4

Put a ⟦?⟧ at the end of each sentence.
Read them to your teacher.

Where is the car
How did he get here
Is it green
Can you run fast

Additional Suggestions: 1. Combine the period and question mark for discrimination and generalization of concepts.

Worksheet #5

Read the sentences carefully. Put a ⟦·⟧ or ⟦?⟧ at the end of each sentence.

This is my chair
Did you tell her
What are you doing
Give her the book
Where is the ball
It is hot today

2. Using pieces of newspaper, have students circle all the periods with a red crayon or pen and all the question marks with a green crayon or pen.

Descriptors:
Structure
Reading Comprehension
Color Words
Number Comprehension

Grade Levels: 1–2
Special
Education
Classroom

Rationale: It is often difficult for classroom teachers to design worksheets for students who lack basic academic skills. Since the classroom teacher cannot spend an excessive amount of time with students who lack basic academic skills when other students need attention too, the students who are deficient in basic skills need to learn to work without constant teacher supervision. The present teaching each helps teachers prepare worksheets to enable such students to work independently and, thus, free up teacher time to be spent helping all students.

Objective: To provide the classroom teacher with basic worksheet ideas for slower progressing students who need to learn to work independently.

Materials:
Ditto master sheets
Duplicating paper
Pencil
Crayons

Procedure:
1. The teacher teaches the student a color word and beginning number symbols (see *Color Word* and *One-to-One Relationships* activities).
2. After preparing very simple worksheets on a ditto master and duplicating the needed copies, the teacher reads the directions with the student. (Note: The student must have sufficient motor control to reproduce simple designs or drawings in order for the activity to be successful.)
3. When the teacher is certain that the student understands the directions and can complete the paper independently, the student is told to work without teacher supervision.
4. As the student completes each paper correctly and independently, s/he is reinforced for the good work (see *Visual Motivation* activity).
5. As the student is taught more skills, the worksheets may be expanded. The student is now comprehending what s/he is reading and following the directions independently. Rebus pictures used in the beginning may later be paired with the written word until, finally, the pictures are replaced by the word only. It may be necessary to sequence the steps as follows: use *concrete objects* (for example, toy car, boat), replace these with *pictorial representations*, and substitute only the *words*.*

*(Note: This technique has been used successfully with students with poor academic skills.)

INDEPENDENT WORKSHEET IDEAS (Student has been taught the word <u>red</u> and the number <u>1</u>)

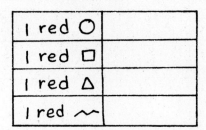

1. Begin with [1 red O] alone on a page, add one more direction, and so on.

2. Expand with more colors and numbers when these have been taught to the student.

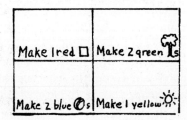

3. Teach the sight word *make* or *draw* and consistently use the same sight word on the paper. Do not mix the two words as they may confuse the student.

Make 1 red □	Make 2 green 🌲s
Make 2 blue Os	Make 1 yellow ☀

4. Teach the sight word *and*. Consistently use it on the worksheets.

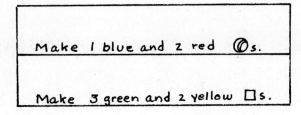

(Note: Do not require the student to reproduce complicated pictures. Geometric shapes and familiar objects are recommended.)

5. Number papers. Teach sight words to match pictures. Teach only one at a time and provide much practice with each newly acquired word.

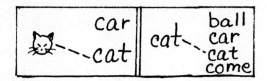

Make 2 Os	
Make 4 Os	
Make 6 blue Os	
Make 8 red Os	

6. Use pictures and words to be matched. Later substitute words for the pictures.

🐱 car ---cat	cat---- ball car cat come

7. Math problems. Teach the student to draw balls to find the correct answers. Leave enough space between problems on a worksheet to allow the student to draw balls.

$$
\begin{array}{r} 2 \\ +1 \\ \hline 3 \end{array} \quad \bullet\bullet \; \bullet
$$

$$
\begin{array}{r} 4 \\ -2 \\ \hline 2 \end{array} \quad \text{✗✗}\bullet\bullet
$$

1 •	3	2
+4 ••••	+2	+1

(Note: A student who is taught to use these strategies can work independently even though the work is different from that assigned to the rest of the class. These activities prepare the student to function better in the regular class by facilitating independence. Allow enough space on the worksheets for beginning students to draw the correct number. It may be useful to use large newsprint and fold into boxes rather than 8½″ × 11″ sheets of dittoed paper.)

Additional Suggestions:

1. Cut and paste. Match the correct word with its corresponding picture. Caution: The student must have the coordination to cut out the words or this activity will become extremely frustrating.

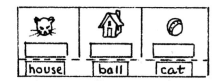

Expand into sentences with pictures explaining them. Example: The cat ran away from John.

2. Cut out four identical triangles. Write picture words on each side of one triangle and draw one corresponding picture on each of the other triangles. The student is to match the picture with the word and make one larger triangle. Feedback must be provided.

3. Fill in the missing blanks. The student may also draw a picture to match each word.

house	ball	sock
1. __ ouse	1. b __ ll	1. soc __
2. __ o	2. __ al __	2. __ o __ __
3. __ o __ s __	3. b __ __ l	3. s __ __ k
4. __ __ __ __ e	4. __ __ __ __	4. __ __ __ __

_____beginning reading activities using visual cues_____

Descriptors: Visual Discrimination
Readiness

Grade Levels: 1–3

Rationale: The following reading activities are appropriate for learners who are best motivated by visual cues. The activities can be used as a segment of the formal reading program in learning centers or as supplementary assignments.

Objective: To present readiness activities using visual cues.

Activity 1: Alphabet Sequence (Grades 1-3)

Materials: Cardboard
Pictures of the letters of the alphabet

Procedure:

1. Two 6″ × 10″ pieces of cardboard are hinged together with tape to form a folder. On the inside of the folder 2-inch squares are drawn with a pocket for each square made by stapling half-inch strips of cardboard at the bottom.
2. The squares are numbered 1 through 78.
3. On twenty-six squares a picture is pasted or drawn to represent each letter of the alphabet; an airplane for A, a balloon for B, and so on.

4. Fifty-two cardboard squares with the capital and the lowercase letters are provided in a box or an envelope.
5. The students place the pictures representing the letters of the alphabet in proper sequence.
6. The students place the small cards with the letters of the alphabet in the pockets with the pictures.
7. Later they may use the letters of the alphabet alone. Put the letters and pictures in the right order.

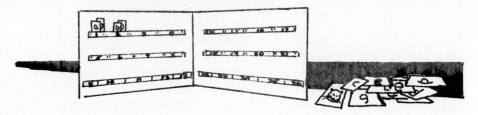

Activity 2: Lacing Game (Grade 1)

Materials: Cardboard
Shoelace

Procedure: Note: The names of the colors can be quickly learned by making cards with the color on one side and the name on the other.)
1. Shoelaces are cut in two, and half a shoelace is connected to each color by making a knot in one end and threading it from the back to the front.
2. A hole is punched beside the color name.
3. The student connects the color and its name with the shoelace.

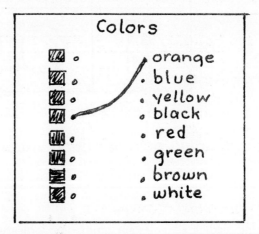

Activity 3: Sentence Completion (Grades 1–2)

Materials: Tagboard
Scissors
Felt tip pen

Procedure: 1. Draw an irregular line lengthwise across each of twenty ovals, 3″ × 4″, with the subjects of a sentence along the line and the predicate on the lower half. The sentences contain words that children encounter in their reading.
2. The student is to match the subject and the predicate.
3. Stories may be made from the sentences. (Note: These activities are excellent for flannel board exercises. Splitting the sentences into two parts is also good for reading comprehension.)

Activity 4: Words That Belong Together (Grades 1-3)

Materials: 20″ × 20″ tagboard
Manila envelope

Procedure:
1. Spaces, 1¾″ × 1¼″, are marked off on 8¾″ × 12″ pieces of cardboard.
2. Categories such as colors, toys, people, time, trees, fruits, food, numbers, home, school, and animals are printed in the top spaces of the oaktag.
3. Words that belong to these categories are printed on 1″ × 1¼″ squares of tagboard.
4. The student is to place the names of the objects under the right category.
5. The material may be stored in a labeled envelope containing the directions for using the game.
6. For self-correction an answer sheet may be provided along with the game.

Which Belong Together?			
Animals	Fruit	Toys	Numbers
cow	apple	doll	1
horse	pear	drum	6

For a readiness activity, replace the words with pictures.

Animals	Fruit	Toys	Numbers

Activity 5: Word Families (Grades 1-3)

Materials: Tagboard
Magic marker
Scissors

Procedure:
1. Cut out balls or squares.
2. Write a word ending on each ball and pull a strip of paper containing the initial consonants through the opening as shown below.
3. This readiness activity can be used with a student and a teacher or with two students.
4. Points may be given to the student who can identify the words.
5. The student who earns the most points receives a prize.

Activity 6: Matching Colors (Grades K-1)

Materials: Colored cloth
Scissors

Procedure: 1. Squares and circles of colored cloth and paper are cut out and distributed to the students.
2. They either sort them into color categories or one student holds up one of his/her pieces and the other students find a similar color among their squares and circles.

Activity 7: Letter Chains (Grades 1-2)

Materials: Paper
Scissors
Magic marker

Procedure: 1. The students make words with paper chains using letters of the alphabet printed on strips of paper.
2. This device is very effective for reversals such as *was* and saw.
3. Entire sentences may be created this way.
4. Two blank links are left between each word.

_____ milk carton "computer" _____

Descriptors: Self-Correction
Motivation
Skill Reinforcement

Grade Levels: 1-3

Rationale: Self-correcting materials are very helpful for individualized skill practice. This computer idea stimulates students' motivation for learning as they receive almost instant feedback by pulling out the answer card.

Objective: To provide question-and-answer practice for academic skills using a milk carton "computer."

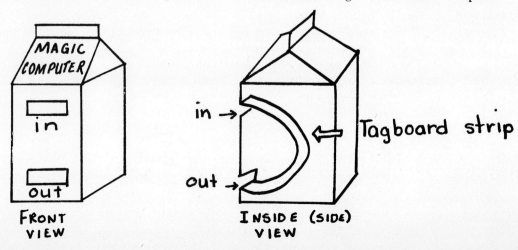

Materials: Empty ½ gallon milk carton
3″ × 5″ blank index cards
Scissors
Masking tape
Black marking pen
Crayons (if appropriate)
4″ × 12″ tagboard strip
5″ × 7″ manila envelopes

Procedure:
1. Construct a computer by cutting two 3½″ × 1″ slots toward the top and bottom of the empty milk carton (see illustration).
2. Open the milk carton and attach the tagboard strip in a curve from the top of the top slot to the bottom of the bottom slot with masking tape. (Note: The strip must be longer than the distance between the two slots in order to be able to curve and serve as a chute that flips the cards as they go through.)
3. Make sets of skill cards from blank index cards. The question/problem is written on one side and the answer is on the opposite side. Place a bright red dot in the upper left-hand corner of each card. The student places a finger on the dot as the card is read in order to ensure that the question/problem side faces up first. The card sets are placed in labeled 5″ × 7″ manila envelopes.

4. The student chooses a card from the appropriate set (as designated), reads the card, and gives the answer as the card is dropped into the top slot.
5. The card, answer side up, is retrieved from the bottom slot for immediate self-correction. (Note: The curved tagboard insert allows the card to turn over to reveal the answer side.)
Examples of skill cards:

Color words:

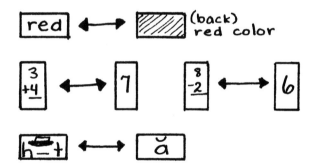

Additional Suggestions:
1. Divide the students into groups and ask them to construct sets of cards for the rest of the class in such subjects as science and social studies. Example:

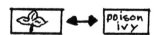

2. Set up a   Do You Know?   computer in the library and construct sets of question-answer cards about the school.

Example: When was our school built?
How many students attend our school?
What is the date of our Christmas vacation this year?

Descriptors: Word Recognition
Spelling
Remedial Reading

Grade Levels: 1–3
Educable Mentally Retarded
Learning Disabled
Personal-Social Adjustment

Rationale: Students do not learn to read in the same way. Consequently, it is beneficial to discover which modalities the student utilizes for the most efficient acquisition of reading vocabulary. Each of the following methods can be used as a starting point to ensure a successful reading experience. The teaching method must be supplemented by other procedures because a good reader needs to have a variety of techniques.

Objective: To discover which reading method appears to be the most efficient for an individual student.

Materials: Tagboard or 3½″ × 5″ blank index cards
8½″ × 11″ newsprint
Lined writing paper (appropriate for the grade level)
Chalkboard (optional)

Procedure:
1. Pick twenty unknown words, five words to teach using each of the following four methods.
2. Use one method one day to teach five words.
3. On the second day use another method to teach a second group of five words. Repeat this procedure for four days.
4. At the end of each daily session test the student on the five newly presented words and record the student's response (see response sheet protocol).
5. On the fifth day test the student on the twenty words presented during the previous four days by flashing word cards. Record the student's response on the protocol sheet. Missed words may be circled to notify the teacher which words need to be retaught.
6. The results may be used as a guideline for checking which methods are the most efficient for teaching a student to read. For example, if a student scores +5 on three methods and +3 on a fourth, it may mean that all three +5 methods were efficient, whereas the remaining method would not be chosen for that particular student.

Caution: These are rather gross assessment methods and the results are merely to be used as a guideline. Sometimes it is better to teach ten words for each method rather than five. The student may remember the words taught on the fourth day better than those from the first day because his/her short-term memory is better than long-term memory. If time allows, in a second week of assessment the sequence of the methods may be varied and again, both the daily and the weekly scores recorded. The third week can also be used to vary the sequence of instruction. If the same methods appear to be more efficient for the student regardless of which day they were presented, the teacher may assume that those methods are likely to be the most effective.

NAME: John Jacobs			DAILY TEST	WEEKLY TEST
DATE	METHOD	WORDS PRESENTED		
3/17	V-A	ran, jump, cannot, look, day	+5	+5
3/20	VAM	then, which, (gold), look, happy	+4	+3
3/21	K	city, come, running, play, up	+5	+5
3/22	Ph	silly, here, (when), (how), upon	+3	+3
3/23		All words		+16/20

Additional Suggestions: Train a volunteer parent or teacher aide to help assess the students as these activities are time-consuming.

Method 1: Visual Auditory Method

In one set, each card includes a picture illustrating a familiar noun with the identifying word printed under it. On another set of cards the words are printed without pictures. The student is first tested on the cards with the words alone to make certain that they are not already known. After the five unknown words are selected, present a picture card, pointing to the word and pronouncing it. The student is now asked to say the word several times while looking at it whereupon s/he finds the corresponding nonillustrated card containing the same word and places it next to the picture-word card. After ten minutes, the student is tested on the nonillustrated cards and the results are recorded on the protocol sheet. This method denotes a "look-and-say" method of teaching word recognition.

Method 2: Visual-Auditory-Motor Method

Prerequisite skill: The student must be able to write letters.

Choose five words unfamiliar to the student and present each word separately as follows: Print the word on a card and pronounce it. Suggest that the student look at the word carefully and then shut his/her eyes trying to picture the word in his/her mind with eyes closed because the student will be asked to write the word from memory. The student opens his/her eyes and takes another look if necessary. Ask that student to name the word as an aid to later recall. Sometimes it is necessary to show the card several times before the student can remember the word clearly enough to write it. The card is finally removed and the student writes the word from memory. If one word is particularly difficult, another should be tried. If the student reproduces the word correctly, s/he is to write it several times while covering up the words that have previously been written to be certain the word is being recalled from memory. After ten minutes, the word is retested. This method illustrates a visual-auditory-motor approach to word recognition.

Method 3: Kinesthetic Method

Prerequisite skill: The student must be able to write letters.

Print an unfamiliar word on lined paper, each letter being approximately 2 inches high. The student is told that s/he is going to learn a new way of reading by using fingers as an aid. The child looks at the word and traces it with the index finger while simultaneously pronouncing it very slowly. The trace-

and-say process is repeated several times, whereupon the student is asked to write the word from memory without reference to a model. Fold the paper down over the stimulus word. The student then writes the word from memory. After ten minutes, the word is tested by flashing it to the student for word recognition. This method is an example of visual-auditory-kinesthetic or visual-auditory-kinesthetic-tactile method of word recognition.

Method 4: Phonics Method

Prerequisite skills: The student must know sound-symbol relationships and be able to write letters.

Ask the student to make new words by substituting beginning consonants: change *run* to *fun, sun, bun,* and so on. Next ask the student to combine the sounds to make a word: k-a-t blends to *cat.* Ask the student to substitute final consonants in short-vowel words using the letter sounds previously taught: *fat* to *fan, cat* to *can, run* to *rub.* Finally, ask the student to read in mixed order the words learned through the phonic approach: *run, cat, rub, man.*

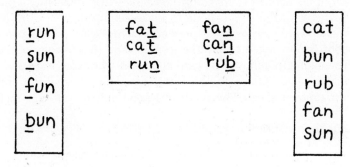

tagboard tachistoscopes

| Descriptors: | Sight Words | Grade Levels: | 1–3 |
| | Phonics Practice | | Resource Rooms |

Rationale: Students having difficulty separating figure from ground often experience problems when asked to read from word lists. In word practice with such students it is helpful to flash one word at a time to them by using a teacher-constructed tachistoscope. The tachistoscope may also be used to reinforce many other types of skills (for example, math, spelling, phonics). The tachistoscope described in this activity is easily constructed from tagboard folders.

Objective: To teach students to decode vocabulary words rapidly using a tachistoscope.

Materials: Tagboard folders
Black marking pen
Scissors
Cellophane tape

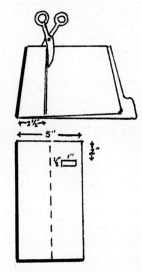

Procedure:

1. Measure 2½ inches from the folded edge of a tagboard folder and cut a strip the length of the folder, thus producing a 5-inch wide strip.
2. Open the strip and cut a ½″ × 1″ window 2 inches from the top of the strip. The window must be wide and long enough to expose one word at a time.
3. Tape the long open sides together leaving the top and bottom edges open.
4. Cut 1 inch off the bottom of the tachistoscope so it becomes 1 inch shorter than the individual strips to be pulled through it.
5. Use the remaining pieces of the manila folder to cut 2 inch wide strips the length of the folder.
6. Write the word lists to be studied on the tagboard strips with a black marking pen making certain that the words are spaced so that only one word at a time will be exposed through the window.

7. The student inserts the appropriate word list strip and reads one word at a time to the teacher, aide, or peer tutor. A percent correct numbered word list may be used to record progressive feedback for both the student and the teacher.

Additional Suggestions:

A tachistoscope for practicing "silent e" words is also useful.

1. Using a tagboard folder, slit two vertical lines approximately ½-inch apart parallel to the right of a written word list.
2. Cut a 1-inch tagboard strip wider than the word list strip and print the letter *e* in the center using a red marking pen.
3. The student first reads the short vowel sound root word aloud and then pulls the strip to expose the letter *e* next to the word and proceeds to read the new long vowel sound word. The following words may be used for this procedure:

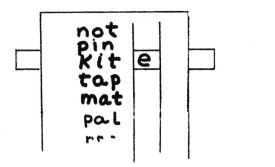

pin	mat	fat
kit	rod	nap
tin	rot	mop
cop	pal	gap
not	rid	hat

_____ **picture vocabulary cards** _____

Descriptors: Sight Vocabulary   **Grade Levels:**   1–3
Word Games
Independent Study

Rationale: Reading and learning new vocabulary words is tedious and unsuccessful for many poor readers. The following idea offers a change of pace for such reluctant learners.

Objective: To increase basic sight vocabulary, particularly nouns, in first- through third-grade students having a reading deficit and lacking a basic sight vocabulary.

Materials: Magic marker
Colors (if desired)
3½″ × 5″ blank index cards cut into thirds or halves (The word to be learned is printed on one side, and the word with the picture above it is printed on the reverse side. Clipping a certain corner of the card makes it easier to keep the cards right side up.)

Procedure: The child is asked to study each word, using the side with the picture. Point out how the word begins and how it ends. This is the time to analyze word structure with the student who may otherwise only gaze at the picture and ignore the printed word. After studying two or three words, the student turns the cards over and sees if s/he can correctly pronounce the written word without the benefit of a picture. The child then uses self-correction by turning over the word card.

Picture Word Card Game to Increase Basic Sight Vocabulary Words

Prerequisite Skill: To know how to count and make tally marks in groups of five. (Example: **ᚼᚼ ᚼᚼᚼ**)

Objective: To win the game by having the most points.

Players: one to six

Procedure:

1. Deal three cards to each player, picture side up. (Increase this to five cards or more as reading skills improve.)
2. Appoint one child to be the scorekeeper.
3. Insist that each student arrange the cards in a left-to-right sequence.

4. Study the words with the students for a few minutes. Say them aloud. Look at the beginning of each word. Look at the ending.
5. When each student feels ready, turn over the cards.

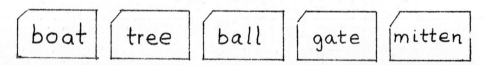

6. Mix up the order ("scramble the eggs"), but rearrange in a *left-to-right* sequence.

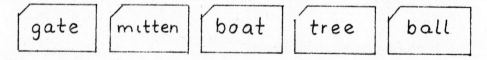

7. Each student has a turn to pronounce each of his five words (*left* to *right*) turning over each word card as s/he says it.

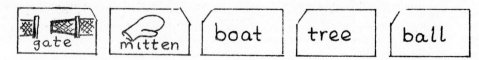

8. The student scorekeeper makes one tally mark for each correct response beside that student's name.

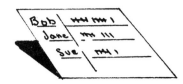

9. If a word card is missed, the student retains that card for the next round. The correctly pronounced cards are placed at the bottom of the dealer's deck to be reshuffled and used again. The missed cards are relearned with the new cards, thus giving the child more practice on words that are difficult.

Example: Five cards   Missed one   Retain one   Add four new cards

10. The student who has the most total points is declared the winner.
    (Note: Commercial picture-word cards are available, for example, Dolch, Milton Bradley.)

Additional Suggestions:

1. For one or two players, it may be more fun to retain all word cards correctly pronounced in one separate pile instead of making tally marks. At the end of the game, it is very reinforcing for a student to count the correct pile of word cards at one time, whereupon the winner is declared.

2. Once the teacher has explained the game and played one round with the students, further teacher supervision is usually not required because the word cards are self-correcting. In the beginning it is important to establish the ground rules for scorekeeping, left-to-right sequencing, retention of missed cards, and so on.

3. Older students may use the same principle in learning vocabulary words and science and social studies vocabulary.

4. Action words.

5. Number words.

6. Color words.

Descriptors: Sight Vocabulary   **Grade Levels:** 1–4
Word Games

Rationale: It is important for students to learn at an automatic level so that when reading they can concentrate more on comprehension than on decoding unfamiliar words.

Objective: To increase students' sight vocabulary recognition to an automatic level.

Materials: Colored construction paper
Black marking pen
Tagboard
Chalkboard
Dice or spinner

Procedure: Decide which words your students need to learn for assignments related to reading, workbook, math, science, social studies, or seatwork. Be sure that the words are at each child's present skill level. Divide the work into short sequential lists and design simple games that can be played at home or at school for additional practice. Overlearning of vocabulary words is very important for improvement of reading skills, that is, students are more confident when they do not stumble over unknown reading words.

The Dolch 220 Basic Sight Word lists divided into levels from pre-primer through grade 3 is another good source for determining appropriate sight vocabulary. These words make up approximately 70 percent of primary reading material and 50 percent of all adult material. You may obtain this list from the reading teacher in your district. Start with only a few words at a time and increase to ten at the most. In this way students can realize greater progress and thus increase their motivation to learn more words. Regular reviewing of words printed on regular index cards (five to ten) tied together with a rubber band is an effective method of improving and increasing the recognition of sight words.

Practice Games

1. *Fish.* Place the words on colored paper cutouts of fish and scatter on the floor. If a student is only assigned four to five new words make multiple copies of each word.

A student is allowed to continue fishing (picking up the paper fish) as long as s/he can pronounce the words. Count the number of fish caught by each student at the end of the game.
Variation: Attach metal paper clips to each fish and use a fishing pole stick and string with a magnet attached to the end. When a fish is "caught" the student must correctly pronounce the word or throw back the fish.

2. *Fill the Gumball Machine.* Construct the outline of a large gumball machine on the bulletin board or on the floor using large drawing paper with empty circles. Cut out colored paper circles and write words on each of them. If the student can read the word, it can be added to the machine until all circles are filled. The reverse procedure is then initiated whereby the machine is emptied by students correctly reading each of the words.

3. *Climb the Ladder.* Draw a ladder on paper or on the chalkboard and fill the spaces with words. A student points to and pronounces each word as s/he "climbs the ladder."

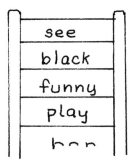

4. *Balloon Pop.* Draw circles on the chalkboard and write a word in each of them. As the student pronounces each word a string is drawn. Reverse the procedure by erasing (popping) the balloons as each word is correctly pronounced.

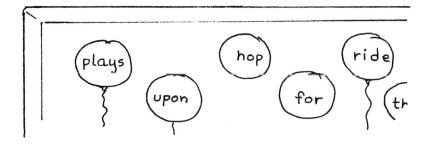

5. *Word Bingo.* Construct bingo cards with words written in each square. Have a larger pool of words than spaces on the cards so that no two students' cards are alike. The caller calls out words from a separate pile of word cards and students play "blackout" by covering the matching word on their cards with colored paper. All squares on a bingo card must be covered before the game is won.

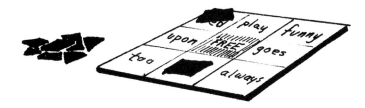

6. *Gameboards.* Adapt gameboards to word lists and use a pair of dice or spinners. The student rolls the die and then moves the number of spaces and pronounces each word as the marker is moved. For example: The die show four. The student pronounces *see, run, play,* and *can* before placing the marker on that space. The first player to reach the treasure chest wins. If a word is missed the student returns the marker to the previous position.

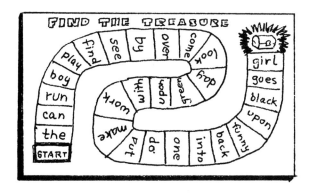

(Note: The two main points to remember in teaching sight words is to monitor the students in the early stages of practicing new words to be certain that they are correct, that is, don't let them reinforce a wrong response, and *not* to introduce more sets of words until a student has mastered the present list. It will be necessary to individualize instruction for your students as they do not all learn at the same pace.)

Additional Suggestions: Dittoing teaching ideas for notebooks to be shared among your faculty makes a good inservice project.

_____ **outlaw words** _____

Descriptors: Nonphonetic Words   **Grade Levels:** 1–4+
                      Bulletin Board

Rationale: Poor readers often experience difficulty learning nonphonetic words. This activity is challenging for the students, yet fun at the same time.

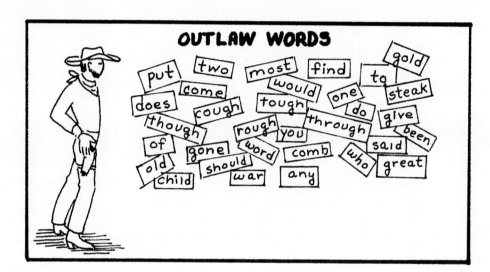

Objective: To enable the student to read orally the nonphonetic words presented on the bulletin board during the year with 85 to 100 percent accuracy.

Materials: Construction paper (various colors for word cards)
                   Black felt marking pen (broad line)
                   Cartoon drawing or poster of an outlaw

Procedure: 1. The teacher prepares the bulletin board by putting up a few of the nonphonetic "outlaw words." These are printed on strips of construction paper 1½ inches wide and as long as necessary to write the word. Marking pens are used for big bold print that can be seen across the room.
                   2. The students pronounce the words as the teacher points to each one. The students may then take turns pronouncing the words individually.
                   3. The teacher may say, "There are many words that cannot be sounded out. As you read or work on your written lessons, and you think you have found a word that cannot be sounded out, bring it to me and we will write the word card to place on the bulletin board."

Additional Suggestions: 1. This makes an excellent game for using as a "pronunciation round-robin" conducted as a spelling bee. The children line up (two or three rows) in front of the bulletin board. If a student cannot pronounce a word, s/he will have to sit down. The team with the most remaining players wins the game.

The teacher should avoid pointing to the words in any lineal order so that the student cannot anticipate which word will be his/hers.

2. The words may also be placed on 5″ × 8″ cards in a notebook or on two large rings. As the teacher flips over each card, the students take turns pronouncing the words using the same rules as above.

_____**"pick it"**_____

Descriptors: Sight Vocabulary   **Grade Levels:** 1–6
                Reading Game

Rationale: Many students need additional practice in quickly recognizing words that have been previously introduced as vocabulary words. In this game, which is a fun way to practice such words, the stimuli are presented visually and auditorily, and the student is asked to make a motor response.

Objective: To reinforce and to expedite the recognition of known words.

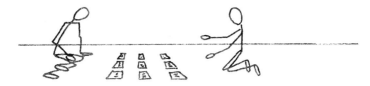

Materials: A list of vocabulary words written on index cards, one word per card. (Words may be taken from Dolch Basic Vocabulary words or the reading vocabulary words from a basal reading series.)
                Stopwatch

Procedure: 1. The twenty to thirty words used in the game should be introduced to the players before the game begins. The words may be familiar ones, which are presently recognized too slowly. (If appropriate, some new words may be introduced.)
              2. One to four students may play this game.
              3. Nine word cards are placed on the floor or table in rows of three. The teacher (or one student familiar with the words) calls out a word on one of the cards. The player next in line is given a short time to point to the correct word (three to seven seconds depending on their skill). If the student picks the correct card, s/he may keep it and replace it with a card from the unused pile. The teacher then calls out another word for the next player. If the students are calling the words, the player that just picked up the card calls a new word for the next player in line.
              4. If a player misses a card, that card is removed from the set, put at the bottom of the unused pile and replaced with a new card. That player loses a turn.
              5. The player having the most cards after the pile is gone is the winner.

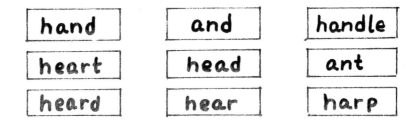

**Additional
Suggestions:**   For variation words may be used that have similar spellings (hit, hut, hat), number words (eight, twenty, fourteen) or science words (miscroscope, telescope).

_____**simplify written directions**_____

Descriptors: Independent Seatwork   **Grade Levels:**   1–6
                   Reading Comprehension

Rationale: Many students have the skills necessary to complete certain seatwork assignments but do not attempt to do so, as they are unable to read the accompanying written directions. Thus the teacher may erroneously assume that the entire task is too difficult for the student whereas, in reality, the student has the prerequisite skills but does not understand what s/he is supposed to do.

Objective: To present strategies for simplifying written student directions.

Materials: Ditto master
                  Duplicating paper

Procedure: 1. Start by reading directions on worksheet assignments to determine whether or not they are too difficult for specific students in the class.
2. In general, the directions may be simplified by breaking them down into small, sequential steps, or using simpler vocabulary.
   a.   Read each sentence two times.
   b.   There is a missing word in each sentence.
   c.   Read the three words underneath each sentence.
   d.   Only one word will fit into the sentence.
   e.   Choose the correct word for each sentence.
   f.   Circle the correct word.

3. Underline the key words in written directions.

   a.   In each of the following pairs of sentences a word has a *line under it*.
          1. "I got a new *watch* for my birthday."
          2. "Ted likes to *watch* airplanes land."
   b.   In each sentence the underlined word has a *different meaning*.
          1. Look at closely
          2. A timepiece
   c.   *Write the number* for the meaning of each word in front of the sentence in which it is used.

          Example: _2_ I got a new *watch* for my birthday.

              1. Look at closely   2. A timepiece

   The students must read each step in the directions and explain what each means.
4. Use a cover sheet or marker to block out the written directions. The student exposes one line at a time and directs attention to that line.

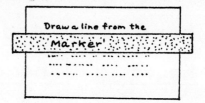

5. Add rebus pictures for more difficult vocabulary.

Example: I got a new watch for my birthday.

I got a new  for my

(Note: The teacher must be certain that all students fully understand what they are expected to do on each worksheet before asking them to complete the assignment independently.)

Additional Suggestions:

1. Read the directions to the student while underlining the written directions using a finger as a pacer for poor readers.
2. Record the directions on a cassette tape and allow students whose auditory skills are better than their visual skills to listen to them before beginning the assignment. The student may replay the tape as many times as necessary.
3. Ask another student to read the directions to the special student if a tape recorder is not available. This may also foster more social interaction.

the fernald method of teaching reading and spelling

Descriptors: Multisensory Reading Approach   **Grade Levels:** 1–6
Remedial Technique

Rationale: Some students do not learn reading vocabulary or spelling words through conventional classroom teaching methods. The Fernald[1] method has been successful with students who have serious reading problems. This multisensory approach to teaching reading and spelling is built on the premise that stimulation of several avenues of sensory input reinforces learning. Thus kinesthetic and tactile stimulation is emphasized along with the auditory and visual modalities. The description presented here is a simplified visual adaptation of the original method described by Dr. Grace Fernald & RG Heckleman.[2].

Objective: To teach students how to read or write a word from memory using a multisensory approach.

Materials: Crayons
Large newsprint
Typewriter
5″ × 7″ index cards
(Note: This whole-word approach is taught in four stages. The student must always write the word from memory without consulting the model to avoid looking back and forth from the student's paper to the model word and, thus, breaking up the word into small meaningless units. The teacher removes from sight or crosses out any errors made in writing the word, and the word is started over again. The student checks his/her written word against the model. Each word is learned as a whole, not letter-by-letter, and immediately placed in a context that is meaningful to the student.)

Stage 1: Tracing—VAKT: Visual, Auditory, Kinesthetic, Tactile

Procedure:

1. Ask the student to select a word s/he wants to learn or choose an unknown reading or spelling word.
2. Write the word in 2-inch high manuscript (cursive, if age appropriate) letters at the top of the piece of newsprint.

---

[1] G. Fernald, *Remedial Techniques in Basic School Subjects* (New York: McGraw-Hill, 1943), p. 53.
[2] R.G. Heckelman, *Solutions to Reading Problems* (Novato, Calif.: Academic Therapy Publications, 1978), pp. 29–42.

3. Say the word as a whole and by syllable (never letter by letter).
4. The student pronounces the word.
5. Ask the student to trace the word with one or two fingertips (index and middle fingers) in contact with the paper saying each part of the word as it is traced. The student traces the word and says "to ge ther" and then "together."

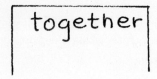

6. Repeat this procedure several times until the student is ready to write the word from memory without a model.
7. Cover and model by folding down the paper. The student says and writes the word without looking at the copy, then compares what is written with the model by lifting up the paper.

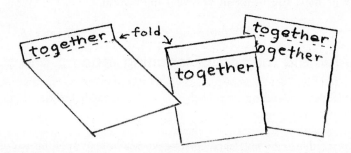

If the student makes an error, steps 2 through 7 are repeated until the student is ready to try again. Attention is not drawn to the incorrect word.

8. If the first try is correct, the student must write the word a second time from memory. Fold the paper down once more and ask the student to write the word again. The new word is checked against the previous two models.

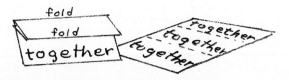

9. The new words are written on blank 5″ × 7″ index cards and filed in a file box for later reference when needed for written expression.
10. Write student-dictated stories on paper including any new words learned by the VAKT technique. Afterwards type the story and present it to the student to determine if it can be read by the student as it would appear in print.

Stage 2: Writing from Teacher's Model—VAK: Visual, Auditory, Kinesthetic

The tracing of words is eliminated at this stage. All the steps listed in Stage 1 are followed with the exception that the teacher writes the word in normal-sized script.

Procedure:

1. Write the selected word on a card or on a piece of paper in normal-sized script and pronounce the word.
2. The student studies the word by looking at it and pronouncing it as long as necessary in order to learn it.
3. The student covers the model and writes the word from memory. The student checks the student's written word against the teacher model.

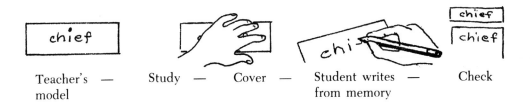

Teacher's — Study — Cover — Student writes — Check
model   from memory

4. Again, all dictated stories are typed for the student to simulate print rather than script. All new word cards (see Stage 1) are filed in the student's file box.

Stage 3: Writing from Print—VAK: Visual, Auditory, Kinesthetic

This stage is reached when the student can write the word after looking at the printed form of it. It is no longer necessary for the teacher to write the word for the student; instead it is pronounced. The student reads silently from the book before attempting oral reading. The student is told any word not known. After each reading session, the student reviews the new words and writes them again.

Procedure:
1. The student looks at the printed word and says it after the teacher has pronounced it.
2. The student writes the word from memory without looking at the printed word.
3. The student checks the written word against the printed copy. (Note: If the student is unable to make the transfer from print to script, the teacher goes back to Stage 2 and writes the word for the student.)

Stage 4: Comparing New Words by Relating Them to Already Familiar Words— VA(K): Visual, Auditory (and Kinesthetic if needed)

The student is now beginning to solve new words by relating them to already acquired words. As reading ability increases, the student reads more difficult materials.

Procedure:
1. The student glances through the reading material rapidly and underlines with a light pencil mark the words not recognized.
2. Pronounce the selected words.
3. The student writes the new words from memory.
4. The student reads the material.
(Note: According to Dr. Fernald, "The child is never made to sound the word when he is reading nor is it sounded out for him by his teachers. He points to the word and is told what it is.")

Review:
Stage 1—Student traces word with finger before writing it from memory.
Stage 2—Student writes word after looking at copy prepared by the teacher.
Stage 3—Student looks at printed word in the book and writes it from memory.
Stage 4—Student reads silently. Unknown words are underlined and pronounced by the teacher, then written by the student. The student finally reads orally.

important points to remember

1. Few students require this type of guidance.
2. Words are *never* spelled orally.
3. Words are always written as a whole, never in separated syllables.
4. Student never copies the word; it is always written from memory.
5. Correct form of the word is emphasized; the incorrect form (that is, an error) is always crossed out or covered up.
6. The word is always written twice in succession (correctly) from memory.
7. The student is asked to read the newly learned words correctly for three successive days.

Additional
Suggestions:
1. Let the student write the word in sand or salt by tracing over the teacher's model. Although the student can write the word from memory in the sand, the teacher must still provide a written model for comparison.
2. Use this method to teach spelling words. The sentences or story formats may be eliminated if desired.

_____reading program supplement_____

Descriptors: Vocabulary Practice   Grade Levels: 1–6
                  Peer Tutors
                  Individual Practice

Rationale: Traditional developmental reading activities may not provide enough practice with new reading vocabulary words for students experiencing difficulty in learning to read new material. Such students require supplementary material that can be practiced with peer tutors, parents, aides, or the classroom teacher. Initially it is time consuming to construct such supplementary aids, but once they have been created they may be used repeatedly with other students.

Objective: To provide a series of vocabulary word activities.

Materials: Tagboard for 3″ × 5″ flash cards and wall charts
                  Black marking pen
                  Lists of new vocabulary words
                  Language master machine and blank cards (if applicable)
                  Scissors
                  Paste
                  Ditto master
                  Duplicating paper

Procedure: 1. Construct materials for activities described in the selected teaching idea.
                  2. Decide if peer tutors, aides, parents, or the classroom teacher will guide the student through the activity.
                  3. Evaluate each student's progress as a result of the activities by noting the student's daily reading patterns, basal reading test scores, accuracy of daily workbook assignments, and so on.
                  4. If the student does not appear to be successful based on the evaluation procedures outlined above, reconsider the level of reading material and determine the student's exact reading level by means of an Individualized Reading Inventory (see *Informal Reading Inventories* activity.)

Activity 1: Flash Cards

Make flash cards of all new vocabulary words introduced in each story using the black marking pen. The flash cards may be used in the following ways:
1. Peer tutors or aides work with the students using the flash cards.
2. The teacher uses the flash cards for drill or for pre-/ or posttesting.
3. The teacher uses the flash cards to introduce new words in the reading group.

Activity 2: Dittoed Word Lists

Make dittoed word lists of all new vocabulary words introduced in a story or unit and give them to all students who are ready to read that story.

Book B - Unit 2

come
upon
there
look
away
what

1. Use the lists as rate sheets by timing the students for one minute each day. Record the number of words each student can read correctly in one minute.

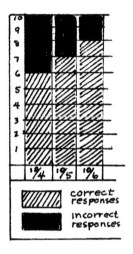
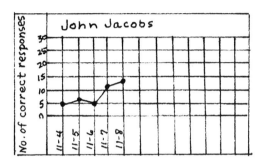

correct responses

incorrect responses

This activity can be adapted by recording errors or percent correct each day. A simple bar graph can also be designed with the students coloring in the number correct and the number missed.
2. Have students make their own flash cards based on words in the lists. The cards may be kept in individual student word banks (made from shoe boxes) and used for future practice.
3. The word lists may be sent home for additional practice. Dittoed directions to parents showing simple games and practice drills using the word lists should accompany the word lists.
4. Put the unit word lists on the bulletin board. Allow the students to challenge a list if they think they can read all the words. If the students can read a particular unit word list with 100 percent accuracy, add a star by the student's name under the appropriate word list number.

FOOTBALL TIGER'S GROUP - VOCABULARY WORDS					
	List 1	List 2	List 3	List 4	List 5
SUE	★	★	★		
JAY	★	★			
CARL	★	★			
MARY	★	★	★	★	

(Note: It is less defeating for the slower students in the class if there are separate starred charts for each reading group, since it is discouraging for a student to see few stars after his/her name and many stars after a brighter student's name. The competitive spirit can work to a student's advantage if the competition is at a student's current skill level.)

Activity 3: Language Master Cards

If the classroom has a language master machine, new vocabulary words may be written on the cards and placed in labeled pocket charts near the language master machine. Students can practice the words at their own pace using earphones. These cards are self-correcting as the correct answer is also printed on the cards.

Cover the blank cards with clear contact paper and write (and record) new words on the cards with a grease pencil. In this way, the words are easily erased and new ones may be added. A pocket chart of clear plastic may also be constructed on the cards with new flash cards easily inserted into the pockets for quick practice. The correct answer must be recorded on each card.

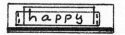

Additional Suggestions:

1. Use sentences instead of individual words.
2. Cut out pictures from old workbooks and paste them on construction paper squares stapled to the bulletin board. Write words or sentences describing these workbook pictures on blank index cards.

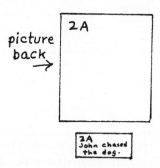

The students may read the sentence cards and pin them under the appropriate picture on the bulletin board. The teacher or aide must check for accuracy or numbered or lettered answers may be coded on the back of each picture for self-correction. Pictures and sentences can be changed frequently as the students progress.

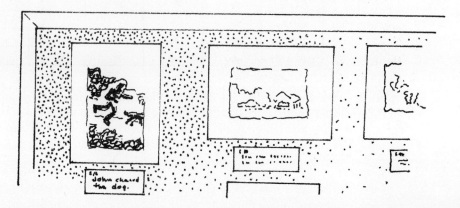

_____ **tachistoscopes** _____

Descriptors: Word Recognition   **Grade Levels:**   1–6
                   Phonics Practice
                   Math Practice

Rationale: Some children have trouble separating figure from ground and, thus, have difficulty reading from lists. For such students, a tachistoscope may be helpful as it allows the child to review only one word at a time. A tachistoscope has many uses in reading and math.

Objective: To teach word recognition or math computation to an automatic level.

Materials: Manila folder or tagboard
                 Black marking pen or primary typewriter
                 Scissors
                 Brass fastener

Procedure: 1. Using a manila folder, measure 2½ inches from the folded edge and cut a strip the length of the folder, thus producing a 5-inch wide strip.

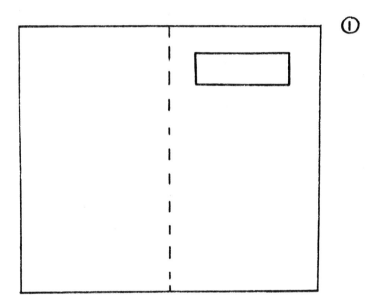

2. Open flat and cut a window 2 inches from the top on the right half of the strip. The window should be long enough to expose one word at a time. (See illustration 1.)
3. Tape the long open sides together leaving the top and bottom edges open.
4. Cut 1 inch off the bottom of the tachistoscope. The tachistoscope should be at least 1 inch shorter than the strip. (See illustration 2.)
5. Use the rest of the manila folder to cut 2-inch wide strips that will pull through the tachistoscope.

② cat
  fat
  him
  pen
  hot
  cup
  hop
  sum

6. Use a primary typewriter to type review lists on these strips or letter with a black marking pen. Be sure that the words are double or triple spaced so that only one word at a time is exposed through the window. (See illustration 3.)

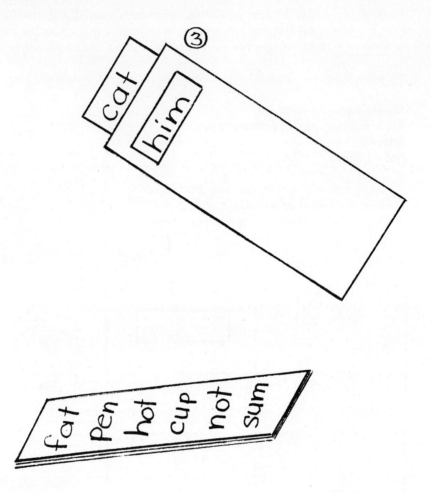

Tachistoscope for Silent e

Procedure: Draw two vertical lines parallel to the list and to the right of it—wide enough for the letter *e* to be inserted. Slit the lines dot to dot, as illustrated. Insert the strip with the letter *e* printed in the center in red. The child reads one word on the list, then pulls the strip to expose the letter *e* next to the word and then reads the new word.

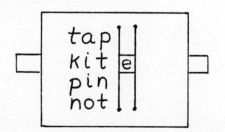

The following words can be used for this procedure:

pin	mat	fat
kit	rod	nap
tin	rot	mop
cop	pal	gap
not	rid	hat

Wheel Tachistoscope—Phonics Wheel or Word Wheel

Procedure:

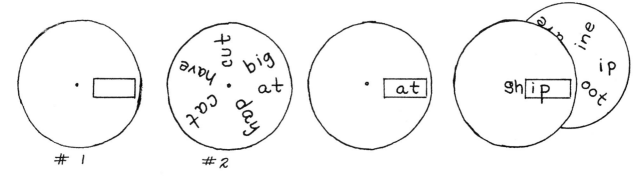

#1   #2

Cut a window in #1 (enough to expose one word), type or letter sight words on #2; for example, from Dolch list at child's level. Attach #1 over #2 with fastener and spin the wheel. Phonics practice with two and three letter blends and digraphs may also be implemented using a wheel tachistoscope. Letter the blend or digraph on the wheel next to the brad fastener. Write word endings on the second wheel.

Additional Suggestions:

1. Use math facts

$$\begin{array}{cccc} 2 & 3 & 8 & 10 \\ +5 & +7 & -2 & -6 \end{array}$$

2. Use prefixes or suffixes for intermediate grades.

informal reading inventories

Descriptors: Decoding Skills
Comprehension Skills
Cumulative Reading Record

Grade Levels: 2–6
Resource Rooms

Rationale: Teachers often want to keep an ongoing record of each student's reading progress as measured by word recognition and comprehension. Since reading achievement tests are usually administered only at the end of the school year, whereas basal reading tests may only be administered after the completion of each book, daily or weekly informal assessment is more useful for determining current student progress. Such information may be the basis for review or reteaching of certain reading skills.

Level	Decoding	Comprehension
Independent	97% to 100%	90% to 100%
Instructional	93% to 96%	70% to 89%
Frustration	Below 93%	Below 70%

Objective: To enable teachers to design and implement informal reading inventories (IRI) for a daily or weekly assessment of students' word-recognition and reading-comprehension skills.

Materials: Basal readers (appropriate for each student's reading level)
Ditto master
Duplicating paper
Typewriter (or photocopy machine)
Pencil
Stopwatch (See Additional Suggestions)

Procedure:

1. Choose several 100-word selections from each story in the basal program. The selections may be typed on a ditto master or photocopied from the text. One consumable copy of the reading selection is required for each student. The student may read orally from the actual book with the 100-word segment to be read properly identified. Ten comprehension questions including facts, vocabulary, and literal and inferential meaning are typed at the bottom of each consumable page.

2. You may choose to have each student read one selection per week or may ask the students to read the 100-word selection from each story. The latter method requires more time if the student reads several stories per week. Finally, it may not be as useful as one weekly assessment.

3. As each student reads the 100-word selection aloud, record any errors on the consumable worksheet using the following guide:

Error	Mark	Definition
Substitutions	black b̀àçk	A student mispronounces an entire word or part of it, or substitutes another word.
Word pronounced for the student	P jockey	The examiner pronounces the unknown word for the student (after five seconds).
Insertions	Jane can ^not go	An extra word is added.
Omissions	Bob fell (down)	Words and/or punctuation are omitted.
Repetitions	Dad said, "Let's go."	Two or more words are repeated.

4. Count the number of word recognition errors recorded using the guide in step 3.

5. Calculate the percentage of word recognition (WR) accuracy by dividing the number of errors by the number of words in the reading selection. Multiply the answer by 100 for percent of error rate. Subtract the results from 100 percent to determine the accuracy rate.

Example: 102 words   4 errors

$$\begin{array}{r} .039 \\ 102\overline{\smash{)}4.000} \\ 306 \\ 940 \\ 918 \end{array} = 3.9 \text{ or } 4\%$$

$$\begin{array}{r} 100\% \\ -\ \ 4\% \\ \hline 96\% \end{array} = \text{error rate}$$
= word recognition accuracy.

A percent of 96 would indicate that the passage is at the student's instructional level. (See chart at the beginning of this activity.)

6. Record the word recognition accuracy percentage by the student's name on a class chart to keep a cumulative record. (See end of this activity.)

7. As each student completes the oral reading selection, ask the ten comprehension questions. Compute the percent of accuracy and record the information both on the individual consumable sheet and on the cumulative class record. It is important to note the type of comprehension questions missed by the student (factual, vocabulary, or inferential) in order to remediate consistent comprehension-error patterns. Example: Student missed two questions out of ten.

$$10\overline{)\begin{array}{c} .20 \\ 2.00 \end{array}} \qquad .20 \times 100 = 20\% \qquad \begin{array}{r} 100\% \\ -20\% \\ \hline 80\% \ \text{comprehension} \\ \text{accuracy.} \end{array}$$

A percent of 80 would place the reading material at the student's instructional level. (See chart at beginning of this activity.)

8. Check the results of the informal reading assessment to make certain that the students are consistently reading at their instructional level rather than frustrational (material is too difficult) or independent (material is too easy and perhaps not challenging enough for the student) level.

class chart: wr = word recognition   comp = comprehension

	Story 1		Story 2		Story 3	
	wr	comp	wr	comp	wr	comp
Joe	90%	80%				
Susan	95%	100%				
Harry	80%	90%				
Kay	100%	100%				

Additional Suggestions:

1. Time the students with a stopwatch and divide the number of words read by the number of seconds it took the student to read the selection. Multiply the answer by 60 to calculate the words per minute (wpm) rate.

Example: 200 words read in 20 seconds.

$$20\overline{)\begin{array}{c} 10.0 \\ 200.00 \end{array}} \qquad 10. \times 60 = 600 \ \text{wpm}$$

2. Choose 200-word rather than 100-word selections. Long passages make it easier to design ten comprehension questions.

decoding letter clusters

Descriptors: Sound/Symbol
Letter Groups
Remedial Reading

Grade Levels: 2–6

Rationale: Students without good decoding skills become poor readers. As students do not learn in the same way, teachers need to try different instructional techniques. The Glass Analysis[3] is a procedure by which decoding skills are taught separate from reading. Reading is here defined as dealing with word meaning, whereas decoding is considered the act of correctly determining the acceptable sound connected with the printed word.

Objective: To teach students how to decode words by identifying letter clusters.

Materials: Blank index cards
Black marking pen

[3] G.G. Glass and E.H. Burton, "How Do They Decode? Verbalizations and Observed Behaviors of Successful Decoders." *The Reading Teacher*, 26 (1973), 645.

Procedure: 1. The Glass Analysis technique consists of five steps.

> *1.* Whole word
> *2.* Give sound
> *3.* Give letters
> *4.* Take away letters
> *5.* Whole word

The teacher writes a word on the blank index card and presents it visually and auditorially to the students using the following procedure:

`nation`

a. Present the word card *nation*. Identify the whole word, the letters, and the sound of the target cluster. Say, "This word is nation. What is this word?" Spell the cluster, "We are going to learn the t/i/o/n sound that says *tion* (shun)."

b. Give the sound(s) and ask for the letter or letters. "In the word, *nation*, what letters make the *na* sound?" "In the word *nation*, what letters make the *tion* sound?"

c. Provide the letter or letters and ask for the sound(s). "In the word *nation*, what sound do the letters *na* make?" "In the word *nation*, what sound do the letters *tion* make?"

d. Take away the letters and ask for the remaining sounds. "If I took away the *na* letters, what sound would be left?" "If I took away the *tion* letters, what sound would be left?"

e. Ask for the whole word. "What is the whole word?"

2. Repeat steps a through e with other *tion* words such as creation or election.
3. The teacher must ensure that the students see the whole word without covering any parts of the word. Correct letter clustering must be seen with letters before and after it as in actual reading.
4. The teacher tells the students the word making certain that they look at the word at all times—not at the teacher.
   Glass emphasizes the following points:

a. Use words whose meaning the students understand. Teaching decoding is separate from teaching word meaning.

`nation`

b. Do *not* teach decoding out of the context of a word or sentence, or using pictures or drawings.

c. Words are seen first as wholes, then as parts. The parts are *letter clusters*, not separate letters.

d. Teach students correct visual and auditory *clustering* for decoding.

e. Learned correct mental sets cause the decoder to see and respond to appropriate letter-sound structures.

Additional Suggestions: To teach "at sight" decoding (reading in a book) use the following procedure:

a. The student orally reads from a book to gain practice in letter clustering with words met randomly. Start at a reading level where the student is able to decode correctly 90 percent or less of the words.

b. Decoding should be emphasized, not vocabulary, comprehension, or other nondecoding activities. If an unknown word occurs containing common letter clusters, the teacher asks what sounds the letters represent. If the student cannot identify the cluster, the teacher says it. If the student still cannot identify the word, the teacher says it and the student repeats it. If the word does not contain common clusters (*laugh* or *what*), the teacher simply voices the word.

oral reading repetitions

Descriptors: Word Analysis
Oral Reading
Repetitions

Grade Levels: 2–6

Rationale: Repetitions or regressions occur in reading when the student rereads words, phrases, or sentences. The cause of such repetitions may be poor word recognition, poor word analysis skills, or a bad habit. Students who repeat many words take longer to read assignments and may become socially ostracized in the classroom. If the problem stems from:

1. Poor word recognition—the student needs instruction and practice in basic sight words.
2. Poor word analysis—determine in what area the problem occurs: phonics, structural analysis, or use of context clues. Instruction in the specific area of weakness is necessary.
3. Bad habit—give the student reading material at his/her level and note the number of repetitions. Then give the student a much easier passage and note whether or not repetitions decrease. If the repetitions continue to occur at a high rate, the problem is probably a bad habit.

Objective: To eliminate a student's habit of repeating words during oral reading.

Procedure:
1. Help the student become aware of the repetitious behavior. Focus the student's attention on setting goals for smooth nonrepetitive reading.
2. Ask the student to use his/her hand as a pacer when reading. Have the student set a smooth, steady, rhythmic pace for the eyes to follow going left to right from margin to margin. The student is not pointing at words but is smoothly pacing the eyes across the page. Initially, you may need to use your own finger as a pacer to demonstrate the technique.

3. Have the student read into a tape recorder and then play it back for self-monitoring while looking at the reading material with you. The student is to listen for repetitions and underline them on a copy of the reading material if possible.
4. Have the student read orally with the teacher, an aide or another student (see *Neurological Impress Method* activity).
5. Have the student read aloud along with a tape recording of the reading passage. (The teacher, aide, parent volunteer, or student peer can record the material on cassettes. Some commercial materials provide tape recordings for poor or nonreaders.)
6. Use easier or more familiar material so that difficult vocabulary is not a problem.
7. Recognize the student's improvement with praise and encouragement. Example, "You're doing better. Yesterday there were five repetitions. Today, only three!"
8. Design a progress graph. Record the number of repetitions in three-minute time limits. Have the student graph daily progress. Increase the difficulty of the material as regression errors are eliminated.

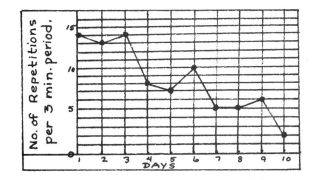

**Additional
Suggestions:**   1. Use a controlled reading machine that structures the reading, sets a pace, and prevents regressive eye movements. Start at a slow pace so that the student does not become frustrated. Be sure the pace does not exceed the student's normal reading rate.

The boy is si⟩

2. Ask the student to read simple stories to younger students in kindergarten or first grade as the student gains more confidence.

neurological impress method

Descriptors: Oral Fluency   **Grade Levels:**   2–6+
Multisensory Approach to Reading

Rationale: Many poor readers suffer from poor oral fluency and erratic eye movements when reading. Such characteristics may cause erroneous comprehension as well as a dislike for both oral and silent reading. The Neurological Impress Method (NIM) by R. G. Heckelman,[4, 5] uses a multisensory approach to reading and is most effective when used in one-to-one tutoring sessions. Although sometimes tiring for both the instructor and the student initially, this method has been used successfully with many students with poor oral fluency. The major concern is with the style of reading, rather than with reading accuracy. One of the reasons for the success of the NIM appears to be due to the enormous exposure students have to words.

Objective: To increase the student's oral fluency as measured by number of words read per minute (words/minute).
(Note: Begin with reading material at the student's independent reading level—99 percent accuracy in word pronunciation with 90 percent comprehension—and gradually introduce the student to more difficult reading material. Choose reading materials that are interesting to the student.)

Materials: Reading material
Stopwatch
Photocopy of three 200-word reading selections

[4] R. G. Heckelman, "Using the Neurological Impress Reading Technique," in *Solutions to Reading Problems* (Novato, Calif.: Academic Therapy Publications, 1978), pp. 28–32.
[5] R. G. Heckelman, "Using the Neurological Impress Remedial Reading Technique," *Academic Therapy*, 1, no. 4 (1966), pp. 235–39.

Procedure:

1. The teacher asks the student to read aloud a selection of 200 words in the book selected for NIM instruction. On a photocopy of the same passage, the number and type of reading errors made by the student as well as the oral reading speed as measured by a stopwatch are recorded. The total number of words in the passage is divided by the number of seconds it took the student to read the passage. The result is multiplied by 60 to determine the words/minute rate.

Example:

$$5 \times 60 = 300 \text{ wpm}$$
$$40 \overline{\smash{\big)}\, 200 \text{ (words)}}$$
$$\text{(sec)}$$

2. The student is seated slightly in front of the teacher so that the teacher's voice is close to the student's ear. The teacher and the student read the same material out loud together. The teacher sets the pace by underlining the spoken words with a finger and synchronizing the voice with the pace of the finger.
3. The student is urged to read while ignoring any mistakes. At no time during the reading does the teacher ask any questions or resort to any form of testing to determine whether the student is mastering the words in terms of word recognition or comprehension.
4. The daily sessions should last approximately fifteen minutes and take place consecutively for a total of eight to twelve hours (thirty-two to forty-eight daily sessions or six to nine weeks of five days/week).
5. The pace of the oral reading should be periodically increased to force the student to achieve higher reading rates This is done only for a few minutes at a time but should become part of each session.
6. The teacher and the student reread the initial lines or paragraphs several times together until a fluid, normal reading pattern is established. In most cases two to three minutes of repetitious patterning is sufficient. At this point more reading material may be introduced.
7. After four hours (sixteen daily sessions) of the Neurological Impress Method of oral reading instruction, the teacher assesses the student's progress by repeating step 1 using a new 200-word selection. Again, the teacher records the number and type of word errors plus the reading rate in words per minute. If the student has made little progress toward meeting the teacher-determined criterion (Example: 15 percent increase in reading speed), either the criterion or the reading material may need to be adjusted to kinesthetic or motor methods. Care must be taken by teachers to try not to push students beyond their intelligence-expectancy grade level in using the NIM.
8. Reassess in the same manner again at the end of eight hours (thirty-two sessions) of NIM instruction to determine whether or not to continue for forty-eight sessions.

Additional Suggestions:

1. A parent or aide may be taught to use the NIM. It is important that the sessions be consistent and consecutive for maximum efficiency.
2. The NIM can be used in a group setting. Students are equipped with earphones and the teacher uses a microphone and overhead projector that projects his/her finger as a "pacer." When using the NIM in a group situation, it must be remembered that this instructional method cannot easily be adjusted to the individual needs of the students. Consequently, the instruction may become frustrating to the students as the pace may be too fast for some, while too slow for others. (Note: Particular attention must be paid to the ending of the lines when the finger must move very rapidly back to the beginning of the next line. Since many students read poorly due to poor erratic eye movement, finger movement, voice, and words must all be synchronized.

prefixes and suffixes

Descriptors: Prefixes
                     Suffixes

Grade Levels: 3–6

un able   cupful

Rationale: Many students have difficulty understanding the concept of prefixes and suffixes. The first step in helping to remediate this problem is to provide the student with a definition of the terms.

Objective: To teach students the meanings of prefixes and suffixes and how to read or write them using worksheets and practice aids. (Note: Lists of prefixes and suffixes are provided at the end of this teaching idea.)

Materials: Tagboard
Red and black marking pens
Scissors
Ditto masters
Duplicating paper
Brass fastener

Procedure: 1. Teach students the meaning of prefix and suffix.
2. A *prefix* is a letter or several letters added to the beginning of a root word to change the meaning of the word.
3. A *suffix* is a letter or group of letters added to the end of a root word to change the meaning of the word.

Activity 1: Word Wheels

Procedure: 1. Cut two circles with a 6-inch diameter.

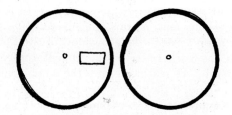

2. Cut a 1½″ × ½″ window in #1, type or print the root words on #2.

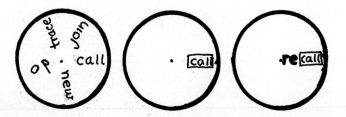

3. Attach the two circles with a fastener. Word wheels may be adapted to teach suffixes in the same manner.

Activity 2: Color-Coded Words

Procedure: Write a list of words with prefixes and suffixes for the student to practice. Prefixes are written in *red*, the root word in *black*, and the suffixes are written in *blue*. This helps the student to see the individual word parts via color cues. The color cues can be faded and finally completely removed as the prefixes and suffixes are mastered.

Activity 3: Word Cards

Procedure: Tagboard 3″ × 6″ word cards may be used for practicing prefixes and suffixes. Fold the card after the prefix or before the suffix so that the child can see the separation of the root word from the affixes. The prefix and suffix will be written on the back of the card.

Activity 4: Practice Exercises

Procedure: Have the student write the correct word in a sentence to fit the meaning of the words in parentheses. Examples:

> ly   mis   un
>
> The teacher said to _____ (not cover) the papers.
>
> The spelling words must not be _____ (spelled wrong).
>
> Sports cars raced _____ (in a smooth manner) on the track.

Additional Suggestions: Make a chart for each suffix and prefix that you plan to teach. These charts show the meaning and the use of a prefix or suffix in several words.

> **un – not**
> unable
> unarmed
> unlike
> unbroken

> **ful – full of**
> cheerful
> wonderful
> painful
> awful

The prefixes and suffixes on the charts may be color-coded to aid learning.

PREFIXES

ad	to; toward; near	inter	between
anti	against	intra, intro	into; within; inward
be	about; near, make	ir	not
bi	two; double	mis	wrong; bad
co	with; together	multi	many
com	with; together	non	not; without
con	with; together	ob, op	toward; against
de	from; down	out	outside; more than
dis	not; apart	per	through
du, duo	two	post	behind; after
em	in	pre	before
en	in; into; on	pro	forward; in favor of
ex	out; out of	re	back; again
for	away; against	semi	half
fore	before; in front of	sub	under; lower
il	not; into	trans	across; through
im	not; into	ultra	beyond; exceedingly
in	into; not	un	not; negative

SUFFIXES

able	capable of	ical	like; related to
age	act of; state of	ion	act of; state of
al	relating to	ish	like; similar to
an	relating to	ism	act; belief in; result of
ance	state of; act of; process of	ist	one who
ar	related to; one who	ity	state; character; condition
ate	make; do	ive	having the quality of
eer	one who	ize	cause; make; become
en	to make; made of; past time; plural of	less	without
		ly	like
er	one who; that which	ment	result
ess	feminine ending	ness	state or condition
est	most; superlative	or	agent; doer
ful	full of	ory	relating to; used for
fy	full of	ous	full of
fy	make; cause	tion	act of; state of
hood	condition of; quality of	tude	quality of
ial	pertaining to	ty	quality of; state of
ian	relating to; belonging to	ure	result of an action; process; being
ible	capable of being		
ic	connected with	ward	direction; course

_____the cloze readability procedure_____

Descriptors: Readability Formula   **Grade Levels:**   3–6
                   Group Assessment

Rationale: To save time, it may sometimes be desirable to administer a group test to assess the readability levels of a group of students rather than having each student read individually. The procedure may also be used to ascertain whether a new student understands a social studies or science text, for example. The teacher may construct a test on a given book ahead of time and use it when necessary.

Objective: To teach a teacher to use a Cloze[6] test procedure to determine a student's independent, instructional, and frustration level of reading comprehension.

Materials: Textbook with publisher's suggested grade level (for example, social studies, science)
Ditto master
Duplicating paper
Pencil

Procedure:
1. The teacher chooses a selection of approximately 150 words from the middle section of a textbook and rewrites the passage on a ditto master deleting every fifth word.
2. The student reads the passage and fills in the missing words using context clues.
3. The teacher scores the text by counting as wrong every incorrect word. The exact words may be read aloud by the teacher and scored by the students. The *exact* word must be used in the blank. Synonyms are not counted as correct.
4. The percentage correct is computed by dividing the number of correct responses by the total number of blanks in the passage of 150 words.

_____

[6]A. Burrow and A. Claybaugh, *Basic Concepts in Reading Instruction* (Columbus, Ohio: Charles E. Merrill, 1972).

Example:

.30 or 30% correct

30 |¯10.00
(blanks)   (correct
           responses)

5. The formula 50 - 30 - 20 is important: 50 percent corresponds to an *independent* level; 30 percent corresponds to an *instructional* level; 20 percent corresponds to a *frustration* level. Thus, if the social studies text was identified as being at fifth-grade level and the student scored 30 percent correct on the test, the student's instructional level is fifth grade. If the student had scored 20 percent (frustration level), the fifth-grade book would clearly be too difficult. A lower level text must be chosen instead or the curriculum must be adapted. Example: Recording the material to allow the student to listen to it, or asking an aide to read the fifth-grade material to the student.

6. After determining each student's reading level for a particular text, the teacher may proceed to plan the correct curriculum for the class.

(Note: A tightly written text obviously loses much comprehensibility. The latter would signify a less difficult "readability" level. Since The Cloze test is often very frustrating to students, the teacher should acknowledge this and remind them that they can miss 50 percent of the words and still score at an independent readability level.)

Additional Suggestions:

1. Use the *Informal Reading Inventory* (IRI) technique as described in this book to determine each student's readability level.
2. Use other formulas: Fry, Spache, and Dale-Chall (see the remedial reading teacher in your school district for further details).
3. Use passages from books at several grade levels. Example: If a student demonstrates a *frustration* level using the fifth-grade textbook, the teacher cannot assume that the next lower level (fourth grade) is automatically appropriate. The lower level may also be too difficult. Thus, passages from several textbooks may be necessary to determine an accurate readability level for each student.

CLOZE TEST:

As festival time grew _____, John was very busy. _____ practicing with the school

_____, he had to train _____ dog to pull the _____ he had made. The

_____, made from a wooden _____ and the wheels of _____ old roller skate,

would _____ a doll dressed in _____ Dutch costume.... and so on.

Level: fifth grade

_____**prolonged silent reading**_____

Descriptors: Independent Reading   **Grade Levels:** 3–6
Recreational Reading

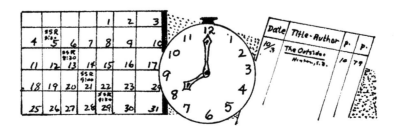

Rationale: Many students never have time to read for pleasure without interruption. This is especially true of slower readers who need more time to complete regular assignments and, thus, rarely find much time for recreational reading during class time. "Prolonged silent reading" (PSR) time is designed to provide *every* student with an opportunity to read without interruption for a specific length of time.

Objective: To provide students an opportunity to read silently for thirty minutes per week.

Materials: Multilevel trade books (appropriate for each student's reading level)
Clock
Ditto master with a log book
Duplicating paper (for student logbook, for each student)
Pencil or pen

Procedure:

1. Explain that a thirty-minute period each week will be planned to enable all students to read a book of their choice without interruption.
2. Pass out a dittoed logbook page to each student. Explain that at the end of each thirty-minute period the student must record the date, title, author of the book, page started, and page ended in the logbook.
3. Decide with the students which weekly thirty-minute period is the most appropriate.
4. Ask each student to choose a book from the library. (Note: The teacher must make sure that each student's book is at the student's reading level.)
5. Advise the students that the signal to begin reading will be given by the teacher or a student. The classroom clock is used as a guide.
6. Ask the students to remain seated and read silently until signaled to stop.
7. At the end of the weekly PSR time, students record their individual reading data in a logbook (see step 2).
8. Provide time for the students to share ideas or reactions to their reading material.

Additional Suggestions:

1. Nonreaders or poor readers may listen to a story record through earphones while reading silently in their book.
2. Students who are assigned book reports may use PSR time to read such books.
3. The teacher should also use PSR time for recreational reading rather than grading of papers, and so on, thereby providing an adult model for good reading experiences.
4. The entire school population might plan a weekly PSR time with the signal to begin and end announced over the school intercom.

"tell back" procedure

Descriptors: Reading Comprehension
Verbal Expression

Grade Levels: 3–6

Rationale: Many students have difficulty concentrating when they read silently. Others cannot remember or verbally describe what they have read. The "tell back" procedure requires students to read a selection and then summarize it by "telling it back" to the teacher using a list of *wh* questions as a guide.

Objective: To establish a specific purpose for students' silent reading in order to improve reading comprehension, recall, mental organization, and verbalization of reading materials.

Materials: Reading selections from short stories, commercial reading labs, or reading skill cards, preferably with illustrations at the student's independent reading level (99 percent word recognition; 90 percent comprehension)

24″ × 36″ tagboard
Black marking pen
Ditto master
Duplicating paper
Individual record forms
Chalkboard and chalk (optional)

Procedure:

1. The teacher prepares a list of *wh* questions on the chalkboard or on a large 24″ × 36″ tagboard chart.

   What is this story about?
   Who is in it?
   Where does it take place?
   What happens?
   When did it happen?
   Why did it happen?

   The teacher reads the list aloud to the students who are told that they are to read the assignment to answer the six questions.
2. A dittoed copy of the six *wh* questions is given to each student for personal references as needed.
3. The students are advised to first read the title of the reading selection, then to look at the illustrations, and finally to read the first sentence and the last paragraph.
4. The teacher may say, "As you read the story, think of answers to the six *wh* questions on the list. Try to visualize in your mind who is there, where they are, and what they are doing. After reading the story and finding the answers to the questions, I want you to tell me the story you have just read."
5. The students are allowed time to read their independent reading selections and to "tell back" the story to the teacher.
6. The teacher evaluates the stories by determining whether the student answered the six *wh* questions; included the main ideas and details of the story; and told the story sequentially.
7. The teacher provides positive feedback to the students at the end of each "tell back" session at which time suggestions for improvement may be offered. Individual student records may be kept of the title of each reading passage. (Note: Students need repeated practice with the lessons to develop good reading comprehension and verbal recall skills. Finally, the teacher needs to be familiar with the reading material to evaluate the verbal sessions.)

Additional Suggestions:

1. The teacher may decide to limit the "tell back" sessions to three or five minutes. With shorter time limits the student develops greater skill in extracting the important facts and main ideas of the reading passage. An egg timer or a stopwatch may be used for a visual record of the length of time allowed.

_____**hard and soft g words**_____

Descriptors: Decoding   **Grade Levels:** 4–6
                     Phonics
                     Sight Words

Rationale: The phonetic rule for the hard and soft *g* sound in words is often taught without sufficient opportunities for students to practice. Thus, many students have difficulty decoding initial and medial *g* sounds. This activity is designed to provide students practice reading words containing hard and soft *g* sounds.

Objective: To provide students with word categorization practice for hard and soft *g* sounds.

Materials: 11″ × 20″ colored construction paper
Black marking pen
Blank index cards—30 (or more as needed)
Bulletin board and thumbacks
Scissors

Procedure:
1. Cut two houses out of light colored construction paper and pin them to the bulletin board.
2. Using the colored construction paper, draw and cut out two figures—one male and one female. Place one by each house and label the female figure's house "Gayle's House," the male figure's house "George's House."
3. Write thirty hard and soft *g* sound words on the blank index cards and mix them together in a word pile.
4. Review the phonetic rule for the hard and soft *g* sound with the students ("When *g* is followed by *e, i,* or *y,* it has a soft sound"). Explain that George's house is supposed to hold the soft "g" sound words (like George), where as Gayle's house is to hold the hard *g* sound words (like Gayle).
5. Two to four students take turns drawing word cards from the word pile. Each student reads the word card aloud and pins it to the appropriate hard or soft *g* sound house.
6. The other students must decide whether or not the word is placed correctly. If correct, the student earns one point. If incorrect, the word card is removed and reshuffled in the pile. The student earns no points.
7. The points are tallied for each student when all cards have been pinned to the bulletin board. The student with the highest number of points wins.

Additional Suggestions:
1. Provide a blank dittoed sheet of the figures and the hard and soft *g* houses. Ask the students to write as many words as possible on the correct house. They may use dictionaries if necessary.
2. Draw two pairs of *g* houses on the chalkboard (one set for each team). Divide the class into two relay teams. At the Go signal, one student from each team runs to the chalkboard and writes a *g* word in either the soft or the hard *g* house. When finished, the student runs back to his/her seat and the next student continues in the same manner. One point is scored for each correct answer. The team finishing first gains three extra points. The team with the highest number of points wins the relay.

3. Follow the same procedure to practice hard and soft *c* words. Example: Cyrus's House   Carol's House

George's House

gentle   strange
ginger   stranger
angel   gem
cage   magic
courage   tragic
agent   gym
danger   giraffe

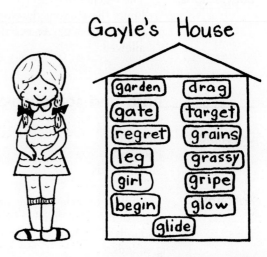

Gayle's House

garden   drag
gate   target
regret   grains
leg   grassy
girl   gripe
begin   glow
glide

Descriptors: Reading Skills
Compound Words
Motivation

Grade Levels: 4–6

Rationale: Learning compound words is part of the curriculum in all intermediate schools. This activity makes learning such words more fun by illustrating them in booklet form.

Objective: To enable the student to identify the two words that make up compound words.

Materials: 12″ × 18″ pieces of colored construction paper
Pencils
Colored flair markers or crayons

Procedure
1. Have each student choose a piece of 12″ × 18″ colored construction paper. Draw a very light pencil line in the middle (9 inches from edge). Fold both outside edges in to touch the pencil line.

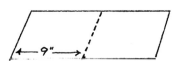

   This forms a "booklet" that opens to the full page.
2. Instruct the students to "close up" the booklet and write on the outside the following: "Did you ever see a".

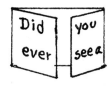 

3. Each student chooses a compound word that can be the basis for a humorous picture when the two words are separated. Suggestions are

milkshake	bridgework	hatband	iceskate
eardrum	offhand	catfish	windmill
horsefly	snapshot	lunchbox	sawmill
sidestep	overalls	antibody	earring
doorway			

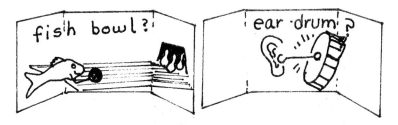

Additional Suggestions:
1. Create an exhibit of illustrated compound words for the school library.
2. Ask the students to write short paragraphs including as many compound words as possible. The paragraphs may be read aloud to the class or posted on the bulletin board.

Descriptors: Reading Comprehension   **Grade Levels:** 4–6
Independent Reading

Rationale: Many intermediate-level students may know how to decode reading material but have not yet mastered efficient methods of reading assigned chapters for specific information. Although some students automatically learn how to implement study skills, others need specific instruction. This activity may be used as a guideline for improving study skills. Such skills become particularly important to students as they progress into junior and senior high school.

Objective: To teach students how to preview a chapter of content area reading material (for example, history, social studies, science) in order to learn efficient study skills.

Materials: Notebook paper
Pencil or pen
Reading material

Procedure: This previewing method requires the following steps:
1. *Table of contents.* Read over the table of contents to get an idea of what the book is about and to understand the relation of your topic or assignment to the rest of the book.
2. *Preliminary outline.* Look over the section headings and make a short outline or list of the headings that are usually printed in darker ink or in larger type.
3. *First and last paragraphs.* Read the first and last paragraphs of the assigned chapter, being certain to review the section headings again.
4. *Pictorial aids.* Study the pictorial aids such as maps, charts, graphs, pictures, and read what is printed underneath.
5. *Inventory.* "Inventory" the information you have just read by asking the following questions: What have I found out about this chapter? and What do I know at this point? You will be pleasantly surprised to discover you already know a lot.
6. *Read/study.* Now you are ready to read/study the chapter.

**Additional
Suggestions:**   1. Review the outline (step 2) after reading and studying the assigned chapter.
2. Divide the class into small groups. Appoint a temporary leader for each group who will lead a discussion about the material read. Students who have better auditory than visual skills may benefit more from the oral discussion than from reading the chapter independently. The discussions also help provide a forum for comparing students' understanding of the material with others who have read the same assignment.

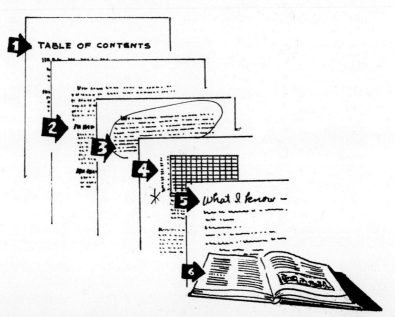

Descriptors: Reading Comprehension
Language Arts
Getting the "Main Idea"

Grade Levels: 4–6
Resource Room

Rationale: Since all students are exposed to newspapers, the use of word puzzles, cartoons, and departmental columns from the daily paper is helpful for teaching youngsters better reading, writing, and general language skills. This activity focuses students' attention on the local newspaper and creates interest in learning.

Objective: To teach students how to use the language, purpose, and general organization of their local newspaper to improve their own reading and writing skills.

Materials: Local newspapers
Paper and pencil
5″ × 7″ blank index cards
Black marking pen
12″ × 18″ colored construction paper
Stapler and staples
Scissors
Regular white business envelopes

Activity 1: Junior Jumble

Procedure:
1. If the local newspaper publishes a word puzzle, the teacher may show it to the students and ask the following questions:
   "What does the word *jumble* mean?"
   "What would a "Junior Jumble" be?"
   "What would you need to know to be able to work a "Junior Jumble"?"
2. Initially, the teacher introduces each jumbled word individually by writing it on the chalkboard.

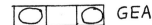 GEA

3. Individual letter cards may be used to help students arrange the letters in different combinations before writing the letters in the spaces provided by the jumble.
4. When all the words are unscrambled, the circled letters must be rearranged to solve a puzzle. The activity may be carried out by the entire class or by small groups who later compare answers. Since a subsequent edition of the newspaper will print the correct answer, the students are stimulated to watch for the answers as well as a new puzzle.

Activity 2: Cartoon Capers

Family-oriented cartoons (such as "Family Circus") are an excellent way of introducing new vocabulary and inferential thinking skills to students.

Procedure:
1. The teacher presents the cartoon to the students and asks specific questions about the picture designed to lead them to the correct conclusions about the cartoon.
   "What time of day is it?"
   "Where are the children playing?"
   "What are they doing?"
   "What did Jeff say?"
   "What do you think happened next?"
2. Students may answer the questions in large- or small-group settings.

Additional Suggestions: Cartoons may be passed around the class in envelopes. Students are asked to write down the meaning conveyed by each cartoon. Answers may be graded by the teacher and later used as a focal point for a class discussion.

Activity 3: Headlines

This activity aids students in learning to summarize the contents of a news article by asking them to design a headline describing it.

Procedure:
1. The teacher cuts out brief articles from the local newspaper and removes the headlines.
2. The articles (minus headlines) are pasted on separate, individually numbered cards.
3. Answer cards are designed by the teacher who pastes the individual headlines on cards numbered to match the articles.
4. After reading the article cards, students write appropriate titles for each on notebook paper.
5. On completion of all articles, students may check their answers against the actual headline cards.
6. To complete the activity, the teacher should discuss with the class how individual students arrived at their headlines, for example, what to look for.

Activity 4: Newspaper Mini-Units

The following mini-units are developed by using the different newspaper departments, columns and services, such as weather forecast, want ads, "quotable quotes," editorials, political cartoons, personal advice columns, book reviews, and travel news.

Procedure:
1. Folders are made by folding 12″ × 18″ colored construction paper in half (12″ × 9″). The bottom edge should be folded up 2 inches and stapled in the middle and at both ends to form two pockets.
2. The teacher pastes newspaper clippings from one category on 5″ × 7″ index cards and places three or five of them in a folder labeled with the appropriate category. Example: World News, or Food.
3. The teacher adds a study card to each folder containing guide questions about the category. These questions can only be answered after reading the clippings in the mini-unit folder.
4. Blank response sheets are also included on which students are to write their answers to the study card questions.
5. Finally, an answer card is included for self-correction by the student who is asked to compare written answers on the response sheet to those on the teacher's answer card.

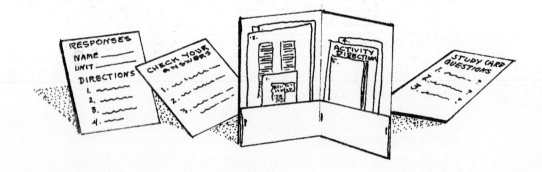

Additional Suggestions: For variation, use the school newspaper or commercial magazines designed for specific grade levels (for example, *Scholastic*).

_____dictionary skills_____

Descriptors: Guide Words   **Grade Levels:**   4–6
                     Entry Word
                     Key Word Meaning

Rationale: Efficient dictionary skills are very important to intermediate-level students who need quick retrieval of information in order to complete assignments.

Objective: To enable students to locate the answer quickly to a given question by teaching the use of guide words, entry words, and key words.

Materials: Dictionary for each student
                     A collection of questions, each printed on separate cards

Procedure: 1. Divide the students into two teams, each consisting of three to five students.
                 2. Each student has a dictionary, closed, on the table in front of him/her.
                 3. The teacher reads the question.
                 4. When the teacher lays the card containing the question on the table, it is the signal for the students to open their dictionaries to find the answer.
                 5. Students on both teams must find the answer to the question by pointing to the key word in the definition on the appropriate dictionary page. The teacher must approve the correct answer.
                 6. The team whose members all find the correct answer first is the winner and scores a point.
                 7. Each member of the winning team takes turns reading the answer aloud.
                 8. Students may not help each other because the goal is to practice independent dictionary skills.

The following are examples of questions:

   1. Is a *pike* a bird, a fish, or a person?
   2. Is an *arena* a person, a building, or an animal?
   3. Is a *gale* a girl, an animal, or a strong wind?
   4. Is a *prank* a jewel, a trick, or a building?
   5. Is an *imitation* a trick, a copy, or a strong wind?
   6. Is a *vision* a dream, an animal, or a building?
   7. Is a *desert* sweets at the end of a meal, a building, or a region without water? (Write *desert* on the board; do not pronounce it.)
   8. Does *vacant* mean to build, empty, or valuable?
   9. Is a *code* a building, a system of secret writing, or a witch?
  10. Does *scrawny* mean skinny, fat, or tall?
  11. Is a *nugget* an apple, a valuable lump, or a dog?
  12. Is *gravel* fruit, fish, or pebbles?
  13. What does *etc.* stand for?
  14. What does *U.S.A.* stand for?
  15. What does *N.W.* stand for?
  16. What is the plural of *wife*?

17. What is the plural of *leaf*?
18. Is *gruel* an animal, a food, or a chemical?
19. Is a *pagoda* a bird, a building, or a person?
20. Is a *pallet* soup, clothing, or a bed?
21. Is a *constellation* a group of boys, a herd of cattle, or a group of stars?
22. Is an *omelet* clothing, furniture, or food?
23. Does *unique* mean without cola, always the same, or only one of a kind?
24. Is a *biography* a story of a person's life, a country's history, or a fairy tale?
25. Does *elongated* mean to get longer, get shorter, or get fatter?

The list of questions is unlimited. Make up questions to fit whatever topics have been studied.

Additional Suggestions: As a variation, shuffle the cards and deal four cards to each student. The students will find the answers for each question in the dictionary and write the correct answers on their paper. Again, the teacher checks the answers.

BEAT THE CLOCK

Using the above procedure, set a timer after the last card is dealt. Any student who answers the questions correctly before the timer rings will receive extra bonus points as an added incentive. Example: One point for each correct answer. Double the points if the student beats the clock.

integration of nonreaders into regular reading groups

Descriptors: Self-Image
Auditory Learning
Mainstreaming

Grade Levels: 4–6
Learning Disabled

Rationale: Students with very low reading skills often do not fit into the existing reading groups in a classroom and, therefore, receive all reading instruction individually from the regular teacher or in a resource room. Such youngsters may become socially isolated from the other students if they are never included in the more traditional reading activities. Despite poor reading skills, these students can benefit from hearing stories, discussions, and vocabulary exercises presented in regular reading groups. They may understand the meaning of language concepts presented in the grade level reading curriculum without being able to recognize such words in print. This activity allows such students to join the traditional reading groups within the regular classroom.

Objective: To mainstream a nonreader into regular reading groups within the classroom.

Materials: Basal reading books
Tape recorder
Blank cassette tapes

Procedure:
1. The teacher identifies the students who find reading frustrating at any level and explains that they may join the reading group (or groups) of their choice.
2. The student may rotate between groups depending on the skill or concept being presented, or just for positive peer interaction.
3. The student may listen to the story read aloud by other group members and may take part in the ensuing discussion without being expected to complete written work (workbooks) or to read aloud.

(Note: The nonreader's interest in learning new skills and concepts tends to become highly stimulated by this activity.)

Additional Suggestions:

1. The teacher tape records the story and allows the nonreader to listen to the tape while the other students read the story silently during seatwork assignments. Verbal questions may be recorded to which the student is asked to record appropriate tape-recorded answers. The teacher checks the taped answers at a later time.
2. The teacher assigns a peer tutor to read the story aloud while the nonreading student follows along using a finger as a pacer (see Neurological Impress Method activity).

oral book reports

Descriptors:
Creativity
Poor Writing Skills
Positive Self-Image

Grade Levels: 4–6
Resource Room
Special Education

Rationale: Many students described as "reluctant" or poor readers are resistant to reading library books because they are required to write grammatically correct written reports on completion of the book. Such students may be stimulated to read more books when oral reports are assigned. While allowing the student an alternate way of reporting on a book and thus giving the teacher a better impression of the student's reading and comprehension skills, this activity also helps to improve a student's self-image.

Objective: To describe alternative methods for giving book reports.

Materials:
Library trade books
Tagboard
Blank index cards
Notebook paper
Scrapbook
Paste
Scissors
Pencil

Activity 1: Academy Awards

Procedure:

1. The teacher asks the students to nominate their favorite books based on those they have read or have heard described during class discussions.
2. The teacher or a student lists the top ten nominations on the chalkboard and asks the students to vote for their favorite on a secret ballot. The second-, third-, fourth-, and fifty-place books will be chosen as runners' up.
3. The students may design a bulletin board featuring the five most popular books. The display may include book jackets along with a short synopsis of each book written on index cards and pinned beneath each book jacket.
4. The students count the votes and the winner is announced at the end of the day.

(Note: This activity stimulates the students' interest in reading other popular books besides creating excitement over the anticipated outcome of the nominations.)

Activity 2: Quiz Show

Procedure:

1. The teacher explains that the class is going to produce a quiz show similar to the popular television shows, "What's My Line?" or "Twenty Questions."
2. Students are asked to read their books, which are later discussed in class as oral book reports.
3. The students are asked to choose a favorite character from their story for the quiz show activity.
4. Each student has a turn at pretending to be a particular character while the class tries to determine who the character is by asking questions that may only be answered by a yes or no. Examples might be, "Are you an athlete? Do you live in the United States? Are you a rock singer?"
5. A limit of twenty questions is set. If the class is unable to guess the correct character within twenty questions, the correct answer is given.

ADAPTATIONS:

a) Set a time limit using an egg timer rather than a question limit. This makes the game much faster.
b) Play charades by silently acting out an important scene from the book.
c) Ask the students to create a costume to wear to class. The costumes alone provide the clues to the book title.
d) If time is limited, the quiz show may be used with small groups implementing the activity simultaneously.

Activity 3: Scrapbooks

Procedure:

1. The students may make a scrapbook about the book they have just read. If the book is fictional, appropriate pictures may be chosen. If the book is about a famous living person, the student may cut out newspaper and magazine articles and pictures to add to the scrapbook.
2. Students may briefly describe their scrapbooks during a class discussion.
3. All scrapbooks may be placed on a library table where the students can look through them during free class time.

(Note: This activity also stimulates students to read other library books.)

ADAPTATIONS:

a) Other classes may be invited to visit the classroom library table or the scrapbooks may be loaned to other classes for a specific period of time.
b) The scrapbooks may be displayed in the school library for the benefit of the entire school.

Additional Suggestions:

1. Students may draw or paint a poster depicting an event from the life of the person about whom they read. The posters may be displayed in the school library, or the hall bulletin board, on hallway walls or in the cafeteria.
2. Several students may design a short skit called "Guess Who?" based on a book character whose identity the other students are asked to guess.
3. Musically talented students may compose or perform a song about a favorite book character. The songs may be tape recorded and later played for the entire class.
4. The class may be turned into a book store where each student becomes a book salesman and takes turns trying to "sell" his/her book to the other students by sharing short, appealing sections of the book.
5. The book reports may represent a small-group effort as skits or radio shows are planned around the theme of a book. Appropriate background music may be played during the oral report. Example: Rock music if the book is about a rock star, or basketball or football background noise (recorded from an actual television or radio sportscast) if the book deals with a sports hero.

Descriptors: Low Reading Skills
                   Sight Vocabulary

Grade Levels: Intermediate–Jr./Sr.
                       High School
                       Learning Centers
                       Remedial Reading Class

Rationale: Some older students are so seriously retarded in reading that there is little chance of their ever using reading for anything but the most essential tasks. Such students learn best through auditory channels, such as listening to lectures, tapes, videotapes. In terms of reading, they profit most from sight-vocabulary instruction directed toward survival in society. The students involved in a reading "survival" program are not normally placed in other types of reading situations. Goals for these students must be short and realistic.

   The following are basic guidelines for a survival program:

   a. The program should enable students to learn as much as possible via listening, pictures, and demonstrations.
   b. Text assignments should be read orally or taped for the student.
   c. Tests should also be read to the student or recorded on tape.
   d. Essential vocabulary is taught using the visual, whole-word approach.

Objective: To teach very poor readers survival vocabulary words using a visual, whole-word approach.

Materials: 3½″ × 5″
                 Black marking pen
                 Chosen at discretion of the teacher:
                    Driver's manual
                    Road signs
                    Menus
                    Television listings
                    Essential vocabulary list (included in this activity)
                    Occupational sight words in an area of interest
                    Newspaper ads
                    Employment contracts
                    Income tax forms
                    Social Security forms
                    Newspaper headlines
                    Telephone books

Procedure: 1. Print the words to be learned on cards having the word on one side and a picture on the reverse side.
   2. Point to the first picture and matching word and pronounce it for the student.
   3. Ask the student to use the word in a sentence (if unable to do so, use it in a sentence for demonstration purposes).
   4. Ask the student to look at the word; see if s/he notices anything about it that would help to remember it (such as double letters, length of word).
   5. Have the student say the word again.

6. Create a pictorial chart of survival words on one topic. Example: Road signs.
7. Review the learned word cards daily using flashcards and picture charts. Flash the words without picture clues as the student becomes more confident.

Additional Suggestions:

1. Plan displays of important survival words on colorful picture charts for the library.
2. Allow older students to teach primary students some of the survival words using charts and flashcards.
3. Group the survival words according to *places* where they occur, *people* to whom they apply, or *circumstances* under which they will be seen. Teach the words that have some relationship to the student. Example:

PLACES

The teacher says, "Today we are going to imagine ourselves going to buy gas at the service station. On our way there, we will see many signs giving us directions." (Introduce signs.)

Ask Attendant for Key
Do Not Block Drive
Employees Only
Exit
No Smoking

a. Print the words on 5″ × 7″ index cards and attach to a drawing of a service station on a board or felt board just as they might be found in a daily situation.
b. Read the word for the student, then ask the student to read the word by sight. Cover the word and ask the student to remember what word was just read. Repeat the procedure until the student is reading the sign at sight.
c. Remove the sign from the picture of the service station on the felt board or chalkboard and ask the student to choose that word from a pile of various signs, and to place it on the drawing in the appropriate place.
d. Have the students enact a role-playing activity where they assume the roles of various service station attendants and consumers, using the signs to communicate information to each other.

ESSENTIAL VOCABULARY LIST

ADULTS ONLY	DEAD END	ELEVATOR
ALL CARS (TRUCKS) STOP	DEEP WATER	EMERGENCY
AMBULANCE	DEER (CATTLE) CROSSING	EMERGENCY EXIT
ANTIDOTE	DELAYED GREEN	EMPLOYEES ONLY
ASK ATTENDANT FOR KEY	DENTIST	END 45
	DETOUR	END CONSTRUCTION
BEWARE	DIM LIGHTS	ENTRANCE
BEWARE OF CROSS WINDS	DIP	EXIT
BEWARE OF THE DOG	DOCTOR (DR.)	EXIT ONLY
BRIDGE OUT	DO NOT BLOCK WALK (DRIVE)	EXIT SPEED 30
BUS ONLY	DO NOT CROSS (USE TUNNEL)	EXPLOSIVES
BUS STOP	DO NOT CROWD	EXTERNAL USE ONLY
	DO NOT ENTER	
CAUTION	DO NOT INHALE FUMES	FALLING ROCKS
CLOSED	DO NOT PUSH	FALLOUT SHELTER
COMBUSTIBLE	DO NOT REFREEZE	FIRE ESCAPE
CONSTRUCTION ZONE	DO NOT SHOVE	FIRE EXIT
CONDEMNED	DO NOT STAND UP	FIRE EXTINGUISHER
CONTAMINATED	DO NOT USE NEAR HEAT	FIRST AID
CURVE	DO NOT USE NEAR OPEN FLAME	FLAMMABLE
	DOWN DYNAMITE	FLOODED
DANGER	DRIFTING SAND	FLOODS WHEN RAINING
DANGEROUS CURVE	DRIVE SLOW	FOUND

FOUR WAY STOP
FRAGILE
FREEWAY

GARAGE
GASOLINE
GATE
GENTLEMEN
GO SLOW

HANDLE WITH CARE
HANDS OFF
HELP
HIGH VOLTAGE
HOSPITAL
HOSPITAL ZONE

IN
INFLAMMABLE
INFORMATION
INSPECTION STATION
INSTRUCTIONS

JUNCTION 101A

KEEP OUT
KEEP TO THE LEFT (RIGHT)

LADIES
LANE ENDS
LAST CHANCE FOR GAS
LEFT LANE MUST TURN LEFT
LEFT TURN O.K.
LEFT TURN ON THE SIGNAL ONLY
LISTEN
LIVE WIRES
LOOK
LOOK OUT FOR THE CARS (TRUCKS)
LOST

M.P.H.
MECHANIC ON DUTY
MEN
MEN ONLY
MEN WORKING
MERGE LEFT (RIGHT)
MERGING TRAFFIC
MILITARY RESERVATION

NEXT
NEXT WINDOW (GATE)
NO ADMITTANCE
NO CHECKS CASHED
NO CREDIT
NO DIVIDE
NO DOGS ALLOWED
NO DUMPING
NO FIRES
NO FISHING

NO HUNTING
NO LEFT TURN
NO LOITERING
NO MINORS
NO PARKING
NO PASSING
NO RIGHT TURN
NO RIGHT TURN ON RED LIGHT
NO TURN ON RED
NO SMOKING
NO SMOKING AREA
NO SPITTING
NO STANDING
NO STOPPING
NO SWIMMING
NOT A THROUGH STREET
NOT FOR INTERNAL USE
NO THOROUGHFARE
NO TOUCHING
NO TRESPASSING
NO TRUCKS
NO TURNS
NO U TURN
NOXIOUS
NURSE

OFFICE
ONE WAY—DO NOT ENTER
ONE WAY STREET
OPEN
OUT
OUT OF ORDER

PAVEMENT ENDS HERE
PED X ING
PEDESTRIANS PROHIBITED
PLAYGROUND
POISON
POISONOUS
POLICE
POLICE STATION
POST NO BILLS
POST OFFICE
PRIVATE
PRIVATE PROPERTY
PRIVATE ROAD
PROCEED AT YOUR OWN RISK
PUSH
PUT ON CHAINS

R.R.
RAILROAD CROSSING
RESTROOMS
RESUME SPEED
RIGHT LAND ENDS
RIGHT LAND MUST TURN RIGHT
ROAD CLOSED
ROAD ENDS

SAFETY FIRST
SCHOOL STOP
SCHOOL ZONE
SHALLOW WATER
SHELTER
SLIDE AREA
SLIPPERY WHEN WET (FROSTY)
SLOW
SLOW DOWN
SLOWER TRAFFIC—KEEP RIGHT
SMOKING PROHIBITED
SPEED CHECKED BY RADAR
SPEED ZONE
STEEP GRADE
STEP DOWN (UP)
STOP
STOP AHEAD
STOP FOR PEDESTRIANS
STOP MOTOR
STOP WHEN OCCUPIED
TAXI
TAXI STAND
TERMS CASH
THIN ICE
THIS END UP
THIS LANE MAY TURN LEFT
THIS PROPERTY CONDEMNED
THIS ROAD PATROLLED BY AIRCRAFT
THIS SIDE UP
THREE WAY LIGHT
TRAFFIC CIRCLE
TRUCK ROUTE
TURN OFF ½ MILE
TURN OFF

UNLOADING ZONE
UP
USE BEFORE (DATE)
USE IN OPEN AIR
USE LOW GEAR
USE OTHER DOOR

VIOLATORS WILL BE PROSECUTED

WAIT FOR GREEN
WALK
WANTED
WARNING
WATCH FOR FLAGMAN
WATCH FOR LOW FLYING AIRCRAFT
WATCH YOUR STEP
WET PAINT
WINDING ROAD
WOMEN
WRONG WAY

YIELD
YIELD RIGHT OF WAY

_____talking book service_____

Descriptors: Alternative Strategies   **Grade Levels:**   Junior High
                    Auditory Input   High School
                    Nonreaders

Rationale: A very small group of students do not learn to read during their school careers despite various instructional methods and materials. Obviously, class assignments can be extremely punishing for such students who are not retarded and are able to understand language concepts at their current grade level. These students can function in their classes if adaptations are provided by the instructors. Most importantly, instruction and other communication to such students must be provided through auditory rather than visual channels. Since it may not be possible for teachers, parents, or student peers to tape record all text books, library books, and so on, use of the Talking Book Service is recommended for students meeting certain requirements. The procedure for obtaining the Talking Book Service for qualifying students is offered here to help teachers when consulting and counseling with parents or referral agencies. It should be pointed out that referrals for this service are not very common.

Objective: To outline for teachers the exact procedure for referring nonreaders or learning disabled students for Talking Book Service.

**Background
Information:**   Talking books are available for the legally blind, partially seeing, physically handicapped, reading disabled, and learning disabled.

A doctor of medicine or a neurologist must certify that the reading disability is an organic dysfunction or of sufficient severity so as to prevent reading printed material in a normal manner.

Talking books and magazines are available on discs, cassettes, and open reel tapes. These are sent to the borrowers and returned to the library postage free. Catalogs of existing titles are sent to the borrower after the initial request has been submitted.

A three-month lead time is needed to record books not already on tape, such as textbooks and specialized materials.

Procedure: **Steps for Obtaining Talking Books**

1. Contact the state library nearest you or obtain the number of your state library from the local department for the blind and physically handicapped. The state library will send you an information packet, including an application for the Talking Book Service and a medical certification form.
2. The applicant must have the Talking Book Service form signed by a doctor of medicine or a neurologist certifying the severity of the reading disability.
3. After returning the medical form and application to the state library, the student is placed on the mailing list to receive the Talking Book Service.
4. In case of problems or questions that the state library is unable to handle, contact the Library of Congress, Talking Books Division, Washington, D.C. (202) 287-5000.

The Talking Books will not remediate a student's reading problem. However, it is an excellent way of helping an older student compensate for a disability by altering the mode of information input (auditory rather than visual).

Math:
Readiness
Number Concept
Skill Practice

Descriptors: Auditory Cues
Beginning Writing Patterns
Numbers 1-10

Grade Levels: K-1
Special Education
Resource Rooms

Rationale: Young learners having difficulty remembering how to write the numbers 1-10 or consistently reversing them may need an auditory cue during the initial learning stages. The simple rhymes in this poem also help the student to remember the correct sequence of writing strokes.

Materials: Chalkboard/chalk
Sand or salt tray
Writing paper
Pencil

Objective: To teach a student how to write the numbers from 1-10 using an auditory cue.

Procedure:
1. The teacher presents number 1 and says the rhyme while writing a 1 on the chalkboard. These steps are repeated 4-5 times.
2. The student is asked to write a 1 on the chalkboard and repeat the rhyme aloud with the teacher. This procedure is repeated several times. When the student is able to recite the rhyme alone while simultaneously writing the number, the teacher stops repeating it. Note: It is important to insure that the student follows the correct sequential stroke pattern to prevent him/her from reinforcing erroneous responses.
3. Ask the student to write the number and recite the rhyme using a salt/sand tray. Repeat the procedure 4-5 times. The student gently strokes the pan to "erase" the number each time.
4. Have the student write the number being practiced on writing paper with a primary pencil. Repeat this procedure until the student can accurately reproduce the number from memory.
5. Reassess the student on a given number just learned for two more days to ensure that s/he has learned the number and can correctly reproduce it from memory.
6. Continue teaching new numbers by repeating steps 1-5. Do not introduce a new number until the previous number has been completely mastered. Provide frequent review sessions.

number poem

The author of this otherwise widespread rhyme is unknown:

A straight line one is fun.

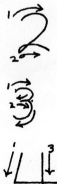

Around and back on the railroad track; Two, two, two!

Around a tree, around a tree; that is how to make a three!

Down and over and down once more;
That is how to make a four.

Fat old five goes down and around. Put a flag
on top
And see what you have found.

Down to a loop, a six rolls a hoop.

Straight across and down from heaven;
That is the way to make a seven.

Make an "s" but do not wait;
Climb right back up to make an eight.

A loop and a line makes a nine!

Make a straight line again
And a ball for a ten.

Additional Suggestions:

1. As the students become proficient at writing the numbers, fade out the auditory cues.
2. Design practice games (after 5 or more numbers have been learned) using the chalkboard. Ask 5 students at a time to go to the board and hand out plain paper for the remaining students to use at their seats. Call out a number and have the students write it down on the chalkboard or on paper. The students at their desks check their work against the chalkboard. After 3 numbers, allow the students at the chalkboard to choose other students to take their place for the next round of numbers. Repeat this procedure until all students have had a turn at the chalkboard.

one-to-one relationships

Descriptors: Math Readiness
Visual-Auditory-Tactile Learning
The Concept of Zero

Grade Levels: K–2
Resource Room
Special Education

Rationale: Beginning students must learn the one-to-one relationship for math concepts in order to progress to higher levels of math understanding. Sometimes these concepts are presented in rapid succession and students misunderstand the information. Consequently, it is not surprising that these same youngsters experience difficulty with addition and subtraction problems. For example, when numbers are presented in order such as 1 2 3 4 5 the student may not understand that the quantity represented as well as the successive order are different, thus,

may be represented as an order rather than differing quantities such as

The activities presented here provide several ways of practicing the one-to-one concept.

Objective: To teach beginning math students the one-to-one correspondence concept.

Materials: Popsicle sticks or tongue depressors
Counters (blocks, beads, poker chips, cardboard circles, buttons, paper clips, dried beans, pennies)
Rubber bands
2″ × 3″ blank slips of paper
Black marking pen
Glue, sand
Sandpaper, pipe cleaners, popcorn, shirt cardboard
5″ × 5″ tagboard squares
Chalk and chalkboard
Shoebox lids

Activity 1: Quantity

Make the numbers 0 through 9 out of sandpaper, felt, pipe cleaners, or white glue dried on cardboard. Securely fasten the numbers on heavy cardboard. Start with the number 1, presenting the numbers in sequence after each preceding number is learned. Present zero last. It is essential that each number be presented consistently in the order listed below.

Procedure: 1. Present the number, saying it.

2. Have the student trace the number as you say it again.
3. Have the student echo the number, saying it as it is traced with a finger. Repeat steps 1 through 3 until the student can say the word without verbal prompting.
4. Present a counter, laying it beside the number saying *1*.
5. Have the student pick up the counter and replace it beside the number saying *1*.
6. Return the counter to a similar group of counters. Ask the student to place one object beside the number, saying *1* at the same time. Repeat this step until the student automatically associates the number 1 with the correct number of objects.
7. Continue introducing a new number but only after the student can consistently correctly identify the previously learned numbers.

Additional Suggestions: 1. Have the student do simple dot-to-dot drawings to reinforce number sequence.

2. Say a number and have the student clap the appropriate number of times.

Activity 2: More Quantity Practice

Quantity should be introduced to the student first through concrete objects such as colored cubes. Three groups of cubes should be introduced at a time and increased as long as the student is interested and responding to instruction.

The three-period lesson should be used in this exercise and all exercises introducing nomenclature.

Procedure: Three-period lesson:
1. First period—introduction.
   Point to the quantity. Say the number quantity and have the student repeat it. Repeat this several times for each quantity. Example: "Two blocks." "One block." "Three blocks."
2. Second period—practice.
   Name a number and ask the student to point to the correct quantity. Repeat this several times. Example: "Show me 3 blocks."
3. Third period—test.
   Point to the quantity and have the student name it.

Student says "2."
4. The symbol should be presented in the same manner as quantity—3 numerals at a time, utilizing the three-period lesson. Numerals made from sandpaper, sand sprinkled on wet glue, pipe cleaners, popcorn glued to cardboard, and so on, can be used. (The important consideration here is that the student can feel the shape of the numeral; visual memory is built up rapidly with the aid of the muscular tactile sense.)

5. When the student can easily work with numbers and numerals up to 5, lay out blocks and ask the student to name the quantity. Then show the student a numeral and ask what it says. Have the student point to the correct quantity. Emphasize that the numeral 5 stands for 5. The quantity is 5 blocks.

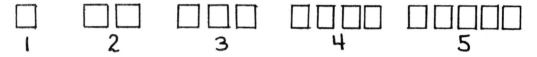

Additional Suggestions:
1. Mix the numbers and ask the student to put the correct number of blocks (or counters) next to each number.
2. Place groups of blocks on the table and ask the student to place the correct number representing each group next to the group of blocks.

Activity 3: Introducing Zero

Procedure:
1. Glue 2 shoebox lids together (small ends) and divide them into 10 sections with a marking pen.
2. Glue cardboard numerals (or write) 0 to 9 in each section.
3. Put 10 rubber bands and 45 popsicle sticks next to the box lids.
4. Ask the student to read the numerals 1 to 9.
5. Have the student count the correct number of sticks for each number and place them in a bundle tied with a rubber band.
6. Direct the student's attention to the compartment with the 0. Explain that it is *zero*, which means nothing. Therefore, no sticks will be placed under zero.

0	1	2	3	4	5	6	7	8	9
	I	II	III	IIII	IIIII	IIIIII	IIIIIII	IIIIIIII	IIIIIIIII

Activity 4: Bead Stringing

Procedure:
1. On 5″ × 5″ cardboard cards write the numbers to be practiced, one on each card.
2. Punch a hole in the bottom of each card.
3. Place a shoelace or yarn with a stiff glued tip through the hole, knotting it to prevent the cord from falling out.

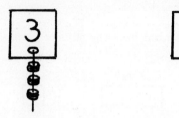

4. Provide the student with a number of beads and ask the student to string the appropriate number of beads on the shoelace or yarn to match the number on each card.
5. Monitor the student and offer reinforcement for correct responses.
6. If incorrect, help the student to count out the appropriate number of beads.

(Note: Reiterate that zero means nothing. Therefore, no beads are added to the zero card.)

Activity 5: Counter's Game: To Introduce Odd and Even

Materials:
2-inch cardboard numerals (1 to 10). These may be obtained from a sign company and spray painted or cut out by the teacher.
55 counters (checkers, cardboard circles, pennies, buttons)

Procedure:
1. Have the student place the numerals in order across the table.
2. Have the student place pairs of counters under each numeral for each quantity—from 1 through 10.

| 1 | 2 | 3 | 4 | 5 | 6 | 7 | 8 | 9 | 10 |

3. Go back and point out that some numerals have equal partners and some have one left over. Tell the student that those with partners are called *even* numbers; those with one left over are called *odd* numbers.
4. Ask the student to say the even numbers out loud (2, 4, 6, 8, 10).
5. Ask the student to say the odd numbers out loud (1, 3, 5, 7, 9).

(Note: After practicing this game several times, the student should be able to recite orally the odd and even numbers from 1 to 10.

Activity 6: Memory Game with Beans

This game is used to reinforce the concept of zero. It helps to build visual memory and reinforces the association of symbol and quantity.

Materials:
2 baskets
55 large white beans
2″ × 3″ folded slips of paper

Procedure:
1. Write the numbers from 0 to 10 on the slips of paper, fold them, and put them in a basket.
2. The other basket contains 55 dried beans.
3. Eleven students sit in a circle.
4. Pass the first basket around the circle and ask each student to draw a slip of paper.
5. Each student should read the numeral silently, refold the paper, and place it behind the student.

6. The basket of beans is now passed around the circle. Students take out the number that matches the drawn number of beans and place the beans in a group in front of them.

7. Ask each student to tell what his/her paper said, to count the beans orally for the group, and to check by showing the slip of paper (the student with no beans should be asked to explain the meaning of zero).

Additional Suggestions:

When the students are able to add or subtract, the same game may be played by writing simple number problems on the slips of paper.

$$\begin{array}{r} \text{Example:} \quad 5 \\ \underline{+2} \end{array}$$

The student shows 7 beans.

Activity 7: Classroom Racetrack

Procedure:

1. On 5″ × 5″ tagboard cards, write the numbers to be learned with a black marking pen. Have at least 3 cards for each number.
2. Select an area, either a classroom or hallway, that has a tile floor.
3. Lay out a "racetrack" with a start and finish line with masking tape or chairs. A minimum distance should be 20 tiles.
4. Plan as many "lanes" as there are students chosen to play the game (2 to 6).
5. Line up the students at the starting line.
6. Thoroughly shuffle the number cards then hold up one card to the student in the first lane.

7. The student must first say the name of the number and then move forward the appropriate number of tile spaces.
8. Any student who fails to do either task correctly loses the turn and must remain where s/he is. The game continues with the student in the second row.
9. The first student across the finish line is declared the winner.

---

counting to ten

Descriptors: One-to-One Correspondence
Beginning Math Concepts

Grade Levels: K–2
Special Education
Resource Room

Rationale: It is important to teach one-to-one correspondence for counting, forming sets, addition, and subtraction. A variety of activities should be implemented to practice each newly learned concept. Some students may need to practice each skill level longer than others. These teaching ideas may be adapted for any skill level. Parents may also be shown how to use the activities at home.

Objective: To practice one-to-one correspondence at each student's current skill level.

Activity 1: Counting: Ordering Numerically

Materials:

Small empty orange juice cans
Pencils
Scotch tape
Tongue depressors
Black marking pen
Pieces of white paper
(Note: Tagboard strips can be used if enough pencils or tongue depressors are not available.)

Procedure:

1. Use a marking pen to draw dots on white paper taped to the front of each can.
2. The student is to place the appropriate number of tongue depressors into the cans as indicated by the dots.

3. Print numerals on the front of the juice cans after these have been introduced to the student. Again, the student is to place the appropriate number of pencils, tongue depressors, or tagboard strips in each can.
4. Ask the student to practice counting the number of objects placed in the cans.
5. Ask the student also to count the objects when they are removed from the cans.

(Note: Buttons, beans, or paper clips may also be used although they would not be as visible and thus make immediate teacher correction more difficult.)

Additional Suggestions:

1. Write simple addition problems on the pieces of paper and tape or glue them to the front of the juice cans. The student places the appropriate number of pencils or tongue depressors in the can to solve the problem. Ask the student to count the number of objects placed in the can. Ask the student to explain how a particular answer was reached.
2. When the student has mastered the addition problems, proceed to subtraction problems.

Activity 2: Clothespin Counting

Materials:

Clothespins and hangers
3″ × 5″ pieces of white paper
Black marking pen

Procedure:

1. Write a number plus the corresponding number of dots on blank pieces of paper that are hooked over each hanger.
2. The student places the corresponding number of clothespins on each hanger.
3. The student should count the clothespins when putting them on and removing them from the hangers.

Activity 3: Pairing Objects

Materials: Egg cartons or apple separators—1 for each student: counters (dried beans, poker chips, paper clips, marbles, screws, small blocks, pennies, washers)

Procedure:
1. Give each student an egg carton or apple separator.
2. Distribute an even number of objects to each student and ask the student to place 1 object in each "cup." (Note: It is suggested that the teacher start with a small number of objects (2) and progress until the student is working with 8 to 10 different groups of 2.
3. Ask the student to place 2 of each object in a cup. Initially it might be necessary to model the activity for the student.
4. When the student completes a grouping of objects, ask the pupil, "How many (objects) are in this cup?" The student responds but may need to be cued the first few times.
5. Finally, ask the student to count the objects in the cup.
6. Give the student an even number of objects and ask him/her to lay them on the table in groups of 2. It may be necessary to model the activity for the student.
(Note: If the student has difficulty making the transition from the egg carton to the table, use a large sheet of paper and draw shapes of circles and squares on it so that the objects can be grouped on the shapes.)

7. Gradually increase the number of objects in each of the groups until the student has reached 10. Remember always to ask the student to count out the number of objects grouped together.

Activity 4: Stepping Out

Materials: 1" × 10" strip of tagboard with the numbers 1 to 10 written on it
10-inch paper circle with footprints labeled L and R drawn on it
Masking tape
Black marking pen

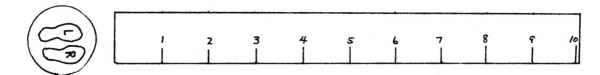

Procedure:

1. Tape the paper strip to the floor.
2. Place the circle in front of the number line and tape it to the floor.
3. Select a student and have the student stand on the footprints inside the circle.
4. Ask the student to move forward along the number line a specific number of steps.
5. The remaining students are instructed to count aloud as the student takes the steps.
6. The students take turns stepping and counting aloud.
7. Let the students take turns giving directions to each other on how many steps to take.

(Note: If the students appear ready for addition, ask 1 student to walk 3 steps and stop. Then ask the student to walk 2 more steps. Ask "What number are you on now?" "Number 5." "Yes, 3 steps plus 2 steps are 5 steps.")

Additional Suggestions:

1. Have the students form a circle. Tell all the pupils to take a certain number of steps. This can also be made a two-point command by asking the students to stop, turn around, or sit down. Allow the students to take turns giving directions.
2. Have the students sit in a circle and let each one name a pair of something they see in the room. For example, the teacher may start with his/her feet. This game can be continued through number 10 if the room is suitable for finding that many like objects. Example: 6 windows or 3 tables.
3. Have each pupil count the number of letters in his/her own name. Let the students compare their names and find the longest and shortest by counting the letters.

how to use the number line

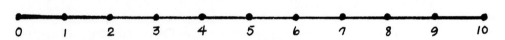

Descriptors: Computation   **Grade Levels:** 1–2
Concrete Math Aid

Rationale: The number line is a beneficial tool for students learning to add or subtract and eliminates the use of fingers, chips, or an abacus. Students must learn to use the number line before given problems to compute. This lesson explains in a simple manner how to use the number line when adding or subtracting.

Objective: To teach students to use a number line.

Assumptions: Recognition of numbers 1 to 10
Number concept 1 to 10
Understanding of symbols and concept (− and +)

Materials: Number line 1 to 10 (commercial or teacher-made) covered with clear contact paper or laminated
Tissue
Red waxed pencil
Masking tape
Plain notecards

Activity 1:

Procedure:

1. Explain to the student that this is a line that has numbers (run your finger along the line, pointing to the dots and counting the numbers as you go).
2. Next show a card with a number on it to the child. Example: 3
3. Have the child draw a circle using a wax pencil around the number on the number line that matches the number on the card.

Example:

Erase with a tissue.

4. Do this activity until the child has successfully found 5 consecutive numbers.

Activity 2:

Procedure:

1. Show the student a card and ask the student to find the number and circle it with a red pencil. Example: 2
2. After the student has found the number 2, look at the second card to make sure you know what number is next. Example: second card is number 5. Tape all of the numbers (not the dots) from 6 to 10 so that the numbers are not showing (cover 1 to 4 with a notecard). If the numbers show, it is confusing to the child when first learning.
3. Present the second card number 5. Tell the student that s/he is now going to hop 5 times like a bunny (jump like a kangaroo, leap like a frog, fly like an airplane).

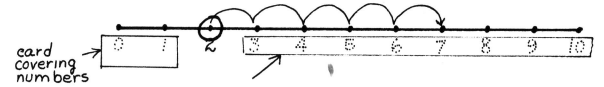

card covering numbers

Taped so as not to be seen, only the dots are showing.

4. Continue steps 1 through 3 until the child has successfully completed 5 problems.

Activity 3:

Procedure:

1. Present one card showing an addition problem using coded symbols.

$$\boxed{③ + \overrightarrow{5}}$$

2. Tell the student, "Circle the number 3 and hop 5 dots. Move the way the arrow shows. In addition, you move this way."
3. Continue steps 1 and 2 until the child has successfully completed 5 problems.

Activity 4:

Procedure:

Give the child 5 addition problems without the coded symbols.

$$\boxed{2 + 6}$$

Activity 5:

Procedure: Do activities 1 through 4 without covering the numbers with masking tape or paper.

Activity 6:

Procedure: Do activities 1 through 5 substituting the subtraction cards.

Additional Suggestions: Construct simple worksheets and ask the student to solve the problems using the number line.

_____task analysis for beginning money skills_____

Descriptors: Beginning Money Skills   **Grade Levels:** 1–2
Trial Teaching

Rationale: Students need to begin learning money skills by starting with penny values and sequentially progressing to nickels, dimes, and so on. It is important to provide students a great deal of practice using simple concepts before teaching higher level skills.

Objective: To teach students physically to combine pennies, nickels, and dimes to equal an amount up to 20¢.

Prerequisite Behaviors: The student must be able to recognize and know the value of a penny, nickel, and dime and add numbers to 20.

Materials: 20 pennies
4 nickels
2 dimes

Procedure: The teacher presents the following sequence to teach beginning money skills. The student models the response by physically putting out the same coins.
 1. Place coins on desk/table.
 2. Pick up 1¢ and place on top of the desk/table.
 3. Pick up 1¢ and place with penny on top of desk. Say to student, "This is 2¢."
 4. Continue same procedure up to 10¢.
 5. Pick up nickel and place on top of desk. Say to student, "This is 5¢."
 6. Pick up 1¢ and place with nickel. Say, "This is 6¢."
 7. Continue same procedure up to 10¢.
 8. Pick up dime and place on top of desk. Say, "This is 10¢."
 9. Pick up 1¢ and place with dime, saying, "This is 11¢."
10. Continue same procedure up to 15¢.
11. Place nickel and dime on top of desk and say, "This is 15¢."
12. Pick up 1¢ and place with coins on top of desk and say, "This is 16¢."
13. Continue same procedure up to 20¢.
14. Continue the procedure by asking the student to show certain different combinations. Example: "Show me 8¢." "Show me 13¢."
(Note: If the student has difficulty mastering money concepts, repeat the beginning steps and teach amounts only to 5¢.)

**Additional
Suggestions:**   1. Use play money.
2. Put price tags on familiar classroom materials such as books, pencils, games, toys, and crayons. Ask the student to "buy" the product of choice by counting out the correct amount of money.

_____**time-telling test**_____

Descriptors: Time Assessment
Criterion-Referenced Test

Grade Levels: 1–3
Special Education

Rationale: The ability to tell time is essential for all students to function independently while in school and later as adults. This skill is particularly useful for the exceptional student who is mainstreamed or entering vocational preparation. The following checklist provides the teacher with a quick survey of students' ability to tell time. The test is arranged in ascending order of difficulty, that is, each succeeding section requires a higher skill level. In addition, within sections items are arranged in the order of increasing difficulty. This format is designed to prevent the tester from frustrating students with continuing item failure.

Objective: To assess a student's current level of understanding time concepts.

Materials: Tagboard
Brad
Scissors
Black marking pen

Procedure: Construct a large tagboard clock face with movable hands fastened to the clock with a brad. Mark five-minute intervals and use individual marks for the sixty minutes with the black marking pen.
In all parts except I and VII, the tester is to move the clock hands to the specified position and ask the student to tell what time the "clock says."
Part I: The questions in this section may be used to evaluate the degree to which the student is aware that events occur in the dimension of time.
Part VII: The questions in this section may be used to evaluate students' ability to pace themselves in time (for example, how much time until a known event or desired activity). This skill is the most complex tested by the checklist. However, it is important for all students including exceptional students who often experience difficulty in efficient time use or punctuality. This skill helps them to be at places and events on time and, consequently, is an important premainstreaming and pre-vocational skill.

name _____	date _____
school _____	examiner _____
grade _____	classroom teacher _____

TIME-TELLING TEST

	Correct	Incorrect	Student's Response

Part I:
Events in Time
Questions:
  1. What **time** do you get up?
  2. What **time** does school start?
  3. What **time** do you eat lunch?
  4. What **time** does your favorite
      TV show come on?
  5. What **time** do you go to bed?			

Part II:
Recognition of Time to the Hour
   12:00
    4:00
    1:00
    9:00
   11:00
    3:00			

Part III:
Recognition of Time to Half-Hour
    2:30
    5:30
   12:30
    8:30			

Part IV:
Recognition of Time to Quarter-Hour
    3:15
    6:15
    7:45
   11:45			

Part V:
Recognition of Time to Ten Minutes
   12:10
    5:40
    2:20
    6:50			

Part VI:
Recognition of Time to the Minute
    4:02
    7:16
    9:43
   11:36			

Part VII:
Time Problems
 	
         Given   **Question**
  1. Clock at 1:00 1. How much time
                          until 2:30?
  2. Clock at 12:15 2. How much time
                          until 4:45?
  3. Clock at 6:27 3. How much time
                          until 6:30?			

_____math movement games_____

Descriptors: Number Identification   Grade Levels: 1–3
               Group Games

Rationale: Once students have been exposed to number identification, they should be provided with many
               practice activities to reinforce the newly acquired skills. Students usually enjoy skill practice using
               game formats. It is important to have the students play games designed for their current skill level;
               otherwise the activity may become too easy or too frustrating for them. Example: Using numbers 11
               to 20 when the student has not mastered numbers 1 to 10 will become frustrating and, thus, not
               provide a good instructional activity.

Objective: To use math movement games to reinforce number identification.

Materials: Chalkboard and chalk
               8″ × 8″ tagboard squares
               72″ × 72″ oilcloth
               Indelible black ink marking pen

Procedure: 1. The teacher explains the rules of the math movement games to the students.
               2. The students should be grouped into appropriate skill levels. Several games may be played
                  concurrently.
               3. The teacher should evaluate the effectiveness of the math movement games by noting if the
                  students can quickly recognize the same numbers in different formats or situations, such as
                  worksheets, math workbooks, and numbered pages in books.

Game 1: Look and Match

Place 2 numbered tagboard squares on the ground in front of 1 or 2 students. The teacher writes a
number on the chalkboard, and the students are to jump on the appropriate maching number in front
of them.

Game 2: Hear, Say, and Jump

An oilcloth number grid is placed on the floor or on the playground. The teacher says a number and
the student must find it on the grid and jump onto the correct matching numeral. (Note: Only use
numbers that the student can correctly identify.)

Game 3: Run through It

Lined configurations are drawn on the floor or on the playground. As a number is called aloud or written on the chalkboard, the student must find it by running through its configuration within the more complex patterns. (Note: Do not use this activity for students with perceptual difficulties. It is fun and challenging for many students, but should be discontinued if too frustrating.)

Game 4: Stretch

An oilcloth number grid is placed on the floor or on the playground. The teacher calls out 2 or 3 digits and the student must use hands and/or feet to touch all digits (like the game "Twister").

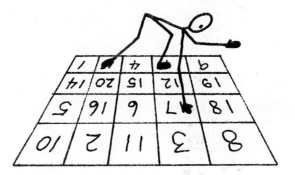

Additional Suggestions:

1. Divide the students into two teams and play a counting relay. Place 2 sets of tagboard number squares in front of 2 groups of students. One member at a time from each team runs over and finds a number (starting with 1), returns to the team with the number, places it on the ground, and tags the next team member, who returns to the number squares, obtains the second number in order, and repeats the process. The first team to finish is the winner.

2. Continue the relay but have the teacher call out a different number each time (not in sequence) the students return to the team.

Descriptors: Criterion-Referenced Test
Language Concepts
Remediation

Grade Levels: 1–3

Rationale: Uncertainty about the use of symbols for greater than and less than is not uncommon among students at the primary level. Often the difficulty lies simply in the writing and reading of the symbols, but unless this can be determined absolutely, sources for the problem should be traced to earlier developmental levels of related mathematical concepts.

Objective: To teach greater than/less than using a sequence of tasks.

Materials: Blocks
Paper and pencil
Black marking pen
Ditto master
Duplicating paper

Procedure: *Questions for the Teacher*

1. Can the student concretely distinguish smaller from bigger quantities, or more from fewer?

   Example: Build a small tower with blocks.
   Now build a bigger one next to it.
   Which has more blocks? Fewer?
   Which has a greater number of blocks?
   Which has less?

2. Can the student count rationally?

   Example: "Give me 7 blocks," or "How many blocks are here?"

3. Does the student have a strategy for comparing the relative quantities in two sets?

   Example: Which set has more?
   Which set has fewer or less?
   Show me how you can tell.

4. Does the student comprehend the order of numerals on a number line?

   Example: On this number line where would you write the big numbers? Small ones?

On this number line where would 3 go?
Could it go on the left of 2? Why?
Is 3 greater than 2 or less than 2?
Is 2 greater than 3 or less than 3?

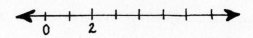

5. Without concrete, pictorial, or graphic representations, can the student name a number greater or less than a given number?

Example: Tell me a number smaller than 4.
Tell me a number greater than 7.
Tell me a number less than 3.
(Note: It is not necessary to name the value that is simply **one** greater than the original. Any number greater than or less than would be correct.)

6. Can the student correctly read and complete word sentencs involving the numerical relationships?

Example: Read this sentence:
3 is less than 5.
8 is greater than 2.
Fill in the blanks with the numbers given:

(3, 6) _____ is more than _____.

(2, 5) _____ is less than _____.

(1, 2) _____ is greater than _____.

7. Can the student read the symbol when it is used in a number sentence?

Example: Read this: 3 ❭ 1
8 ❬ 9

8. Can the student supply the appropriate symbol to complete a true number sentence?

Example: Fill in the blanks with > or < :
2 ☐ 3
5 ☐ 4

(Note: If the difficulty lies only at steps 7 or 8, the remediation involved is not essentially mathematical. In step 7 the reading task is one of fixing sight words (or symbols) so that a student's efficiency is increased as illustrated in the following case history: After further examination of the learning strategy of a student who consistently reversed the >, < symbols it was found that the student considered the "sticks" of the sign to be the pointer ❭. Thus, although she understood quantity, the language concept used to teach the signs was confusing and the student missed all math problems involving >, <.)

Additional Suggestions: Several mnemonic aids have been suggested for helping youngsters determine the correct formation of the symbol. Some techniques utilize a greedy duck who prefers to eat the larger of two quantities and consequently turns his head toward the larger number.

Descriptors: Visual Discrimination
Number Comprehension
Quantity

Grade Levels: 1–3

Rationale: Some students have difficulty recognizing and writing the less than symbol used in math instruction. Many students find it easier to recognize symbols if they can relate them to a caption, riddle, or picture. The method for teaching the less than concept may also be used to teach the distinction between true or false statements. To help students recognize the < symbol, they are told that the small point of the little mouse's nose is next to the small number. Example:

$$1 \quad \text{<} \quad 3$$

Objective: To teach a student to read and understand the less than symbol and to tell if a statement is true or false.

Assumptions: The student understands number concepts and the language concepts smaller than and next to.

Materials: Chalkboard and chalk
Plain drawing paper
16″ × 20″ tagboard
Abacus

Procedure: 1. Introduce each activity as described below after drawing the less than symbol as a little mouse's nose (see Rationale) on the chalkboard.
2. Do not introduce the next higher activity until the student has mastered the present one.
3. Keep a list of students who need more individualized help and design specific practice activities for such students.

Activity 1:

1. On the chalkboard write the symbol < and say, "This is the sign for smaller than—also called less than" (allowing the student the option of which term to use and having the student hear the less than term).
2. Have the student say the symbol while writing it on the chalkboard.
3. Say, "What is this sign? That's right. This is the smaller than or less than sign." (If the student does not know the sign, repeat steps 1 and 2.)
4. Erase the sign. Ask the student to write the smaller than sign again. The student writes it on the chalkboard. Ask, "What is this sign? Yes, this is the smaller than sign."

Activity 2:

1. Draw the less than symbol on the chalkboard.
2. Put a number 1 on the chalkboard to the left of the symbol. Put a large 4 on the right side of the symbol. Say, "We are going to read a sentence just like you would read a book. Read with me: 1 is smaller than 4." Point to each number and the symbol as you read. "The smaller number is next to the small point. Let's check to see if 1 is smaller than 4."

3. Using the abacus, count 1 bead as you push it across the wire, then push 4 beads across. "Which is the smaller group of beads? That's right, 1 is a smaller group than 4. This sentence is true."

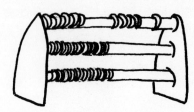

4. Change the number putting the smaller number on the left side of the symbol and read the problem aloud. Follow steps 1 and 2. In this lesson choose numbers that differ greatly in size while staying within 1 to 5 range. Example:

$$0 < 5, \quad 1 < 3, \quad 1 < 4, \quad 2 < 4$$

5. Continue until the student can successfully read 5 problems on the chalkboard and compute the same 5 problems on the abacus. After this is completed, continue with activity 3.

Activity 3:

1. "This time we are going to do 5 problems, but these are not true. Don't let them fool you. If we don't think it is true, we'll check with the abacus. If the abacus shows us that it is not true, let's say 'boo-oo' and erase it. Are you ready? Let's try it."

2. Write on the chalkboard: $2 < 1$

3. "Let's read this together: 2 is smaller than 1."
4. Whether or not the student believes that this statement is right or wrong, use the abacus to check.
5. "No, that's not right. 'Boo-oo!' Erase."
6. Repeat steps 1 through 5 with 5 problems.

Activity 4:

1. Use both true and false problems. Do 7 problems using steps 1 through 6.

Activity 5:

1. Write 7 problems on the 16″ × 20″ tagboard.
2. The student reads the posterboard, which has 4 true and 3 false problems.

2 < 5	
3 < 1	4 < 2
2 < 3	2 < 0
1 < 4	3 < 5

3. When the student has learned both the less than and the greater than signs, prepare a tagboard chart of both types of problems and ask the student to read them aloud.
4. Write 2 numbers on the chalkboard and ask the student to fill in the correct sign between each of the numbers. Example:

5 > 3		1	6
2	7	4	2

Additional Suggestions:

1. Prepare ditto master sheets of less than problems. Ask the student to circle the true statements and cross out the false ones. Examples:

2. Write 2 numbers on the chalkboard with the smaller number on the left. Ask the student to supply the missing sign and read orally all the problems.

_____greater than_____

Descriptors: Math Concepts   **Grade Levels:** 1–3
                 Visual Clues
                 Auditory Clues

Rationale: The symbol for the number concept "greater than" is often confusing for young students experiencing difficulty with math. It may be helpful to provide the students with riddles or clues to help them remember the symbol. If the students can understand the words *bigger than*, the teacher may also want to provide the following clue:

"The big (or fat) space is next to the big number."
Example:

$$ 3 > 1 $$

Objective: To teach a student to read and understand the greater than symbol ($>$) in a sentence and to judge whether or not a statement is true or false.

Assumptions: The student understands number recognition and quantity and the term "next to."

Materials: Chalkboard and chalk
Plain drawing paper
16″ × 20″ tagboard
Black marking pen
Abacus

Procedure:
1. Implement each activity in sequential order.
2. Evaluate the success of each activity by informal tests.
3. Do not present the less than sign while teaching the greater than concept.

Activity 1:

1. Write the symbol $>$ on the chalkboard and say, "This is the sign for bigger than, also called greater than" (the student is given the option of both terms).
2. Ask the student to say the symbol aloud while writing it on the chalkboard. Example: $>$ "greater than."
3. "What is this sign?" "Yes, this is the bigger than or greater than sign." (If the student does not know the correct answer, repeat steps 1 and 2).
4. Erase. Ask the student to write the bigger than sign again. When the student writes it on the chalkboard, ask, "What is this sign? Yes, this is the bigger than sign."

Activity 2:

1. Write a large number 4 on the board to the left of the greater than symbol. Put a small 1 on the right side of the symbol. Say, "We are going to read a sentence just like you would read in a book. Read with me: 4 is bigger than 1. The bigger number is next to the big space. Let's check to see if 4 is bigger than 1."
2. Using the abacus, count out 4 beads and the 1 bead to the right of the first row of beads. "Which is bigger? (or greater?). That's right, 4 is bigger than 1. This sentence is true."

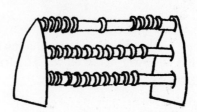

3. Change the numbers, putting the bigger number on the left side of the symbol and read. Follow steps 1 and 2. In this lesson, choose numbers that differ greatly in size while staying within 1 to 5 range.
   Example: 5>0, 3>1, 4>1, 4>2.

4. Continue this procedure until the student can successfully read 5 problems on the chalkboard and demonstrate the same 5 problems on the abacus. After this is completed, continue with activity 3.

Activity 3:

1. Say, "This time we are going to do 5 problems, but these are not true. Don't let them fool you. If we don't think it is true, we'll check with the abacus. If the abacus shows us that it is not true, let's say 'boo-oo' and erase it. Are you ready? Let's try it."
2. Write on the chalkboard 1>3.
3. "Let's read this together: 1 is bigger (or greater) than 3."
4. Whether the child thinks it is right or wrong, use the abacus to check by pushing 1 bead and then 3 beads to the right of the first row of beads.

5. "No, that's not right." Say "boo-oo" and erase.
6. Repeat steps 1 through 5 with 5 problems (as described in activity 2).

Activity 4:

1. Write both true and false problems on the chalkboard.
2. Complete 7 problems using steps 1 through 6 described in activity 3.

Activity 5:

1. Write 7 true and false problems on a 16″ × 20″ tagboard poster. Read the posterboard with the 7 statements (4 true and 3 false).
2. Ask the student to read aloud each statement as it is written.
3. Ask the student to say whether each statement is true or false.

2 >1	
3 >2	4 >1
2 >4	2 >3
1 >5	5 >2

Additional Suggestions:

1. Using a ditto master, duplicate worksheets as described in activity 5. Ask the students to circle the correct statements and cross out the false ones.

2. Following the previous suggestions ask the students to write T for true in front of the true statements and F in front of the false statements.

    T 3>1
    F 2>4

climb the numbered beanstalk

Descriptors: Math
Number Recognition
Addition Facts
Subtraction Facts

Grade Levels: 1–3
Resource Room
Learning Disabled
Mentally Retarded

Rationale: Once number identification has been introduced to students, practice becomes important to ensure that they have mastered this concept. It is fun to practice number identification using a game format. The bean stalk game may be adapted for higher level skill practice, such as addition and subtraction math facts. Although the following description covers the numbers 1 to 10, beginning students would only use the numbers 1 to 5.

Objective: To provide students with a practice activity in number identification from 1 to 10.

Materials: 12″ × 28″ heavy-weight tagboard
10″ × 10″ tagboard
Colored construction paper: green, brown, yellow
Glue
Scissors
Crayons
Black marking pen
Brad fastener
Colored blocks or counters (1 for each student)
¼-inch piece of plastic drinking straw
1 yard clear contact paper (if laminator is not available)
Black wax pencil (optional)

Procedure:

1. Cut "ground" from brown construction paper and glue to the bottom of the heavy 12″ × 28″ tagboard.
2. Cut out leaves and stalk from green construction paper and glue on the tagboard (see illustration).
3. Design a castle from yellow construction paper. Draw details on the castle with a black marking pen and glue to the top of the bean stalk.
4. Randomly mark numerals from 1 to 10 on the leaves with a black marking pen.
5. Add the label "Climb the Beanstalk" to the tagboard and cover the game board with clear contact paper.

6. Cut a 7-inch circle out of the 10″ × 10″ tagboard and divide it into 10 pie-shaped sections with a black marking pen.

Randomly write the numerals 1 to 10 on the sections and cover with clear contact paper.
7. Cut out a 2-inch tagboard pointer and punch a hole on the end opposite the point.

8. Attach the pointer to the numbered circle by placing the brad fastener through the ¼-inch piece of plastic straw and through the hole in the pointer, and finally through the center of the circle. Secure it on the back of the tagboard circle. (Note: The plastic straw acts as a spacer and allows the pointer to turn freely.)

9. The teacher, aide, or a student peer supervises the number game for accuracy.
10. Four students are chosen to play the game. Each chooses a marker and the players take turns spinning the spinner.
11. The player who spins must identify the number on which the pointer stopped.
12. That player may now move a marker to the leaf on the beanstalk with the same number as the one on which the spinner stopped.
    (Note: If the player cannot identify the number spun, that student may not move a marker. If the player moves a marker to an incorrect number, the player must go back to his/her last position.)
13. The first player to reach the Giant's castle is the winner.

Additional Suggestions:

1. Use the game to practice additional problems.

   a. Make a set of 20 cards, 2″ × 3″, with addition up to 10 on them.

   $$3+1=\qquad 2+4=\qquad 8+2=$$

   b. Instead of using a spinner, shuffle the cards and place them face down on the title of the game board.
   c. The student draws a card, reads the equation, answers it, and moves a marker to the correct numeral. (Teacher, aide, or student peer supervises to check for accuracy. An answer card with facts to 10 printed on it might also be used.)

2. Use the game to practice subtraction facts. Follow the same procedure but substitute subtraction problems.

5-3=   6-1=   9-4=

3. Do not number the colored leaves with a black marking pen, but cover the board with clear contact paper. Use a black wax pencil and write numbers and problems on each leaf. The surface marks are easily wiped off and new numbers may be added.

_____using the abacus_____

Descriptors: Place Value
Visual Representation
Concrete Materials

Grade Levels: 1–3
Special Education
Resource Rooms

Rationale: Many students are taught to count by rote with little understanding of quantity. If students are taught the use of a counting abacus, place value, for example, is easily explained, while regrouping (borrowing and carrying) follows in a sequential order. It is important for students to become proficient at one level before a higher level is introduced. Thus, practice activities must be designed and implemented with the students at home and at school.

Objective: To teach students to understand the place value concept to 100 using the abacus as a teaching aid.

Materials: Commercial abacus with 100 counting beads
Chalkboard and chalk
Paper and pencil

Procedure:
1. Introduce the abacus and ask the students to count aloud each row of 10 beads until the students understand that each row contains 10 beads. Slide each bead from left to right across the bar as it is counted. (In this manner, the student is also being prepared for reading left to right.)
2. Teach the students to count to 100 by tens by sliding whole rows of 10 beads across at one time and counting 10, 20, 30, 40, 50, 60, 70, 80, 90, 100. Repeat this step until all students can count to 100 by tens. (Note: If the teacher is standing behind the abacus, the beads must be moved from right to left in order for the students to follow a left-to-right progression.)
3. Ask a student to show the class 10 beads.
4. The student pushes 10 beads from left to right and says "10."
5. Write "10" on the chalkboard with a dotted vertical line between the 1 and the zero to designate the tens and the ones columns.

Example:

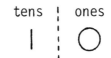

10 means 1 group of 10 and no ones.
6. The same procedure is followed, asking different students to show the class other multiples of 10 by pushing over the correct number of beads and asking the student to write the number on the chalkboard with a dotted vertical line between the 2 numbers.

Example:

tens	ones	tens	ones
4	◯	7	◯

Each time the student repeats that the number means X tens and no ones.

7. Write a number on the chalkboard.

Example:

Ask a student to show the amount on the abacus. Show the students that 80 is 8 rows of 10 and no more.

8. The teacher or a student pushes over a specific number of rows of beads (all multiples of 10). A student is asked to count the beads and to write the number on the chalkboard.

"Show me 30 beads."
Write   on the chalkboard.

tens ┊ ones

3 ┊ O

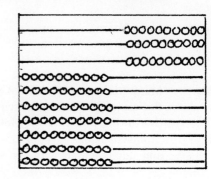

"30 means 3 tens and no ones."

9. The teacher next introduces counting by fives using the abacus and sliding 5 beads at a time left to right from the students' view as previously explained.

10. The teacher introduces tens and ones by sliding several groups of 10 over and adding some extra beads from the next row. (Note: Do not use the numbers 11 to 19 at this time as they are more difficult for the student to grasp.)

Example: "How many beads have I pushed to the side?"
"That's right. I have 34 beads."
"3 rows of 10 and 4 more beads.

Write 34 on the chalkboard. Draw the dotted line to check the tens and ones in the number.

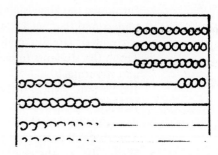

11. Continue this activity using the 3 variations previously explained.

STEP 1.

a. Teacher says number.
b. Student shows correct number of beads on the abacus.
c. Student writes number on the chalkboard with the dotted vertical line between them.

STEP 2.

a. Teacher pushes over a specific number of beads.
b. Student writes number on the chalkboard with a dotted vertical line between the 2 columns.

tens ┊ ones

c. Student orally says the number and states that the number has X number of tens and X number of ones.

STEP 3.

    a. Teacher writes a number on the chalkboard with a dotted vertical line between digits.
    b. Student pushes over the correct number of beads.
    c. Student orally tells the class the number and how many tens and ones the number contains.

12. Vary the game by using the 3 different steps until the students become proficient at understanding place value.
13. Introduce the numbers 11 to 19 in the same manner.
(Note: The abacus provides a visual representation of place value. By writing the number while saying it, students are presented with a sequential program that uses visual, auditory, tactile, and kinesthetic input.)

Additional Suggestions:

1. Duplicate worksheets of abacus beads and ask the students to write the number shown on the abacus.
2. Vary this activity by writing the number and allowing the student to draw the beads. Caution: Students with poor motor control may find this a difficult task.
3. Write numbers and ask the students to fill in the missing blanks under the tens and ones columns.

    Example: 72 is _____ tens and _____ ones.

4. Write a sentence: 9 tens and 4 ones are _____. Ask the students to fill in the blank with the correct number.
5. Introduce the hundreds column in the same manner.

hundreds	tens	ones
2	6	1

6. Teach addition and subtraction using the abacus as a concrete visual aid, "26 − 5 = 21."

place value game

Descriptors: Math Readiness
                    Small-Group Game
                    Chip Trading

Grade Levels: 1–3

Rationale: Many students find the math concept of place value difficult to learn. A gameboard with colored chips represents a visual approach to mastery of the place value concept.

Objective: To teach students the concept of place value through a board game.

Materials: Glue
               4 12″ × 18″ tagboard gameboards
               1-inch diameter colored construction paper circles
               Yellow—40 circles + 1″ × 2″ rectangle
               Blue—40 circles + 1″ × 2″ rectangle
               Green—40 circles + 1″ × 2″ rectangle
               Red—36 circles + 1″ × 2″ rectangle
               A die
               Black marking pen

Procedure:

1. Divide each gameboard into 4 equal sections (4½ inches wide) using a black marking pen.
2. The 1″ × 2″ colored rectangles are glued at the top of each section. From left to right glue red, green, blue, and yellow (see illustration).

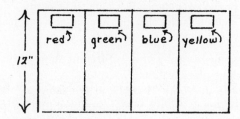

3. Five players are chosen to play the game. One player is designated as the banker who takes care of all colored chips (colored construction paper circles). The remaining 4 players each takes 1 gameboard.
4. Explain that each student is to roll the die and receive a corresponding number of yellow chips on each turn until the number 10 is reached. Ten yellow chips equal 1 blue chip, 10 blue chips equal 1 green chip, and 10 green chips equal 1 red chip. (Note: The place value concept will be more clearly understood as the game progresses.)
5. The player on the right of the banker rolls the die and asks the banker for the number of yellow chips that corresponds with the number on the die. The chips are placed on the student's yellow section (at the right) of the gameboard (see illustration).

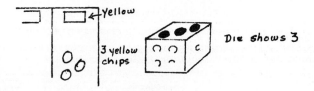

6. Each player continues taking turns in the same manner.
7. On the second turn the first player again rolls the die and asks for yellow chips. Whenever a player has accumulated 10 yellow chips these are traded for 1 blue chip. Trading may only occur at a player's turn.

Example: If a student has 8 yellow chips and rolls a 4 and, thus, earns 4 more yellow chips, s/he exchanges 10 yellow chips for 1 blue chip and retains 2 yellow chips.

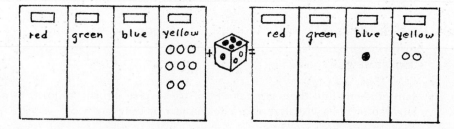

(Note: The color concept demonstrates the place value of 12 although this is not explained to the students as a number value at first.)

8. The game continues in this manner until each student has earned 10 blue chips. The blue chips are turned in for 1 green chip. When 10 green chips are earned these, in turn, are exchanged for 1 red chip.
9. The first player to earn a red chip wins the game.

Additional Suggestions:

1. Using 2 or more dice speeds up the game.
2. Use the game to teach subtraction. Example: If a player has 1 red, no green, no blue, and no yellow chips this would correspond to 1,000 (see illustration).

Thousand (red)	Hundreds (green)	Tens (blue)	Ones (yellow)
1	0	0	0

If a 10 is rolled using 2 dice the student would trade the 1 red chip in for 10 green chips, then trade 1 green chip in for 10 blue chips (leaving 9 green chips), trade 1 blue chip in for 10 yellow chips leaving 9 blue chips and 10 yellow chips. Subtracting 10 as rolled by the 2 dice takes away the 10 yellow chips, that is, 1,000 − 10 = 990.

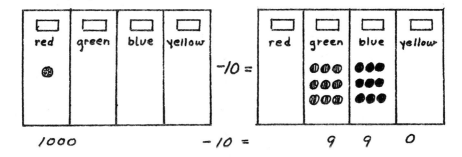

3. To transfer from color symbols to number symbols ask each player to write down the numbers that correspond to the same place value, as chips are added or subtracted. Example:

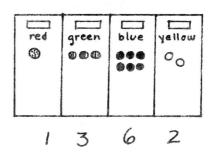

---

the greedy goose

Descriptors: Greater Than Concept
Less Than Concept

Grade Levels: 1–3

Rationale: Students who have mastered number sequencing are ready to learn the greater than/less than concepts and symbols. These concepts are made easier and more fun when a cartoon character is used to present a visual symbol.

Objective: To teach students the concept of greater than/less than. The student will be able consistently to write the correct symbol between 2 numbers designating the larger and the smaller number.

Materials: Chalkboard and chalk
Goose cut out of colored construction paper
Writing paper
Pencil

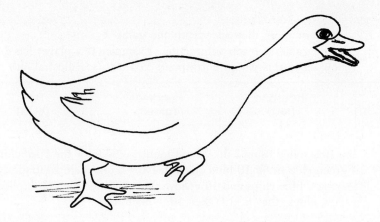

Procedure:

1. Construct a two-sided goose out of colored construction paper and introduce it to the class as "The Greedy Goose."
2. With thumb and forefinger simulate a mouth opening wide to eat something large and closing to eat something small.

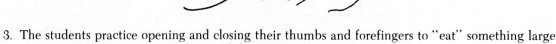

3. The students practice opening and closing their thumbs and forefingers to "eat" something large and something small in imitation of the demonstration.
4. Write 2 numbers on the chalkboard with a space between them (example: 3   5), and ask the students which is the larger number of the two.
5. State that "The Greedy Goose" wants to eat the larger number so it opens its mouth very wide toward the 5. Demonstrate this concept using the construction paper goose.
6. Now write the symbol < between the 2 numbers on the chalkboard. Explain that the symbol is like the goose's mouth. It opens wide for the large number.
7. Continue with examples of more number pairs on the chalkboard. Describe the concept of less than stressing that the goose's closed mouth points to the smaller number of the 2.

   Write   3 < 4   Say, "The closed part of the sign points to the 3 because it is

   smaller than the number 4."

8. Write other number pairs on the chalkboard. Ask students to solve the problem of identifying the larger and smaller numbers by first using the goose and then writing the symbol between the 2 numbers. Other students may copy the numbers on writing paper and use their pencils to solve the same problems a classmate is solving at the chalkboard.

Additional Suggestions:

1. Have students cut out their own geese for individual practice.
2. Ditto worksheets with pairs of numbers. The students are to write the correct symbol between each number pair.

Descriptors: Math Practice
One-to-one Correspondence
Measurement
Motivation

Grade Levels: 1–3

Rationale: Teachers are often looking for procedures to motivate and keep their students "on task." This activity is almost guaranteed to get your students' attention. Before introducing the edibles, any dietary restrictions among the students (such as diabetes, hypoglycemia, or obesity) must be considered. Choose foods that all students can enjoy.

Objective: To teach more meaningful math concepts using edibles.

Materials: Edibles (raisins, cherries, red hots, licorice sticks, graham crackers, sugarless gum, candy corn, chocolate bars, cookies)
Rulers
Scissors
Paper and Pencil

Activity 1: Measuring

Procedure:
1. Each student is given a ruler, a licorice stick, and a pair of scissors.
2. The students are asked to measure specific lengths such as 1 inch, ½ inch, and 4 centimeters with a ruler and cut off the exact amount, which is subsequently eaten.
3. The students continue to measure and cut their licorice stick in the designated lengths until it is gone.

Activity 2: Odd and Even Sets

Assumptions: The concepts of odd and even has previously been introduced. This activity practices the concepts.

Procedure:
1. Each student is given 10 pieces of candy corn.
2. Ask the students to eat an odd number of candy.
3. Ask the students to eat an even number of candy corn. (Note: The students learn that an even number minus an odd number leaves an odd number.

(Note: Experience has shown that most students seem to eat the minimum amount allowed in order to preserve their allotment!)
4. Continue this procedure until all corn is eaten.

Activity 3: Addition and Subtraction

Procedure:
1. Give each student a small box of raisins, cherries, or red hots.
2. Practice addition, subtraction, multiplication, or division problems using the edibles.
   Example: "Show me 3 sets of 3."
   $3 \times 3 = 9.$

"Eat 1 set of 3. What is left?"

"Two sets of 3 (or 2 × 3 = 6) are left." The student may also say, "9 − 3 = 6."

Activity 4: Fractions

Procedure:

1. Give each student graham crackers divided into fourths.

   insert art

2. Say, "Eat one-fourth of your graham cracker. How much is left?"
3. Continue this procedure until the graham cracker is eaten.
4. Give each student chocolate bars divided into 8 squares.
5. Ask the students to give one-eighth of their candy bar to the student sitting next to them (after a vigorous handwashing session). Note: This is a novel way of teaching sharing and all students get the same amount. It is a change of pace from eating one's own.

Additional Suggestions:

1. Cut apples into halves and fourths.
2. Use packages of sugarless gum containing 5 sticks of gum to study fifths.
3. Use packages of cookies or fruits (such as oranges or apples) to study dozen, one-half dozen, one-fourth dozen, and so on.

testing money skills

Descriptors: Criterion Test
Money Value

Grade Levels: 1–4
Mentally Retarded

Rationale: The ability to use money is a prerequisite for independent functioning. Exceptional students often have not acquired this skill even though they have the ability to develop it. This activity contains a quick checklist to be used in determining a student's skill level of understanding money concepts. The checklist examines a student's understanding in 4 subskill areas of money usage. The first area is coin recognition (name and value). The other 3 areas (recognizing value of grouped coins, giving the called for amounts, and making change) are based on arithmetic computations. Not all items on the checklist need to be presented. Items are sequenced according to level of difficulty, an arrangement that prevents the tester from frustrating the student with continued item failure. For example, if the child is unable to make change with amounts to 5¢, there is no need to ask for change with amounts to $5.00. It is suggested that actual money be used in testing, if possible.

Objective: To assess a student's current level of understanding of money concepts.

Materials: Real or play coins:
10 pennies
5 nickels
5 dimes
4 quarters
2 half-dollars
Real or play bills:
5 one-dollar bills
1 five-dollar bill

Procedure: *Money Skills Checklist*

PART I: COIN RECOGNITION.

The teacher presents coins one at a time and asks the student to name each. After all coins have been presented, the teacher again presents the coins and asks the student, "How much is this coin worth?"

PART II: RECOGNIZING AMOUNTS.

The teacher places groups of coins in specified value amounts in front of the student asking, "How much are these coins worth together?" or "How much money do I have?"

PART III: GIVING CALLED FOR AMOUNTS.

The teacher places an adequate amount of change in front of the student asking him/her to give the teacher specified amounts.

PART IV: MAKING CHANGE.

A specified coin or bill is given to the student. A purchase simulation is carried out for differently priced items. The student is asked to tell the teacher how much change s/he should get back. (This procedure can also be reversed to measure both the student's ability 1) to recognize that s/he has received the correct change, and 2) to count out the correct change.

Additional Suggestions: Design games to practice money skills particularly making change. Begin with very simple problems and gradually increase the difficulty. Use concrete materials in a store format (grocery, hardware, clothing, etc.) and place price tags on each item. Use play money and a cash register for both the shopper and the clerk.

name _____ date _____

school _____ teacher _____

grade _____

MONEY SKILLS CHECKLIST

	Correct	Incorrect	Response Value

I. Coin Recognition
  Penny
  Nickel
  Dime
  Quarter
  Half-Dollar			

II. Recognizing Amounts
  3¢
  8¢
  21¢
  36¢
  64¢
  80¢			

III. Giving Called for Amounts
  4¢
  7¢
  12¢
  19¢
  28¢
  51¢
  96¢			

IV. Making Change			

IV. Making Change

Given	Cost	Change
.05	.03	.02
.10	.06	.04
.25	.20	.05
.25	.16	.09
.50	.49	.01
.50	.25	.25
.50	.30	.20
.50	.10	.40
.50	.18	.32
1.00	.50	.50
1.00	.75	.25
1.00	.95	.05
1.00	.80	.20
1.00	.63	.37
1.00	.22	.78
5.00	1.00	4.00
5.00	3.00	2.00
5.00	2.50	2.50
5.00	3.25	1.75
5.00	1.15	3.85

_____informal math checklist_____

Descriptors: Task Analysis   **Grade Levels:** 1–5
                  Specific Skill Levels

Rationale: Sometimes it becomes necessary quickly to assess a student's math skills in order to place the student in appropriate teaching materials. This is particularly true when a new student joins your class in the middle of the year or if previous testing or cumulative records are not available. This informal math checklist was originally developed for use in a clinical setting to determine whether or not further diagnostic math assessment was necessary.

Objective: To assess briefly and quickly a student's current math levels.

Materials: Student Protocol Sheet
                  Test Profile Form
                  Pencil
                  Clock with movable hands
                  Coins:
                      10 pennies
                      10 nickels
                      10 dimes
                       4 quarters
                       2 half-dollars
                       1 dollar

Procedure:
1. The teacher uses the Informal Math Profile checklist to begin testing a student. The teacher must use discretion as to where to begin testing by taking into account the student's age, grade, previous history, and so on. That is, an older student would probably not be asked to identify geometric shapes or to write numerals but, instead, would begin with the math problems.
2. The student proceeds to complete the test as far as possible. The student usually indicates to the teacher when the test materials become too difficult.
3. The teacher circles the symbols missed on the teacher check sheet.

    Example: $+ \quad - \quad = \quad \textcircled{>} \quad \textcircled{<} \quad \times \quad \div$

4. During the testing, the teacher keeps observational notes describing the student's math strategies in order to plan a better program for the student. It is important to note if a student uses fingers during computations or begins working problems from left to right rather than right to left in two-place number problems. Some youngsters subtract the smaller number from the larger number regardless of position, because they have not yet mastered the concept of regrouping. Others may need a cover sheet or a marker to reduce the stimuli by exposing only one row of problems at a time. The student's sequential stroke pattern when writing each number is also important to note to determine if it is erroneous and inefficient.
5. The Time and Money sections of the checklist are very brief and are only designed as a screening procedure. More detailed tests covering both areas are included elsewhere in this book.
6. The teacher scores the test and plans a remediation program based on the test information or implements further in-depth diagnostic assessment measures if deemed necessary.

Additional Suggestions: Use the test protocol sheet to share with parents during Individualized Education Program (IEP) conferences.

INFORMAL MATH PROFILE CHECKLIST

student _____   date of test _____

age _____   grade _____

school _____   teacher _____

Directions: The teacher begins the assessment appropriate for the age, grade, and skill levels of the student. Stop testing each area when the student becomes frustrated by the level of difficulty. Circle the areas needing remediation when several are listed. Example: (Counting: 10s, 5s, 2s)

1. Count by 1s to 10, 20, 30; <30 (if desired).
   Count to 100 by 10s, 5s, and to 20 by 2s.

2. Numeral Identification 1 to 10 and 11 to 20: "What number is this?" Teacher points, student answers orally.

0	5	1	3	2	4	8	6	9	7	10
13	11	14	12	15	18	16	20	19	17	

3. Write numerals 1 to 9. (Assess 11 to 20 if desired.)

   _____

   _____

4. Identify: ◯ ☐ ▭ △

5. Math Symbols: $+$ $-$ $=$ $>$ $<$ $\times$ $\div$ $\$$

6.
$$\begin{array}{cccccc}
2 & 4 & 25 & 42 & 26 & 58 \\
+0 & +3 & +64 & +27 & +15 & +34
\end{array}$$

7.
$$\begin{array}{cccccc}
5 & 7 & 58 & 46 & 37 & 53 \\
-1 & -3 & -22 & -32 & -19 & -26
\end{array}$$

8.
$$\begin{array}{cccccc}
7 & 3 & 21 & 35 & 28 & 30 \\
\times 1 & \times 4 & \times 3 & \times 6 & \times 52 & \times 18
\end{array}$$

9. $3\overline{)9}$ $4\overline{)24}$ $6\overline{)248}$ $22\overline{)75}$

10. Time: Show time on clock face. (Student orally answers.)

Hours	8:00	11:00	12:00
Half hours	2:30	9:30	12:30
Quarter hours	3:45	1:45	8:45
Minutes	1:20	4:10	7:52

11. "Tell me the days of the week."

12. "Tell me the months of the year."

13. Money: "What is this coin?" (Show penny, nickel, dime, quarter, half dollar, dollar.)
    Addition: Teacher places coins on the table and asks the student to add them (use own discretion). Example: 3 pennies + 6 pennies, 2 nickels + 1 dime and 1 nickel, 1 dime and 3 pennies, 2 dimes 1 nickel, and so on.

    Subtraction: Teacher follows the same screening procedure. Example: 8 pennies − pennies, 1 dime, 3 pennies − 5¢, and so on.

INFORMAL MATH PROFILE CHECKLIST		Passed	Needs Help	Date Passed
Oral Counting	1 to 10, 11 to 20, 20 to 30, 30 to 100 by: 10s, 5s, to 20 by 2s			
Recognition	1 to 10, 11 to 20 (identify missed numbers)			
Writing	1 to 10, 11 to 20 (note stroke pattern)			
Identification	circle, square, rectangle, triangle $+, -, =, >, <, \times, \div, \$$			
Math Problems	Addition: 1 place 2 place regrouping (carrying) Subtraction: 1 place 2 place regrouping (borrowing) Multiplication: 1 place 2 place regrouping: 1 place multiplier 2 place multiplier Division: 1 place divided 2 place divided 1 place divisor with remainder 2 place divisor with remainder			
Time	Hours, half hours, quarter hours, minutes Days of the week Months of the year			
Money	Identification: penny, nickel, dime, quarter, half dollar, dollar Addition: pennies, nickels, dime, quarter, half dollar Subtraction: pennies, nickels, dime, quarter, half dollar			

_____dice games for math practice_____

Descriptors: Problem Solving
Multiplication
Addition
Subtraction

Grade Levels: 1–6

Rationale: Many students need repeated practice in order to learn math facts to a rote level. To avoid overuse of flash cards and dittoed worksheets, the teacher may introduce a change of pace by introducing a series of games using dice. Small groups of students can play these games and "painlessly" learn math facts at the same time. The following activities may be used with any grade level. The teacher is responsible for ensuring that students are assigned to groups appropriate for their skill level.

Objective: To practice math skills using dice.

Materials: Dice (commercial or teacher-made)
Chalkboard and chalk
Ditto master
Duplicating paper
Counters (toy cars, chips, paper clips)
Tagboard
Black marking pen

Procedure: 1. Choose an appropriate activity for the age and skill level of the students.
2. Explain the activity to the students and pass out the necessary materials.
3. Plan a specific time for each activity such as before morning recess, end of the day, or noon.
4. Make certain that at least one person in each group (for example, teacher, aide, parent volunteer, older student or student in the classroom who has already mastered the math skills being practiced) knows the math skills required and, thus, is able to correct any mistakes. If not, students may be consistently reinforcing wrong responses.
5. A pre- and posttest should be administered to check the effect of the activities on students' skill levels.

Activity 1: Roll Call

Younger students can make their own dice by writing numbers on 1-inch blocks of wood with a black marking pen. To start, young students may use 1 die with the numbers 0 to 5 on it. The die is rolled and the student calls out the number on top. A die with higher numbers 6 to 10 (add another 0) is used next. Later 2 dice may be thrown at a time; the student now calls out both numbers. Example: "48" (see illustration). Older students may play more complicated games using several blocks or commercial dice. A group leader is appointed to roll the dice. Before rolling them the leader calls out an instruction such as add, subtract, multiply, or divide. Other students in the group compete to be the first one to call out the right answer.

Instruction: Add: +   Answer: 7

Activity 2: Go

Design a game on tagboard with sections marked off between Start and Finish. Each student is given a marker (such as toy car, button, poker chip) and begins by throwing the die and moving the marker the number of spaces indicated on the die. The first student to reach Finish wins the game.

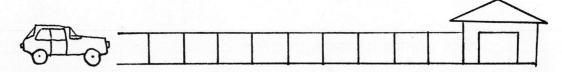

The game becomes more complicated if 2 dice are rolled and the student is asked to add the 2 numbers before moving the marker the total number of spaces. Later increase to 3 dice, and design more spaces between Start and Finish. The designs should be age-appropriate for the students (for example, don't give older students immature or childish-looking game formats).

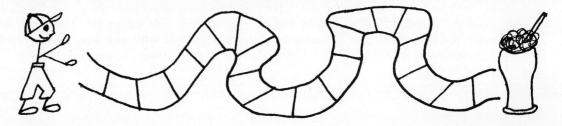

Activity 3: Before/After Sequence

Write a number (2 to 6 or 2 to 12) on the chalkboard and say, "I'm looking for the number which comes before (or after) the one I have just written." The students roll their dice until one of them gets the appropriate number. That student goes to the chalkboard and writes the number in the proper position next to your number.

(Note: When working with older students high numbers may be used and more dice may be added. Also, dots may be added or multiplied to reach the right number.)

Activity 4: Problem Strips

This game is similar to bingo. The student chooses one of the problem strips as illustrated. The first player rolls the die, counts the number of dots showing, and uses a sequence tagboard number to cover the appropriate space. Example: The player rolls a 5 and selects the problem 12-7 on the problem strip to stand for "5." That problem is then covered with a tagboard 5.

The other players follow in turn. If a player rolls a number for which the appropriate space is already covered, the play passes to the next player. The game ends when 1 player has covered all the spaces on a strip. To increase the difficulty level, the number value of the problems may be increased (Example: 6+5 or 11+6) and more dice may be added.

(Note: This game may also be played using a bingo card format instead of a strip.)

Activity 5: Write It

Each student is given a pair of dice and a sheet of lined paper. Students roll the dice and write the addition (or subtraction) problem shown by the dice on the first line. Example: If a student rolls a 2 and a 5, 2 + 5 = 7 or (if subtraction) 5 − 2 = 3 is written on the first line. Each student completes at least 10 problems using this procedure.

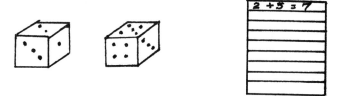

Activity 6: Circle Subtraction

This activity is excellent for students in the beginning stages of subtraction. Ditto a worksheet with a circle and approximately 6 lines underneath it. Give each student a die and 6 dried beans (or other counters), which are placed in the circle. The student rolls the die and removes the number of beans indicated by the die from the circle and counts the remaining beans. Next, the student records the subtraction fact on the first line beneath the circle. Example: 6 beans—roll a 4—take away 4 beans—remaining beans equal 2, thus, 6 − 4 = 2. Continue until 6 (or more) problems have been written. Increase the number of beans to 10 as the students' skills increase.

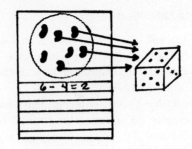

Activity 7: Cross Out

Write the numbers 1 to 9 on a piece of paper. Monitor as the student tosses 2 dice and marks out the sum tossed. Example: If you toss a 5 and 2 you may mark out the 7 or any combination of digits that totals 7 such as 4 and 3. The student continues tossing the dice until the sum tossed from the remaining digits can no longer be marked out. Each student's score is the sum of the remaining digits. The person with the lowest total number wins the game.

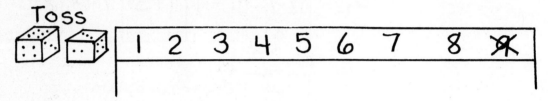

A second game may be started by writing a new line of numbers 1 to 9 beneath the previous one.

Activity 8: Problem Squares

The teacher constructs 3 6″ × 6″ cardboard frames using tagboard and places them left to right with + (or −) and = signs between the frames (see illustration). Three players are chosen. Player A rolls 1 die and places it inside square A. Player C rolls 2 dice and places them inside square C. The sum of the 2 numbers represents the sum of the equation. (Note: If the sum of the numbers in square C is smaller than the number in square A, the dice must be rolled again. Player B uses either 1 die or 2 dice and *turns* them (not rolls them) so that the sum of the numbers on the dice added together with A's number equals C's number.

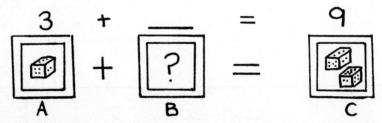

The students may record each equation on paper later to be corrected by the teacher. To practice subtraction each player receives 2 dice. Two players roll their dice. The player with the larger number places his/her dice in square A; the other player uses square B. The third player then uses 1 die or 2 dice to show the correct number to represent the difference between A and B.

$$6 \quad - \quad 5 \quad = \quad 1$$

Activity 9: Tic-Tac-Toe Bingo

Game cards constructed using tagboard and a black marking pen are used to practice addition or multiplication. The game format may also be dittoed and glued to tagboard. Begin with the numbers 1 to 6 both horizontally and vertically. Each player takes a blank card. The first player rolls the 2 dice. Example: 4 and 3. The student then multiplies (or adds) 4×3 and 3×4, writes the answer in the appropriate grids on the card and draws circles around the numbers (see illustration). The second player follows the same procedure. The players take turns rolling the dice and filling in their cards. The first player to completely fill one line across, down, or diagonally (as in bingo) wins the game.

X	1	2	3	4	5	6
1						
2						
3			⑫			
4		⑫				
5						
6						

_____ **puzzle fun** _____

Descriptors: Self-Correcting Puzzles   **Grade Levels:** 1–6
Math
Language
Reading

Rationale: Self-correcting materials are both useful for students practicing newly acquired skills and time effective by freeing the teacher from constant supervision. Puzzles provide a helpful self-correcting feedback system.

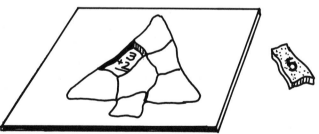

Materials: A commercial cardboard puzzle with a frame or a cardboard puzzle with a piece of sturdy cardboard used as a frame.

Procedure: (For puzzle with frame)
1. Remove 1 piece of the puzzle at a time.
2. Trace the outline of the piece in the vacant space on the frame.
3. Write an arithmetic problem (appropriate for grade level) in the vacant space.
4. Write the answer to the problem on the back of the piece corresponding to the vacant space.
5. Repeat the previous 4 steps for each piece of the puzzle. Write a different arithmetic problem in each space.

Procedure: (For puzzle without frame)
1. Put the puzzle together on a piece of cardboard or other sturdy backing.
2. Outline the parameter of the puzzle.
3. Follow the 5 steps described for framed puzzles.
   (Note: The students' interests and abilities determine the choice of the picture on the puzzle, as well as the number and size of pieces. However, the puzzle itself should be easy enough to prevent visual perception errors in matching a piece with its outline. The purpose is not to develop puzzle skills, but to use a puzzle as a self-correcting feedback device.)

Additional Suggestions: Other skills that may also be taught using the puzzle format include matching color words and colors, rhyming words, opposites, number words and numbers, and upper and lowercase letters.

_____ "worm" your way to multiplication! _____

Descriptors: Math Facts   **Grade Levels:**   3–6
Group Activities
Spelling
Basic Sight Vocabulary

Rationale: This visual and tangible teaching idea appeals to those students who are otherwise difficult to motivate and also serves to aid the teacher in rapidly determining each student's progress. To eliminate unfair competition between high and low math groups in the class, the activity is recommended for small groups of students on the same skill level.

Objective: To help stimulate a student's motivation to learn multiplication facts.

Materials: Colored construction paper
Black marking pen
Scissors
Paste
Pipe cleaners
Apples
Ditto master of 2-inch diameter circles
Duplicating paper
Bulletin board
Thumbtacks

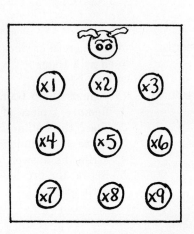

Procedure:

1. Draw a large apple on a piece of red construction paper for each math group in the classroom and attach each apple to the bulletin board.
2. Draw 2-inch diameter circles on a ditto master and duplicate 1 for each student.
3. Each student draws a worm face on a circle with a marking pen, cuts it out, adds pipe cleaner antennae and his/her name, and attaches to bulletin board apple with a thumbtack.
4. As each student masters the various levels of multiplication facts, form a worm by attaching a circle (worm segment) from the duplicated sheet containing the number of the level of the facts mastered to the student's worm face.
5. As the students' worms grow and their mastery level increases, cut away part of the paper apple to demonstrate that the math worms are "worming" their way into the apple.
6. When the students have memorized their facts, the paper apple will be gone and you can reinforce the students by giving each a real apple to celebrate their success.

Additional Suggestions:

1. Use a drawing of a book rather than an apple and ask the students to design "book worms." Each worm segment lists a library book the student has just read.
2. Use the worm idea for spelling word lists mastered.
3. Design individual apples, which each of the students pastes to a black piece of construction paper. The students add circle sections to their own worm faces following the procedure previously outlined, but keep the records in their desks. When completed, the papers may be displayed on the class bulletin board.

Descriptors: Addition Practice   **Grade Levels:** 2–5
Subtraction Practice

Rationale: Many students have difficulty in regrouping (both borrowing and carrying) because they have not mastered the basic math facts 11 to 20 at an automatic level. Although most teachers spend a great deal of class time working on math facts 1 to 10, they allow little practice at the next level, assuming that the students have generalized the previous information and are able to apply it at the higher level.

Objective: To present sequential practice activities with addition and subtraction facts from 11 to 20.

Materials: 5-inch diameter colored construction paper circles
Black marking pen
Manila folders (1 for each student)
Duplicating paper
Ruler
Pencil
Ditto master
Counters (beads, chips, paper clips)
Tape recorder (optional)

Procedure:
1. The teacher designs a blank five-day grid and dittoes multiple copies. Students will receive a new grid each week.
2. Students who need to learn the basic math facts 11 to 20 receive a blank grid and attach it to their folders.
3. The teacher writes in the math fact to be learned each day. This allows the teacher to individualize the math instruction. Students will be working on different problems appropriate for their level.
4. The students look in their folders to see the math facts to be learned on a given day.

Name	Monday	Tuesday	Wednesday	Thur
10/15	9+2=___ 2+9=___	3+8=___ 8+3=___		

5. The addition combinations for 1 number is practiced for a whole week. Example: All addition combinations that equal (2 + 9, 9 + 2, 3 + 8, 8 + 3, 4 + 7, 7 + 4, 5 + 6, 6 + 5).
6. Each student completes the number problems assigned for that day and practices the number combinations using the following procedures:

   a. Solve the number problem by using counters.
   b. Write the number problems on blank pieces of paper and draw balls to illustrate them.

$$2 + 9 =$$
$$oo + \begin{matrix} ooo \\ ooo \\ ooo \end{matrix} = 11$$
$$9 + 2 =$$
$$\begin{matrix} ooo \\ ooo \\ ooo \end{matrix} + oo = 11$$

   c. Write the answers to the number problems on the assignment sheet in the folder.

d. Write the math problems on one side of 5-inch circles cut from colored construction paper and the answers on the other side. The students keep their own circle flash cards (called "math balls") in an envelope at their desks. In this way students have an opportunity to practice and review all previously learned math combinations.

e. Record the day's problems on a tape recorder and play it back to listen to the problem plus the answer.

7. Each day the student reviews all previously mastered number problems by reviewing the flash cards. On Friday the week's problems may be tested using a math problem worksheet or flash cards.

(Note: It is important not to introduce the next higher set of number problems, for example, addition combinations to 12, until the student has completely mastered the previous combinations.)

Additional Suggestions:

1. Follow the same procedure to learn subtraction facts 11 to 20.
2. Ask the students to practice each week's assigned problems with student peers or at home with parents. Daily and weekly review sessions are vital for retention of the information.

---

organize math columns

Descriptors: Structure
Visual Perceptual Aid
Math Practice

Grade Levels: 2–6

Rationale: This aid is designed for a student who has difficulty with visual perception or visually organizing information.

Objective: To organize visually addition math problems in a column with a "magic window."

Materials: 5″ × 8″ index card
Razor knife
Marker
Worksheet of math problems in columns

Procedure: Cut a long slot in the index card. The size of the slot will depend on the level of difficulty of the problem and whether teacher-made or standard worksheets are used. Make the slot long enough so the student can write the answer and "carry." The extra space to the left and on the bottom of the column allows the student to write a two-digit response when completing the problem. Mark an arrow to show the child the direction in which to move the card when adding.

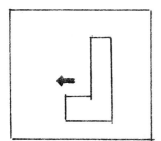 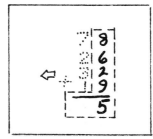 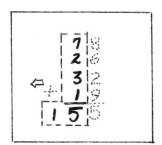

Additional
Suggestions: 1. Use a smaller window for subtraction practice.

2. Use large-squared graph paper.

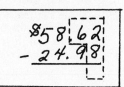

_____ spacy fractions _____

Descriptors: Math Practice   Grade Levels: 3–4
                Visual Aids

Rationale: Many science fiction films and television programs appeal to students who are sometimes not
                motivated to do school work. Capitalize on such an interest by using science fiction to teach fractions,
                for example. Once you succeed in getting the attention of otherwise unmotivated students, you will
                be surprised at how quickly they learn.

Objective: To teach fractions by using visual concepts.

Materials: Chalkboard and chalk
                Ditto master
                Duplicating paper
                Pencil

Procedure: 1. Draw an outer-space robot on the
                   chalkboard and ask the class, "How many
                   robots do you see?"
                2. One student is called to the chalkboard.
                   That student writes the number 1.
                3. Erase half of the robot and say, "An
                   invisible ray gun shot the robot. How much
                   of the robot is still showing?"
                4. A student is called to the chalkboard.
                   The student writes ½.
                5. The teacher draws a spaceship containing
                   two fat robots and asks the class, "If one of
                   the robots leaves the spaceship, what
                   fraction indicates the number of fat robots
                   left to run the ship?"

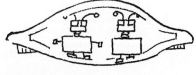

                6. A student is called to the chalkboard to write the answer ½.
                7. Continue by adding more fat robots to the spaceship, for example, 4 robots. Say, "Two leave,
                   thus, what fraction is left to control the ship?" Answer: 2/4 or ½.
                8. Draw 6 fat robots and have 3 leave. Repeat the question in step 7. Ask a student to come to the
                   chalkboard and write the answer (3/6 or ½).
                9. Using a ditto master sheet draw more fraction problems using robots and spaceships. Duplicate 1
                   copy for each student as a seatwork assignment.
               10. Evaluate each student's progress when grading the completed papers. If some students have not
                   grasped the concept of fractions, go back to the chalkboard and work with the students on steps 1
                   through 8.

"Here is a flying saucer with thin robots. How many thin robots are in the spaceship? _____(8)_____ .
If a thin robot is ½ as big as a fat robot, how many fat robots would fill the spaceship _____(4)_____ ."

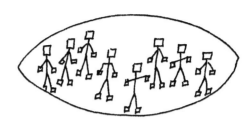

"Here comes a fleet of flying saucers. How many are there in all? _____(6)_____ .
One-half of this number are how many flying saucers? _____(3)_____ .
Five flying saucers equal how many sixths? _____(5/6)_____ .
One-third is how many saucers? _____(2)_____ ."

"Here comes the robot army! How many robots are there? _____(12)_____ .
Color ⅓ of the army orange. How many are ⅓? _____(4)_____ .
Color ⅔ blue. How many are ⅔? _____(8)_____ ."

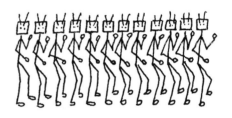

"Here are _____(5)_____ sick robots. Color 2/5 of these sick robots purple. Color the other robots green. What fraction of the robots are green? _____(3/5)_____ ."

After the students finish the problems, they may want to make up their own robot examples on index cards and exchange them with classmates.

Additional Suggestions: Use other cartoon characters or animals that interest your students. By allowing the students to design their own fraction problems, they become actively (rather than passively) involved in problem solving.

Descriptors: Math Skills
Visual Cues

Grade Levels: 3–6

Rationale: Once students have mastered the idea that zero has a very special property in addition and subtraction, namely, it does not change the original quantity, they often tend to overgeneralize this characteristic to the multiplication operation. For example: If $4 + 0 = 4$, and $4 - 0 = 4$, why not expect 4×0 to also equal 4? Effective strategies to prevent such generalization include the realization that confusion with zero, even in addition, may not occur until *after* the multiplication form has been introduced. Hence, even at this stage, it is helpful to require the student to illustrate the symbolic form for addition *and* multiplication by using either concrete or pictorial representations.

Objective: To use a pictorial representation to depict the different role of zero in the processes of addition and multiplication.

Materials: Paper
Pencil
Black marking pen
Chalkboard and chalk

Procedure: *In the set model:*

1. The teacher draws the illustrated diagram on the chalkboard saying, "A set of 3 members plus an empty set equals a set of 3 members: $3 + 0 = 3$."

2. The teacher now draws the next illustrated diagram on the chalkboard saying, "Three sets of no members, or 3 empty sets equal an empty set: $3 \times 0 = \square$, $0 + 0 + 0+ = 0$, $3 \times 0 = 0$. In this representation, the property of multiplication as repeated addition is clear; zero is added 3 times."

(Note: In the developmental progression toward symbolic competency, the next step is often used to illustrate the same process by means of a number line.)

Addition

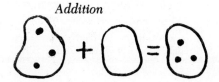

Multiplication

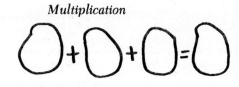

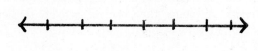

3. The teacher writes the following problems on the chalkboard and draws a large number line.

Addition	**Multiplication**
3 + 0 =	3 × 0 =

Addition

3 + 0 =

This would be interpreted to indicate a start at zero (always the starting point), then a move to 3 followed by an additional move of 0 distance:

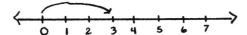

The answer is determined by the stopping point, thus

3 + 0 = 3.

Multiplication

3 × 0 =

This would be interpreted to indicate a start at zero (always the starting point;, then taking 3 jumps of 0 distance each time:

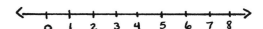

The answer is determined by the stopping point. In this case the 3 jumps involved no distance, thus

3 × 0 = 0.

(Note: The set model is most frequently employed for addition, and the number line strategy for multiplication. One advantage of the number line conceptualization for multiplication is that it portrays jumps of equal length and landing points on multiples of the factor. Hence, it establishes valuable groundwork for later discovery that the process is like "counting by threes" and so on.)

Additional Suggestions:

Instructional approaches advocated by early research at Education Development Center, 55 Chapel Street, Newton, Massachusetts, 02158, successfully utilize a jumping insect for illustration on the number line approach to multiplication with young children. For example, a "3 cricket" is one who is programmed to jump along the number line from zero for a distance of 3 units. Hence, 4 × 3 can be represented as 4 jumps of a 3 cricket.

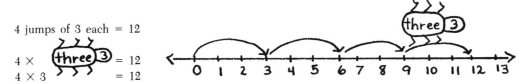

4 jumps of 3 each = 12

4 × (three 3) = 12

4 × 3 = 12

In this mode, 4 × 0 would be represented as 4 jumps of a 0 cricket.

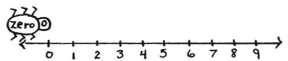

4 jumps of 0 each = 0

4 × (zero 0) = 0

4 × 0 = 0

(Note: The cricket covers no distance from zero on number line.)
Also, 0 × 4 would be represented as 0 jumps by a 4 cricket.

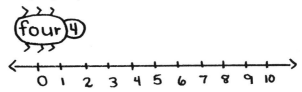

0 jumps of 4 each = 0

0 × (four 4) = 0

0 × 4 = 0

Such a representation provides a conceptual back-up for students as they move into situations that require facility with the effect of zero in addition and multiplication processes.

Descriptors: Pocket Calculators
Multiplication

Grade Levels: 3–6

Rationale: Most elementary math books require students to multiply by multiples of ten before using two- or three-place factors. Thus, it is important to achieve success at this level before the student is expected to proceed to more difficult multiplication problems. Some students have difficulty understanding how many zeros should be placed at the end of an answer. By using a calculator the students learn that the number of zeros that go into the calculator as factors will reappear at the end of the product.

Objective: To teach students how to multiply with multiples of ten before progressing to more difficult problems.

Materials: Pocket calculator
Blank index cards
Black marking pen
Pencil

Procedure:

1. Give the students an index card with the following problem printed on it:

2. Put the equation into the calculator for the student while saying the problem:
   29 × 10 = 290.
3. Clear the calculator.

4. Ask the student to put the same equation into the calculator while saying the problem:
   29 × 10 = 290.

5. Have the student write the answer to the equation on the index card.
6. Ask the student to count orally the number of zeros in the factors.

   $$\begin{array}{r} 29 \\ \times 10 \\ \hline \end{array}$$ Answer: 1 zero.

   Ask the student to count orally the number of zeros in the product.
   290   Answer: 1 zero.
7. Continue working with the student, repeating steps 1 through 6 with the following equations written on index cards:

   $$\begin{array}{r} 29 \\ \times 100 \\ \hline \end{array} \qquad \begin{array}{r} 29 \\ \times 1000 \\ \hline \end{array} \qquad \begin{array}{r} 29 \\ \times 10000 \\ \hline \end{array} \qquad \begin{array}{r} 29 \\ \times 1000000 \\ \hline \end{array}$$

8. Ask the students to do steps 4 through 6 independently with the following problems written on index cards:

   $$\begin{array}{r} 53 \\ \times 10 \\ \hline \end{array} \qquad \begin{array}{r} 53 \\ \times 100 \\ \hline \end{array} \qquad \begin{array}{r} 53 \\ \times 1000 \\ \hline \end{array} \qquad \begin{array}{r} 53 \\ \times 10000 \\ \hline \end{array} \qquad \begin{array}{r} 53 \\ \times 1000000 \\ \hline \end{array}$$

   If correct, proceed. If incorrect, repeat the entire set following steps 1 through 6.
9. Give the students a paper with the following problems and ask them to write the product with a pencil without using a calculator.

   $$\begin{array}{r} 42 \\ \times 10 \\ \hline \end{array} \qquad \begin{array}{r} 42 \\ \times 100 \\ \hline \end{array} \qquad \begin{array}{r} 42 \\ \times 1000 \\ \hline \end{array} \qquad \begin{array}{r} 42 \\ \times 10000 \\ \hline \end{array} \qquad \begin{array}{r} 42 \\ \times 100000 \\ \hline \end{array}$$

Additional Suggestions:

1. When the students know the multiplication facts 2 to 9, use steps 1 through 9 to teach multiplication by other factors that end in one or more zeros. The following series of problems may be used.

SET A

23	23	23	23	23
×40	×400	×4000	×40000	×400000

SET B

56	56	56	56	56
×30	×300	×3000	×30000	×300000

SET C

62	62	62	62	62
×210	×2100	×21000	×210000	×2100000

2. Ideas for calculator games may be found in: E. Schlossberg and J. Brockman, *The Pocket Calculator Game Book*, Science News, Dept. CB-3, 1719 N Street, N.W., Washington, D.C. 20036.

addition and subtraction practice

Descriptors: Games   **Grade Levels:**   3–6
Motivation

Rationale: In order to perform higher level math operations students need to commit the basic math facts to memory. To be proficient, students must be able to recall the facts automatically without the aid of counting.

Objective: To practice math facts until the student reaches an automatic level of proficiency.

Materials: 3″ × 5″ and 5″ × 7″ flash cards
Black marking pen
Graph paper
Ditto master
Duplicating paper
Crayons

Procedure:

1. Administer a practice test that includes all basic addition facts in all combinations (provided they are all appropriate for the student's current level of functioning). The test may be administered with flash cards with the student giving oral answers or duplicated on paper with the student writing the answers.
2. Record the types of problems missed by the student.
3. Begin remediation by working on the lowest numbers missed. Example: If the student had difficulty adding numbers with the digit 6, begin practice with 6 added to all digits 1 through 9.
4. Do not introduce the next level of numbers until the student is proficient with the newly introduced skill. Example: When the student has mastered +6 with other digits (1 to 9) at an automatic level, begin working with the number 7.
5. The following practice activities may involve parents, teacher aides, student peers, and the classroom teacher as sources of help to the student.
6. Administer a postpractice (oral or written) test periodically in order to determine whether or not the student has retained the newly learned skills and is able to generalize to other areas.

Practice Activities

1. *Flash Cards with Charting Graph.* Using flash cards or dittoed worksheets, the student along with the teacher or a tutor practices 20 math problems at his/her level. The number of problems solved correctly each day may be recorded. As the student becomes proficient at answering the problems correctly, a timer may be used and the results may be graphed as number of seconds needed to complete the 20 problems. A visual record of the gradual decrease in time required for each worksheet is very motivating to many students. In reality, a student is competing with him/herself. Caution must be exercised in using timed exercises for students with poor writing skills, who may find such activities very frustrating. These students should practice orally with flash cards rather than writing the answers.

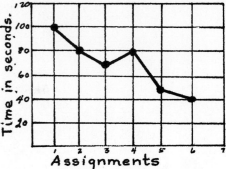

2. *Grids.* Ditto wide graph paper forms to be used by the students in making math grids for addition practice. Number the columns 1 to 10 across the top of the grid and 1 to 10 down the left side. Each number on the left side is added to the top numbers and the answer is written in the corresponding box. (Note: Begin by writing in only the numbers 1 to 5, as the large grids present too many stimuli for beginning learners.)

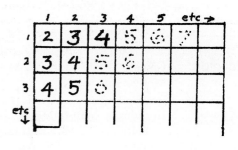

3. *Worksheets.* Ditto a worksheet of math problems at the student's present level of functioning. For example, if a student is working on 6+ addition facts, do not include 7+ or 8+ problems on that particular student's worksheet. Cut the paper in strips if it offers too many stimuli at one time. A blank piece of paper may also be used as a cover sheet to reduce the number of stimuli presented at one time.

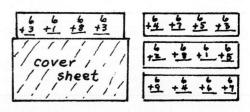

4. *Cross-Out.* Write the numbers 1 to 10 on the chalkboard or on a blank sheet of paper. Ask the student to:
   Cross out the 2 numbers whose sum is 5.
   Cross out the 2 numbers whose sum is 12.
   Cross out the 2 numbers whose sum is 19.

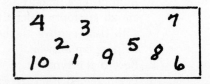

5. *Nineteen Is the Winner.* Two people may play this game. The first says a number that is less than 5. The second repeats the first player's number and adds it to another number less than 5. The total of these numbers is now added to a number less than 5 chosen by the first student. This continues until the total reaches 19. The first student to reach 19 is the winner.

Example: John, "4." Bill, "4 and 4 are 8." John, "3 and 8 are 11." Bill, "4 and 11 are 15." John, "4 and 15 are 19." John is the winner!

6. *Can You Find "N"?* This game may be played by 2 players. On blank cards (5″ × 7″) write the numerals from 1 to 19, 1 on each card. Line the cards up on the chalkboard tray so they are visible to the students. On another chalkboard write several number sentences, such as 6 + 5 = N. At a signal, the 2 players quickly try to match the number sentence with 1 of the number cards. Each correct score earns 1 point. The students' points are totaled with the high scorer being declared the winner.

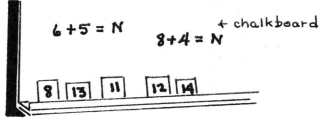

7. *Subtraction Practice: What's the Difference?* A game for 2 players. On white, 3″ × 5″ cards write black numerals from 1 to 10, 1 on each. On 3″ × 5″ white cards write (use crayons) one of the numerals 11 to 19, 1 on each. Shuffle the cards well and deal them all out to the players. The first player turns over a card and so does his opponent. If the cards both have black numbers or both have red numbers, the player showing the lowest number of the two cards scores the difference between the 2 cards. For example, 6 and 10 would mean the player having the 6 card would write down 4 points on his score. Each turns over another card. If the cards show different colored numbers (1 red and 1 black) the player having the higher number receives the difference as a score. (For example, if black 6 and colored 19 are displayed, the player having the 19 card may write down 13 as his score. The sums of the 2 numbers can be used as an alternative game.)

8. *Smart Cards—Magic Tricks.* The student makes 5 "smart cards" exactly like the ones below. Make them big enough so that the whole class can clearly see the numbers. Ask a student to pick any number between 1 and 31. Then the student points to each card in which the chosen number appears. Unknown to the student, you just add the first number of each of the boxes the student points out. It will always be the chosen number.

1	3	5	7
9	11	13	15
17	19	21	23
25	27	29	31

2	3	6	7
10	11	14	15
18	19	22	23
26	27	30	31

4	5	6	7
12	13	14	15
20	21	22	23
28	29	30	31

8	9	10	11
12	13	14	15
24	25	26	27
28	29	30	31

16	17	18	19
20	21	22	23
24	25	26	27
28	29	30	31

    1   2   3   4   5

Example: Chosen number – 15. Student points to cards 1, 2, 3, and 4. You add 1+2+4+8, which equals 15.

Additional Suggestions: Use each of the activities to practice subtraction facts. Follow the same procedure suggested for addition facts. Do not place a student at too high a level. The pre- and postassessment is very important to ensure that the practice activities are successful.

Descriptors: Addition
Coin Identification

Grade Levels: 3-6

Rationale: Grocery shopping is a life skill that should be introduced during the elementary-school years. Many students learn money identification as an isolated skill without transferring that knowledge to areas such as shopping lists, advertisements, or price labels. This activity provides such practice.

Objective: To give students practice in reading words and prices and counting money.

Prerequisite Skills:

1. Students should be able to identify all the coins and know their value.
2. Students should know the ¢ and the $ signs.
3. Students should be able to read words on shopping lists.

Materials: Large piece of tagboard
Black marking pen
Commercial pictures (newspaper ads, magazines, catalogues)
Glue
Clear contact paper or laminator
Real or play coins:
  6 quarters
  10 pennies
  10 dimes
  20 nickles

Procedure:

1. Students cut out large, distinct pictures of food items and prices from newspaper grocery ads.
2. Glue the pictures onto large tagboard posters (22″ × 28″) and write a price and the word beside each picture.
3. Cover the charts with clear contact paper to make them more durable.
4. Print "grocery lists" on 7″ × 9″ tagboard cards using a black marking pen. Design a variety of cards.
5. Laminate or cover each list with clear contact paper.
6. Give the student a "grocery list" and $3.00 worth of real or play coins in varying amounts. Instruct the student to find the cost of each item on the list by referring to the large charts.
7. Have the student count out the correct amount of money for each item on the list. The total amount is not added at this learning stage.
8. Check the amounts.
9. The student may have a second card after completing the first one correctly.
10. If the first card is incorrect, the student recounts the coins with assistance.
11. Construct 2 different posters and a variety of "grocery lists" to keep the student actively involved.

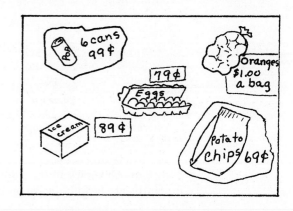

126

Additional Suggestions: 1. Cards may be made up for the students to use as self-correctors. Purchase a money stamp set. Make up identical "grocery list" cards and stamp correct coins beside the food item. Students are then able to correct their own errors. It is necessary to show all coin combinations that add up to the amount of the item.

Pop	⑩ ⑩ ⑳ ⑤ ⑩ ① ① ①	(99¢)
Bread	⑳ ⑩ ⑩ ① ① ①	(48¢)
Eggs	㉕ ㉕ ㉕ ① ① ① ①	(79¢)
Oranges	⑩ ⑩ ⑩ ⑤	(65¢)

2. Students may add the total amount needed for each grocery list card. The totals may be recorded on the back of the self-correcting card. Use a calculator or clicker counter to arrive at the total.
3. Add sales tax to the total. To calculate the amount of tax involves prerequisite multiplication skills.

rate sheets

Descriptors: Graphing Skills   **Grade Levels:**   3–6
Math Drill

Rationale: To increase students' sight recognition of basic math facts and motivate them to improve their performance by graphing their own progress.

Objective: To reinforce a student's knowledge of basic addition, subtraction, and multiplication facts and to teach the student to graph progress by keeping rate charts.

Materials   Ditto master
Duplicating paper
Dittoed math worksheets
Dittoed blank progress graphs
Paper
Stopwatch

Procedure: 1. The teacher dittoes worksheets with addition, subtraction, multiplication, or division problems according to the students' skill levels. Initially, the math worksheets should stay at one level (Example: +for all problems, or ×4). The top row called "mini-practice" is enclosed in a box (see illustration).
2. The students are asked to work the problems in the mini-section first. If all answers are correct (as verified by the teacher), the student is ready to proceed to the rest of the worksheet while being timed. If the mini-section is completed incorrectly, the student needs to restudy the math skills tested by the worksheet before being timed on that skill.
3. The student is allowed one minute, as timed with a stopwatch, to complete the math sheet.
4. The number of problems answered correctly are computed for the one-minute period and added to an individual graph (dittoed by the teacher).
5. The same skill (Example: +3 problems) is timed daily for 5 or 6 days until the student's number correct reaches the criterion set by the pupil and the teacher. This number will vary according to the student's age and skill levels.
6. A new graph is started with the introduction of each new skill level.

(Note: By requiring the student to complete the mini-section with 100 percent accuracy before being timed on the rest of the worksheet, the teacher ensures that the student is not practicing erroneous responses. If the student is to increase math speed, the student will have to memorize the facts rather than look at the answers in the mini-practice section. Eventually, the student will no longer need the mini-practice sections.)

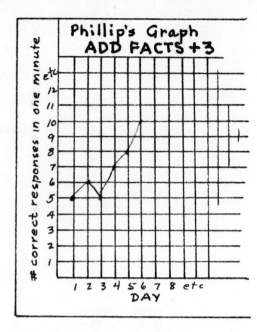

Additional Suggestions: The completed math worksheets and rate sheets may be kept in individual notebooks as a permanent record of established math skills.

multiplication drill

Descriptors: Multiplication
Division
Small-Group Activity

Grade Levels: 3-6

Rationale: Multiplication facts tend to cause some students difficulty long after they are expected to be mastered. It is not true that there are 9 numerals times 9 or 81 facts to learn and remember. Multiplication memory work can be reduced considerably by using the commutative property of addition and multiplication. Actually, there are only 36 facts to remember if one makes use of the commutative principle according to which the order of the factors makes no difference. For example:

$$2 \times 4 = 8 \qquad 4 \times 2 = 8$$

Most of the facts that are difficult to remember make up a very small number of the total 36 facts. The multiplication facts may be considered in terms of their products as well as their commutative partner. *One* is the identity factor. Any number times 1 equals that number. Once students know and remember this, they know the ones.

Objective: To provide further practice with multiplication problems after these have been introduced to students.

Materials: 3″ × 7″ tagboard strips
Worksheets
Blank index cards
Black marking pen

Procedure: 1. Make a list of the following multiplication facts grouped into categories by their product.

Products under 10 (4 facts)	Tens (9 facts)	Twenties (7 facts)	Thirties (5 facts)
$2 \times 2 = 4$	$2 \times 5 = 10$	$4 \times 5 = 20$	$5 \times 6 = 30$
$3 \times 2 = 6$	$3 \times 4 = 12$	$5 \times 5 = 25$	$4 \times 8 = 32$
$4 \times 2 = 8$	$2 \times 6 = 12$	$3 \times 7 = 21$	$6 \times 6 = 36$
$3 \times 3 = 9$	$7 \times 2 = 14$	$4 \times 6 = 24$	$4 \times 9 = 36$
	$4 \times 4 = 16$	$3 \times 8 = 24$	$7 \times 5 = 35$
	$2 \times 8 = 16$	$3 \times 9 = 27^*$	
	$9 \times 2 = 18$	$4 \times 7 = 28^*$	
	$3 \times 6 = 18$		
	$3 \times 5 = 15$		

Forties (5 facts)	Fifties (2 facts)	Sixties (2 facts)	Seventies (1 fact)	Eighties (1 fact)
$7 \times 6 = 42$	$7 \times 8 = 56^*$	$7 \times 9 = 63^*$	$8 \times 9 = 72$	$9 \times 9 = 81$
$5 \times 9 = 45$	$6 \times 9 = 54^*$	$8 \times 8 = 64^*$		
$8 \times 5 = 40$				
$7 \times 7 = 49^*$				
$6 \times 8 = 48^*$				

If you know $3 \times 7 = 21$, you know $7 \times 3 = 21$. This reduces the number of multiplication facts to be learned and may also give the youngsters a head start on division facts. Students appear to have difficulty remembering the facts with the astericks. Be sure to tell the students that the facts with the astericks have always been a little harder for some reason. Provide more drill with the difficult facts.

2. Tell the students that they can learn all the multiplication facts by mastering only 36 facts. Begin with "products under 10." Make flash cards from blank index cards for this category. At this stage make flash cards of the commutative principle of each problem.

Example: $2 \times 2 = 4$ $4 \times 2 = 8$
$2 \times 3 = 6$ $2 \times 4 = 8$
$3 \times 2 = 6$ $3 \times 3 = 9$

3. Ask the students to practice the flash cards in this category until they become proficient.
4. When the students have mastered the "products under 10" category, introduce 3″ × 7″ tagboard flash cards that have been written vertically.

```
   2          3
   4          2
   8          6
```

5. Cover 1 number with your hand. The students are to supply orally the missing number.

Example:

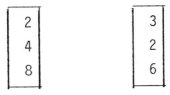

4x2= ?   4x ? =8   ? x2=8

This game provides practice with the relationship of the 3 numbers in the multiplication problem.
6. When the students become proficient with both types of flash cards and can demonstrate this proficiency on dittoed worksheets of number problems, the teacher may introduce the next higher level (products in the tens) following the same procedures.

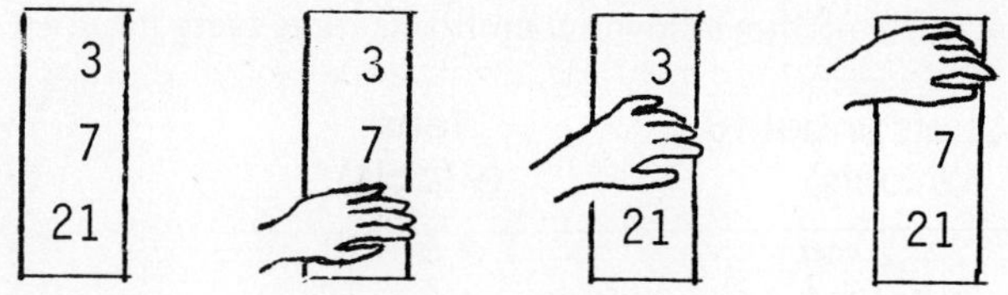

3x7= 21   3x7= ?   3x _?_ = 21   _?_ x7= 21

Additional Suggestions:

1. Introduce division after the student has practiced the multiplication drill cards.

Example: 2 × _?_ = 8   8 ÷ 2 = 4
              3 × _?_ = 21   21 ÷ 3 = 7

2. Allow each student to construct his/her own set of multiplication drill cards grouped by products. Provide rubber bands to keep the cards together, and ask the students to take them home to practice with parents. Add the next set (grouped by products) when the student has completely mastered the previous level.

math visual response cues

Descriptors:
Visual Perception
Poor Motor Skills
Addition and Multiplication

Grade Levels: 3–6

Rationale:
Many students have difficulty with visual perception, motor planning, and the organizational procedures involved in addition and multiplication. Often these students have the computational skills to solve correctly the given problem but arrive at wrong answers because the numbers end up in the wrong column.

Objective:
Visually to cue responses in addition and multiplication problems.

Materials:
Marking pen
Regular pen or pencil
(Note: The marks could also be added to a ditto master.)

Procedure:
Add parentheses above the second column (and additional columns when appropriate) to cue the student to carry. Dashes are used to cue the spacing of the answers to multiplication problems. Once the concept has been established, the cues can be faded out gradually.

Assumptions: Student has mastered place value and addition or multiplication facts.

Additional Suggestions: 1. Use lines for answers to division problems.
2. Use large squared graph paper.

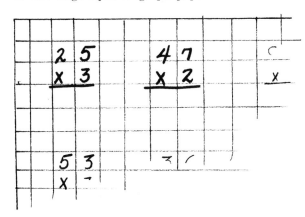

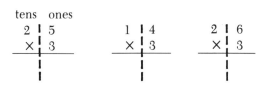

_____task analysis for multiplication_____

Descriptors: Sequential Math Skills   **Grade Levels:**   3.5–6
Multiplication Practice

Rationale: Multiplication problems that appear to be similar, such as $31 \times 3 = 93$ and $87 \times 3 = 261$ are in reality quite different in terms of the demands they make on a student. In the first algorithm no renaming is required for the two-place product 93, whereas in the second algorithm the student is required to rename twice. The student who is able to complete the first algorithm but experiences difficulty with the second, needs further practice with the skill levels required in the second example.

Objective: To teach a student to multiply, sequentially, figures requiring renaming.

Materials: Chalkboard and chalk
Pencil and paper

Procedure: 1. The teacher should consistently use the same multiplier to introduce the task analysis sequence. Example: ×3. The student practices the multiplication table of ×3 using flash cards, games, and teacher-made exercises until proficient.
2. The teacher introduces the following sequential number problems on the chalkboard and asks several students to come to the chalkboard to work them while the rest of the class complete the problem using paper and pencil at their desks. As each step is introduced, the teacher provides a minimum of 3 other math problems at the same level to allow for more practice and to ensure that they understand the process before proceeding to the next step.

SEQUENTIAL NUMBER PROBLEMS

Examples   a.   13   22   32   Practice Problems
× 3   × 3   × 3

(no renaming required)

b.   tens   ones   This problem introduces the computation   tens   ones
1 | 7   of renaming the *ones* multiplicand.   2 | 5   1 | 4   2 | 6
× | 3   × | 3   × | 3   × | 3

c. In order to introduce 1 new element at a time, the second step uses renaming with the *tens* multiplicand but not the ones.

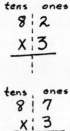

d. This step requires renaming of both the *ones* and *tens* multiplicands.

3. When the students become proficient at using the multiplicand 3, a new multiplier may be introduced following the same procedure.

Additional Suggestions

Following the same procedure, design worksheets with 1 row of problems to be completed for each step.

decoding math word problems

Descriptors: Computational Math Skills
Reading Comprehension

Grade Levels: 4–6

Rationale: Many students can read and solve computational math problems presented in a number format, but are unable to read and translate word problems into basic algorithms. The teacher needs to use a task analysis procedure to teach students how to decode math word problems and translate them into more familiar computations. Word and number cards are used in this activity to accomplish this task.

Objective: To teach a student how to translate and solve math word problems.

Materials: 12″ × 18″ tagboard sheets or 5″ × 7″ blank index cards
Contact paper or laminating material
Colored marking pen (washable ink)
Black magic marker
Scissors
Paper and pencil
4 cards for each of the following signs: +, −, ×, ÷, ?, =

Procedure: 1. Select a word problem from a math text, write the problem on index cards and cover with contact paper or laminate. If tagboard charts are used instead of index cards, cut the cardboard so that each card contains only 1 word or number.

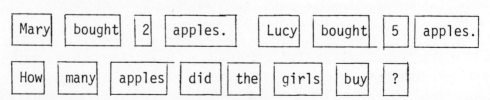

2. Read the problem aloud to the class 2 times.
3. On the second reading underline the important words with a bright colored magic marker.

2	apples

4. Take the underlined words out of the word problem and place them into a new equation.
5. Place the process signs in the appropriate places.

6. Write the equation on paper and solve.

    2 + 5 =   or   2
                    +5   (teacher corrected)

7. Choose another similar problem and repeat steps 1 through 6 allowing the student to talk through what s/he is doing.

(Note: After some practice the student should be able to do the underlining him/herself and form the equation, underline important words on a worksheet and form equation, and solve word problems independently.)

Sample Problems

ADDITION:

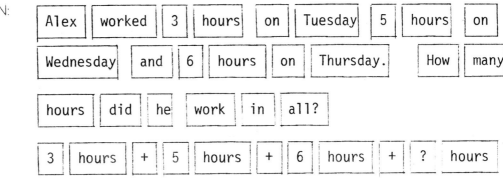

Write as 3 + 5 + 6 =   hours or   3
                                       5
                                      +6
                                     ‾‾‾‾‾
                                      hours

SUBTRACTION:

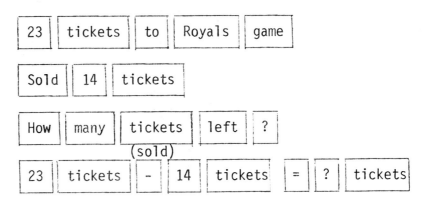

Write as: 23 − 14 =   tickets or   23
                                      −14
                                      ‾‾‾‾‾
                                      tickets

MULTIPLICATION:

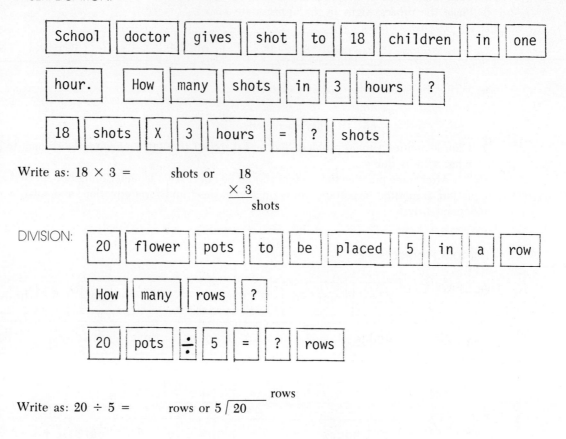

| School | doctor | gives | shot | to | 18 | children | in | one |

| hour. | How | many | shots | in | 3 | hours | ? |

| 18 | shots | X | 3 | hours | = | ? | shots |

Write as: 18 × 3 =   shots or   18
                                    × 3
                                 ‾‾‾‾‾‾‾ shots

DIVISION:

| 20 | flower | pots | to | be | placed | 5 | in | a | row |

| How | many | rows | ? |

| 20 | pots | ÷ | 5 | = | ? | rows |

Write as: 20 ÷ 5 =   rows or 5 ⟌ 20‾‾‾‾ rows

Additional Suggestions:

1. Put all words and number cards for each word problem in an envelope marked with a colored number. Example: Problem #1 is identified with a red 1. All cards belonging in that envelope are marked with a red 1 on the back for easy sorting. The complete word problem is written or typed on a slip of paper and added to the envelope to save time when placing the cards on the table. The correct answer is also included inside a folded card to be used for self-correction.
2. Design student graphs to chart students' daily progress in computing word problems.

models for decimal fractions

Descriptors: Visual Reference
Concrete Manipulation

Grade Levels: 5–6+

Rationale: Many upper-intermediate youngsters require concrete and pictorial representations in preparation for symbolic decimal concepts. These students need to work through sequential stages to reach a grasp of such concepts. Among the numerous commercially available materials in this area are: Cuisenaire[1] Powers of Ten, Dienes[2] Multibase Blocks and the related stamp kits that precede the use of place value charts, and the more abstract worksheets containing only numerals. If such commercial materials are not available, three-dimensional forms can be inexpensively made by pasting large-grid graph paper over cardboard solids to represent the shapes commonly used. In trying to master the concept of decimals, it is helpful for slower students to use manipulatives.

---

[1]The Cuisenaire Company of America, 12 Church Street, New Rochelle, N.Y. 10805.
[2]Creative Publications, 3977 East Bayshore Road, P. O. Box 10328, Palo Alto, Calif. 94303.

Objective: To teach students the decimal concept by using concrete forms.

Materials: Cardboard boxes: large cube, thin box (1/10 the size of the large cube), 1 rectangle (1/10 the size of the thin box), and 1 cardboard cube
Tagboard and masking tape (optional)
Large-grid graph paper (centimeter squares)
Glue
Black marking pen

Procedure: 1. The teacher constructs 4 box sizes (see illustration) by covering commercial boxes with large-grid graph paper. As relative size is very important to the decimal concept, it may be difficult to obtain the needed boxes. Consequently, the teacher may need to use pieces of tagboard and masking tape to construct one.

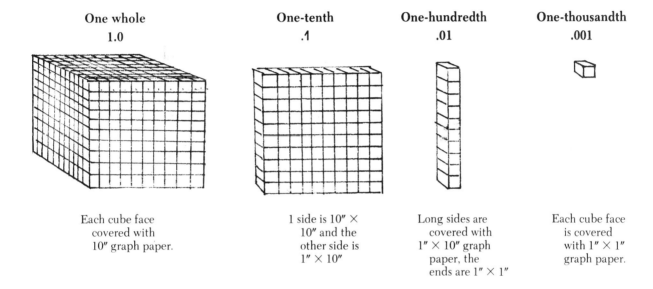

One whole 1.0	One-tenth .1	One-hundredth .01	One-thousandth .001
Each cube face covered with 10″ graph paper.	1 side is 10″ × 10″ and the other side is 1″ × 10″	Long sides are covered with 1″ × 10″ graph paper, the ends are 1″ × 1″	Each cube face is covered with 1″ × 1″ graph paper.

2. Explain to the students that the base-ten place value concept underlying decimal notation can be effectively demonstrated by the blocks themselves (for example, 10 one-tenth squares can be stacked to represent the same quantity as 1 whole: $10 \times 1/10 = 1$ or $10 \times .1 = 1$).
3. The teacher provides each student with a duplicated pictorial chart representing the blocks with appropriate reference labels. The chart combines pictorial, verbal, fractional, and decimal fractional expressions.

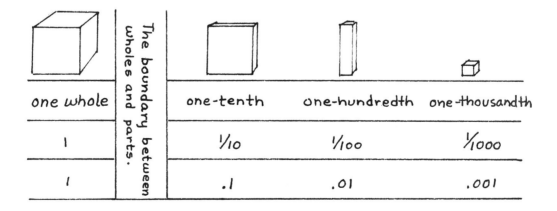

4. The teacher demonstrates how graphically to represent a decimal on the chalkboard.

5. The teacher duplicates the following decimals and asks the students to draw visual representations for each of them and to insert 0 as a place value holder when necessary. Tasks that require ordering decimals that appear to be similar numerically can be graphically represented. For example, to order the following quantities from least to greatest, the students first draw the representations.

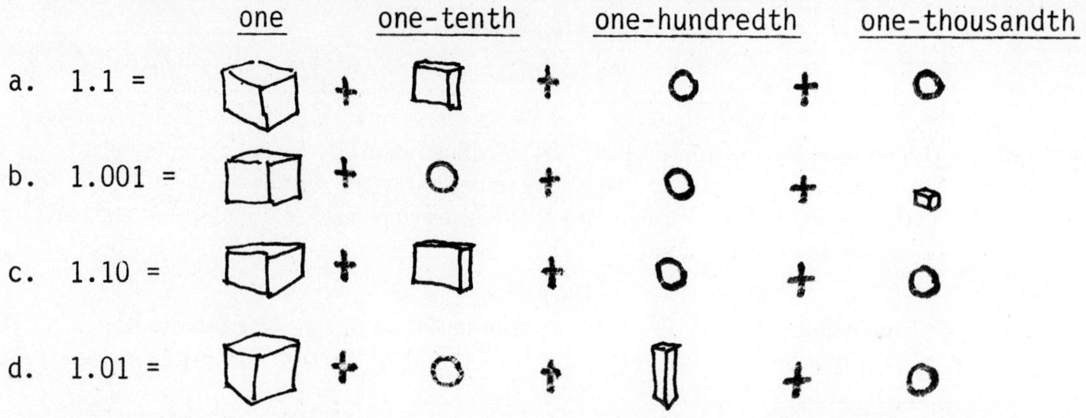

	one	one-tenth	one-hundredth	one-thousandth
a. 1.1 =	+	+	O +	O
b. 1.001 =	+	O +	O +	
c. 1.10 =	+	+	O +	O
d. 1.01 =	+	O +	+	O

6. By inspection it is possible to determine that the *least* quantity is b. Next is d. Values for a and c are equivalent. If this relationship is not clear by visual inspection, of course, manipulation of the actual forms would reveal that b, for example, simply has the least bulk.

Additional Suggestions: Design more worksheets and allow space for the students to draw the pictorial representations and to write both the fractions and the decimals.
Example:

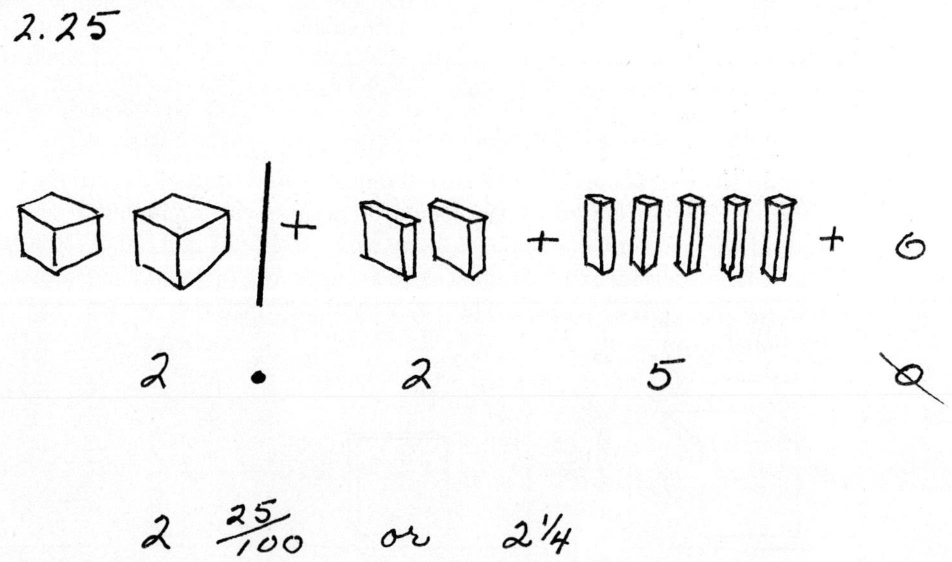

2.25

2 . 2   5   0

2 $\frac{25}{100}$ or   2¼

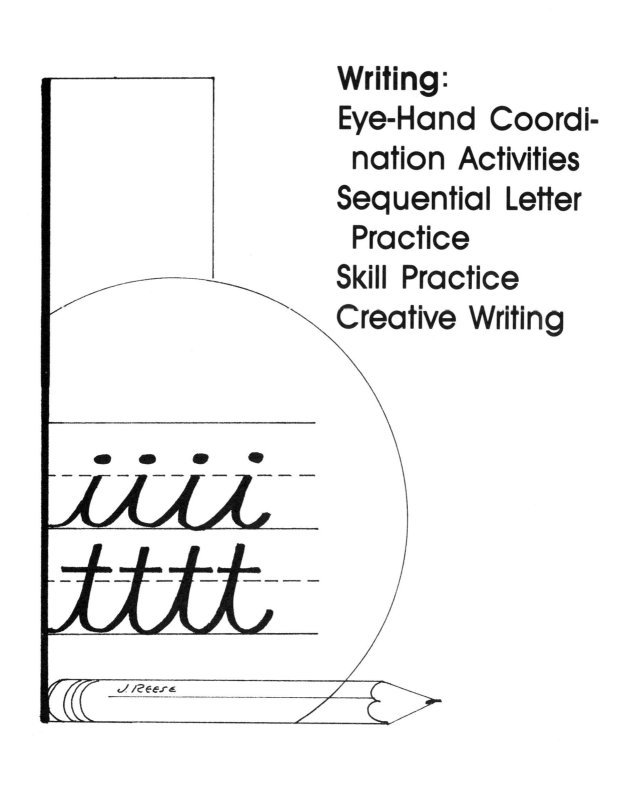

Writing:
Eye-Hand Coordination Activities
Sequential Letter Practice
Skill Practice
Creative Writing

development of opposition
finger-thumb movement

Descriptors: Fine-Motor Coordination
Readiness

Grade Levels: K–1

Rationale: Development of opposition movement of the thumb and fingers is essential to many areas of a child's daily life. Many self-help tasks (buttoning, snapping, tying) are impossible to carry out if thumb and finger do not work in opposition of each other. Cutting, coloring, and writing as well as many functional tasks, such as turning a door knob or using feeding utensils, require opposition movement. This skill is difficult for many children with motor problems or mild cerebral palsy.

Objective: To present a list of activities designed to aid the development of oppositional movement and later a pincer grasp (use of the thumb and forefinger only in opposition, as in holding a pencil).

Materials: See each activity.

Procedure:
1. The teacher chooses an activity to be introduced to the students.
2. The teacher evaluates the success of each activity before introducing a new one.
3. Suggested activities

   a. turning pages of a book
   b. picking up small pieces of a sponge with clothespins
   c. putting clothespins in a bottle with a small mouth
   d. playing with toys that have knobs or wind up
   e. picking up and sorting small objects (such as seeds or coins)
   f. stringing beads
   g. putting coins in a bank
   h. lacing boards
   i. playing finger games ("Where is Thumbkin?")
   j. putting toothpicks in styrofoam
   k. string painting (this utilizes both hands at once)
   l. snapping activities
   m. pinching clay, shaping it with the fingers
   n. gluing seeds on pictures
   o. cutting simple lines
   p. cutting out simple pictures—the teacher draws a circle around each picture

(Note: Specially designed scissors are available for children having problems with opposition movement and weakness in their hands. The scissors are easy to cut with and reinforce oppositional movement. They are available from: University Publishing Company, 1126 "Q" Street, P. O. Box 80298, Lincoln, Nebraska 68501, (402) 432-2761.)

Easy-Grip Scissors

_____**fold and cut**_____

Descriptors: Following Directions   **Grade Levels:**   K–1
Eye-Hand Coordination
Fine-Motor Skills

Rationale: Many young students have difficulty learning to fold and cut shapes such as circles, triangles, and hearts, activities that are often required in kindergarten. Such students become very frustrated when their art project, for example, is a disaster because the cut-out circle or heart ends up in two pieces. Many beginning teachers find it very hard to teach folding and cutting of heart designs for Valentine's Day projects. The following activities present easy-to-follow directions for folding and cutting shapes.[6] For example, the "ice cream cone" idea used in this teaching idea stimulates a familiar visual image and enables the youngsters to complete otherwise complicated hearts with no difficulty.

Objective: To teach young students how to fold and cut out designs from paper according to teacher directions.

Materials: Colored construction paper
Scissors
Paste

Procedure:

1. At the beginning of the school year, show the students how to cut out a circle from a square of paper. Fold the square in half. Show the students the difference between the folded side and the open side. Say, "Pinch the fold with your fingers and thumbs. Put your scissors on the folded corner. Cut up, up, up and around your thumb. Cut back down to the other corner. Open up the paper and you have a circle."

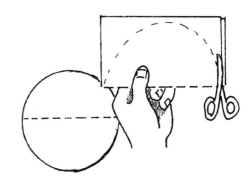

2. Allow the students to continue cutting out circles until they have mastered the skill. Some students may have difficulty in the beginning, but with additional practice they will become successful.

3. Demonstrate art projects that can be created from the circles the students have learned to cut out. Example: The colored circles may be pasted to a piece of colored construction paper and arranged in various shapes and designs.

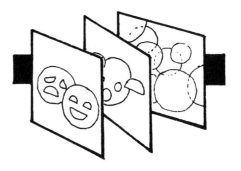

4. Teach the students how to cut out an oval in the same way but using a rectangular rather than a square piece of paper. Continue to allow students to create their own art projects based on the cut-out shapes.

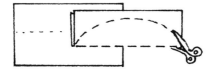

[6]Ginger Porter, kindergarten teacher, Olathe, Kansas, shared this idea with the author.

5. Teach the students to cut out triangles by folding and cutting a square (or rectangle) from one open corner across to the opposite folded corner. The students can create people, witches, birds, Christmas trees, jack-o'lanterns, and so on, by using these basic shapes.

Additional Suggestions:

1. For Valentine's Day, teach the students to cut out hearts by folding and cutting red construction paper hearts. Give the students rectangles of red paper and say "Fold the paper in half. Start cutting from the folded corner up and across to the open corner just the way you did when cutting out a triangle. But when you get almost to the top, come around and back to the fold so it looks like an ice cream cone! Open the paper up and you have a heart."

2. Use the hearts to design valentines, animals, and people.

visual discrimination strips

Descriptors: Readiness Activities
Language Training
Eye-Hand Coordination

Grade Levels: K–1

Rationale: Teachers tend to bombard young students with dittoed sheets of readiness activities. Such papers often contain too many stimuli at one time for some students who, consequently, are not sure exactly what to do or where to look. Tagboard strips containing individual components of the directions may be used over and over again as teaching tools for such students. As the students understand the directions and can correctly follow them, the teacher may proceed to introduce the dittoed worksheets confident that all students will know what to do.

Objective: To teach students the readiness skill of following directions using visual discrimination comparisons and language concepts.

Materials: 3″ × 10″ tagboard strips
Black marking pen

Procedure: 1. Using a black marking pen the teacher prepares 3″ × 10″ tagboard strips to illustrate a language or visual-discrimination exercise. The strips are presented to the students one at a time in order to isolate the concept being taught.
2. The teacher or aide presents one strip to the student saying, for example, "Point to the large triangle." "Point to the small triangle." "Which one is the middle-sized triangle?"

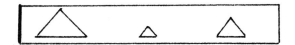

3. Continue practicing with similar strips illustrating sizes and shapes.

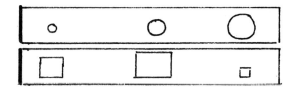

4. When the student can successfully follow the oral directions using one strip at a time, introduce dittoed worksheets that require the student to mark a specific size stated by the teacher. (Note: This activity promotes independent work habits.) Example:

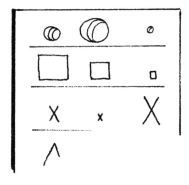

"Draw a line under the largest ball in the first line."

5. Proceed to ask the student to draw the shapes (large, small, and so on) on paper. It may be necessary to demonstrate motor planning for some students (when to start and where to stop). Allow the students to first practice on the chalkboard.

Additional Suggestions: 1. Use the tagboard strips to teach visual discrimination for "same" and "different."

Example: "Which symbol looks just like the first one?"

2. Progress to more difficult exercises on strips

3. Proceed to worksheets.
4. To teach copying skills ask the student to reproduce the figure presented.

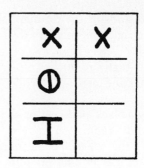

_____developing finger muscles_____

Descriptors: Fine-Motor Coordination
Pincer Grasp Practice

Grade Levels: Preschool
Kindergarten
Educable Mentally Retarded

Rationale: Young students need to develop fine-motor muscles in their thumb and forefinger in preparation for buttoning, zipping, holding a pencil, and so on.

Objective: The student will be able to pick up a clothespin, open it, and place it on the designated areas of a bowl.

Materials: Clothespins
Small bowl
Colored tape

Procedure:
1. Place tabs of tape at 1-inch intervals around the edge of the bowl.
2. Put a small piece of tape on the end of each of the clothespins. (Number of clothespins corresponds to number of taped sections.)
3. The student is shown how to pick up the clothespin with a thumb and forefinger.
4. Demonstrate how to push the ends of the clothespins together and place them on the taped sections of the bowl.

Additional Suggestions:
1. Use different-colored tape to practice matching colors.
2. Write numbers on the clothespins and the tape on the bowl. The student is to match the numbers.

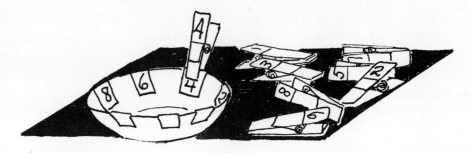

tying shoes

Descriptors: Backward Chaining/Shoe Tying

Grade Levels: Preschool
Kindergarten
Educable Mentally Retarded
Orthopedically Handicapped

Rationale: Some students respond better to a step-by-step instructional process when the first step they undertake is actually the last step of the instructional process.

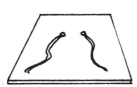

Objective: After daily practice using this sequential training activity, the student will be able independently to tie a shoe.

Materials: Tying board (plywood)
2 different-colored shoelaces
Old shoe (optional)

Directions: Construct a tying board with two holes or use an old shoe nailed to a board. The tying board can be made using a 1-inch thick plywood board cut to the desired length. When cut to 10- or 12-inches, the board has more stability. Use two different-colored shoelaces for easy visual discrimination. Drill two holes 1½ inches apart, bring the laces up from the bottom, and secure them on the back of the board by tying knots.

Procedure:
1. Demonstrate the following steps while the student observes the entire process without participating.

    a. cross the laces
    b. bring one under the other
    c. pull laces tight
    d. make loop, hold with thumb and forefinger
    e. bring lace over thumb and around loop
    f. remove thumb, push lace through opening
    g. pull bow tight

2. Go through steps a through f with the student completing step g.
3. Praise the student for completion of his/her part of the task.
4. Untie the board and repeat step 2. Repeat the process until the student completes the task independently.
5. When the student demonstrates competency on step g, begin again and complete steps a through e allowing the student to complete steps f and g.
6. Continue this backward progression until the student completes steps a through g independently.

Additional Suggestions: The teacher may want to transfer from the tying board to a regular shoe for more realistic assimilation of the skills being taught.

Descriptors: Eye-Hand Coordination
Following Directions
Cutting Skills

Grade Levels: Preschool–1
Orthopedically
Handicapped

Rationale: Many youngsters need repeated practice in order to develop good eye-hand coordination skills that are required in most readiness and primary curricula. The following activities may be duplicated for parents who can provide the needed experiences at home.

Objective: To provide a teacher or parent with visual perceptual activities that may be used with a young student before more formal educational experiences are introduced.

Materials: Wide black marking pen
Student scissors
Drawing paper
Newspaper (comic section and news section)
Household items (see activity 4)

Procedure:
1. Read each activity and obtain the materials needed for the activity.
2. Describe the activity to the student. (Note: It is important that the student possess the prerequisite skills for the activity. Example: If a student cannot cut with scissors refer to the *Cutting with Scissors* activity in this book for ideas on how to teach the student to cut before involving the student in an activity presupposing such skills.)
3. Complete the activity and provide a similar follow-up activity later on to determine whether or not the student has completely mastered the previously taught skill.

Activity 1:

Draw straight lines, curves, and spirals with a wide black marking pen making it easier for the student to discriminate picture outlines. Ask the student to cut along the lines.

Example:

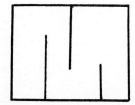 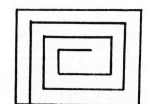 

Activity 2:

Outline pictures from the newspaper or magazines with a wide black marking pen. Have the student cut out the pictures. The pictures should be fairly large at first.
Example:

Activity 3:

Glue a large magazine picture or a simple color book picture to cardboard. Mark off puzzle shapes with a black marking pen. Have the student cut along the lines. Start with two or three pieces and increase the number as the student develops the necessary skill.

Activity: 4:

The student should be given an opportunity to manipulate objects with his/her hands and describe verbally likenesses and differences of the objects. For example, after grocery shopping have the student stack the cans in the cupboard according to contents (all the beans together, all the corn together, all the pears together). Young children may be asked to sort the silverware into the silverware tray (knives together, forks together, teaspoons together, tablespoons together).

Activity 5:

Have the student complete missing parts of pictures.

a. a tree without a trunk
b. an elephant without a trunk
c. a car without a wheel
d. a face without a feature (nose, eye, mouth)

Examples:

Activity 6:

Dot-to-dot pictures. Start with pictures that have large dots and numbers. As the student develops this skill, increase the number of dots and make them smaller.

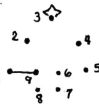

Activity 7:

Draw geometric shapes on drawing paper with a black marking pen and ask the student to tell which ones are the same and which are different. The student may then be asked to copy a given shape or to cut it out depending on the student's current skill level.

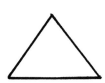

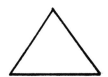

Activity 8:

Fold a piece of paper into two sections. Open it and have the student trace over the folds first with a finger and then with a crayon.

Later fold the paper into fourths and follow the same procedure.

Activity 9:

Have the student trace comic strip characters from a newspaper. As s/he traces, ask the student to describe what was traced; for example, body part or article of clothing.

writing one's own name

Descriptors: Eye-Hand Coordination   **Grade Levels:**   K–1
                    Letter Sequence

Rationale: Although most kindergarteners begin to learn how to write their own name, many students are still unable to do so by the time they enter first grade, where mastery of this skill early in the school year is important as students are required to write their name on a multitude of papers.

Objective: To teach students to write their own name correctly.
(Note: It is recommended that beginning writers learn to write their name in both capital and small letters instead of all caps as is a common practice in kindergarten. By first learning to write their name in capital letters, students must relearn writing their name in first grade.)

Materials: Chalkboard and chalk
                  Salt or sand tray
                  Cardboard or styrofoam meat trays
                  Pencil and paper
                  Masking tape
                  Salt or sugar
                  White glue
                  Tagboard
                  Colored marking pens
                  Optional: paintbrushes, watercolor paint, finger paint, crayons, Exacto knife

Procedure: 1. Provide each student with a correct model of his/her name written on a piece of tagboard with a black marking pen. The name cards are taped to the top of each student's desk for quick reference.
    2. Help each student print his/her name letter-by-letter. It is important that the student learn the correct sequence of strokes at this time (see *Manuscript Letter Writing* activity) to avoid practicing erroneous response patterns.
    3. Send home the student's name on a card with a sequential stroke pattern for each letter. Example:

Parents may help the student master the writing of the students' name following the teacher's directions (see *Parent Help with Writing Skills* activity).
    4. Do not teach the student's last name at this time as this will involve too many stimuli for immature learners. When two or more students have the same name, teach the beginning initial of their last name, for example, Bill S., Bill B.

5. Label coat hooks, lockers, art materials, and so on with each student's carefully printed name. The labels provide good models for the students.

The following activities offer additional practice for students learning to write their own name.

Activity 1: <u>Writing</u> <u>in</u> <u>Air</u>

Write the model letter on the board. With your back to the students. Write the letters in the air while pronouncing the letter name for each student's name. Example: *S a m* Sam.

Activity 2: <u>Gross-Motor</u> <u>Activities</u>

a. Write the student's name on a chalkboard.
b. Write the student's name in a box filled with sand, salt, or cornmeal.

The student may also write with a finger, a stick, or another object. Erase the writing by gently shaking the pan. Guide the student's hand while writing the entire name. Eventually ask the student to write the name without help.
c. Write on a large piece of newsprint or paper with magic markers or crayons.
d. Write with finger paints and/or paint brushes.
e. Sandpaper names can be made from white glue squeezed into letters on tagboard. Sprinkle salt, sand, or sugar over the wet glue. Sandpaper names can also be cut from sandpaper and glued onto a piece of cardboard.

Activity 3: <u>Stencils</u>

This step is designed for students who are having difficulties with hand coordination. If used, cut a stencil of the student's name using meat trays, tagboard/cardboard, and an Exacto knife. (Note: There will be no centers in such letters as P, B, R, O, or D.)

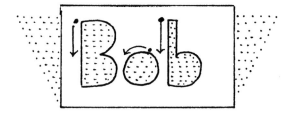

When using the stencil, place a dot at the starting point and eventually fade it out.

Activity 4: <u>Roads</u>

Construct double lines and have the student practice making "roads" between the double lines. If necessary, use arrows and numbers to show directions and sequence of lines. Have the student continue to say the name of the letter while writing it. After each student has written the name, ask the student to spell it.

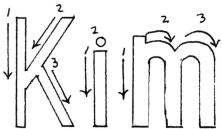

Activity 5: Dot-to-Dot

Provide a dot-to-dot drawing of name. Have the student connect the dots. Eventually place the dots farther apart gradually fading them out altogether.

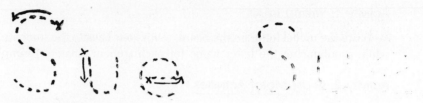

Activity 6: Tracing—Visual Closure

Write the student's name and have him/her trace it. Write the first part of name and have the student trace the first part and then complete the remainder of name. Finally, reduce the cues. Continue to name the letters.

Additional Suggestions:

1. Teach the student to write his/her name from memory. Provide the student a paper with the name on it. Ask the student to trace the name with a finger several times. Fold the paper over and ask the student to write the name without a model. The student continues to name letters while writing the name.

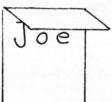

2. Reinforce the student each time the name is correctly written, for example, reward with a sticker by the name on the paper if correct and another sticker for the correct work completed on the paper.

$$\begin{array}{ccc} & & \\ \begin{array}{r} 3 \\ +1 \\ \hline 4 \end{array} & \begin{array}{r} 1 \\ +0 \\ \hline 1 \end{array} & \begin{array}{r} 2 \\ +2 \\ \hline 4 \end{array} \\ \begin{array}{r} 2 \\ +1 \\ \hline 5 \end{array} & \begin{array}{r} 1 \\ +3 \\ \hline 4 \end{array} & \begin{array}{r} 3 \\ +0 \\ \hline 3 \end{array} \end{array}$$

progressive coloring skill

Descriptors:
Fine-Motor Practice
Eye-Hand Coordination
Coloring

Grade Levels: K–2
Educable Mentally Retarded
Orthopedically Handicapped

Rationale:
It is essential for children to develop eye-hand and fine-motor coordination in preparation for academic tasks, such as handwriting.

#1   #2   #3   #4   #5

Objective: To develop fine-motor skills and eye-hand coordination by learning to color within the lines of a given object or design.

Materials: Teacher-prepared worksheet
Crayon

Procedure:
1. The student is presented with worksheet #1 and a crayon and asked to color in all the white space. Remind the student to color only the white area and to try not to color on the shaded area.
2. After the student is finished, check the paper and praise the student for his/her efforts. Point out any areas that have not been colored and tell the student to go back over such areas. Call attention to shaded areas that have been colored and stress the importance of staying within the lines. (Note: This procedure should be repeated daily until the student begins to color all of the white space.)
3. Worksheet #2 is presented next following the same procedure. The shape to be colored now has a thinner border. While progressing from wide to narrow borders, the student's eye-hand coordination skills improve and the student gains greater awareness of how to color within the border areas.
(Note: By beginning with the wide margin and gradually reducing it, the student is given more room to work with and less chance of making errors.)

Additional Suggestions:
1. Use a beginning coloring book. Progressing from wide to narrow widths, black out the areas bordering the figure to be colored.
2. Initially it may be necessary to guide the student's hand to demonstrate how to color within the margins.

cutting with scissors

Descriptors: Eye-Hand Coordination
Hand Dominance
Art Projects

Grade Levels: K–2

Rationale: Many primary activities require students to have mastery of cutting skills. Readiness skills for cutting with scissors include hand dominance, arm-hand, and eye-hand coordination. It is important to select scissors that cut well and ones that are appropriate for the right or left hand. Some students may still have difficulty with such activities even in grade 2, thus they must be taken through a sequential program to teach cutting skills.

Objective: To teach a student how to cut with scissors using a sequential progressive skill program.

Materials: Paper
Primary scissors
Clay
Black marking pen

Procedure: Lay scissors on the table and let the student choose them with the hand s/he prefers.

1. *Snips (three years old)* Let the child make snips across a narrow strip of 4″ × 1″ paper. Using this procedure the child cuts through the paper in one snip. Hold the blades of the scissors at a 90 degree angle to the paper so that they actually cut and do not just slide over the paper. Clay can also be cut into little pieces. Unlike paper, clay can be held in any position to be cut. At first, it does not have to be held at all.

   If necessary, manipulate the child's hands through the releasing and closing movements of using the scissors.

   Training Scissors may be used for those children who experience difficulty in learning to manipulate scissors. The child's fingers are placed in the inside holes, the teacher's fingers in the outside holes. Be sure and choose right- or left-handed scissors, whichever is appropriate. Do not use paper for this activity. Say "open" and open the scissors; then "close" and close the scissors. Later on, fade into "open" and wait until child opens, then say "close" and wait until child closes.

2. *Consecutive Snips* Let the child make snips along the side of a paper 4″ × 6″ and then begin to increase to two or three *consecutive* snips, eventually cutting through the wider piece of paper.

3. *Straight Line (four years old)* Draw a thick straight line using a black marking pen. Do not use crayons. A thick waxed line drawn with crayons might cause the scissors to slip.

   If the child has difficulty following the thick black line, make a wider "road," using two lines, and have the child cut down the middle.

   Gradually narrow the road into a heavy straight line. Emphasize the straight line by making it thicker, making it a different color, and providing tactile guidelines for a seriously handicapped child by mounting two strips of cardboard on a sheet of paper and having the child cut between them.

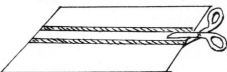

   Once the student cuts along a straight line with someone else holding the paper, the student should begin to hold the paper in his/her nondominant hand so that cutting becomes a bimanual process. The "holding hand" should have the thumb side on top of the paper.

4. *Curved Line (five years old)* Follow the same procedures as in Step 3.

Road   Heavy Line

   The paper must be turned continuously when cutting curved lines and circles. Have the child start by cutting short, curved lines clearly drawn on paper. Next, let the child cut out large circles and gradually decrease the size as more skill is developed.

5. *Angled Lines (five years old)*

Road   Heavy Line

Follow the same procedures as step 4.

6. *Cutting Easy Figures* When cutting out a pictured object, the child may have as much trouble deciding on which line to cut as with the manipulation of the scissors. The following aids may be useful:

1. Use a definite color to outline the object.
2. Run the child's finger around the outline before s/he starts to cut.
3. Color the figure to make it easier to recognize the whole form.

Additional Suggestions: Some youngsters are frustrated because they want to cut out complex forms before they are ready to control the scissors. Solve this problem by drawing a circle, square, or triangle around the complex figure. By cutting on these easy lines, the child has the satisfaction, for example, of having "cut out a doll."

manuscript writing

Descriptors: Eye-Hand Coordination
Readiness

Grade Levels: K–2

Rationale: Many students first learn to write by copying models presented by the teacher on the chalkboard or by using a commercial workbook format. Although the students' efforts may look like the original model, the students may be using inefficient stroke patterns unless the teacher demonstrates how sequentially to write a letter showing where to start and stop the strokes. It is helpful to begin with simple strokes gradually proceeding to more difficult strokes.

Objective: To teach students the prerequisite strokes for the manuscript capital and small letters of the alphabet.

Materials: Chalkboard and chalk
Overhead projector
Colored marking pen
Clear transparency
Ditto master
Duplicating paper
Manuscript writing paper
pencil for each student

Procedure:

1. The teacher demonstrates simple strokes to the students using a chalkboard or an overhead projector. Each student is given a piece or writing paper. The students watch the stroke before copying it in the air and on paper. The suggested sequence of strokes is:

   a. vertical lines (tall and short)

   b. horizontal lines ➡ _ _ _ _ ⎯

   c. slanted lines ↘\ \ \\ ↗////

   d. counter-clockwise circle ⟲ ◯ ◯

   e. up-and-over semicircle ⌒ ⌒ ⌣ ⌣

   f. clockwise circle ⟳ ⟳ ⟳

2. When the students are proficient at performing the prerequisite writing strokes, the teacher introduces letters using the same procedure as described in step 1.

3. The teacher designs a dittoed worksheet of the letter. The students are provided with a dotted model that can be traced. The dots are faded until the students are asked to reproduce the letter without tracing over a dotted model. The capital and small letters should be introduced at the same time. The students may say the letter name as they write it in the air and on paper. Example:

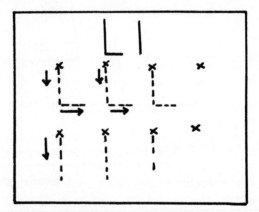

4. The teacher should consistently review the letters previously learned by the students before introducing a new letter. (Note: Begin teaching letters with vertical lines. A suggested order is

Ll	Ii	Tt	
Oo	Cc	Aa	Ee
Mm	Rr	Uu	Nn
Ss	Dd	Ff	Hh	Bb
Vv	Kk	Ww	Xx	Zz
Yy	Pp	Jj	Qq.)

Additional Suggestions:

1. Use salt or sand trays and magic slates to practice the letters.
2. Teach the students to write their names. It is important to show the students the sequence of strokes as the word is demonstrated, especially if not all the letters have been introduced.
3. Teach the students to write simple words beginning with each letter.

Descriptors: Eye-Hand Coordination   **Grade Levels:** 1–3
               Letter Practice

Rationale: Many students who experience difficulty in school as years go by have developed inefficient writing patterns. These are the students who do not complete their work on time (or never finish it). Their worksheets are sometimes illegible and, whenever possible, such students avoid writing altogether. Time spent teaching correct letter formation at the early learning stages is a good investment and may prevent having to remediate poor handwriting habits later on.

Objective: To present alternative techniques for students beginning to write letters.

Materials: Chalkboard and chalk
Box of salt or baking pan 9″ × 12″ × 1½″
Newsprint
Styrofoam meat trays
Exacto knife
Black, green, and red marking pens
Sandpaper or glue with sand, salt, or sugar
Tagboard
Crayons
Pencils

Procedure:

1. Begin by teaching letters that use the basic "pull down" stroke.

2. Teach letters that have a circle or half circle.

3. Teach letters that drop below the baseline.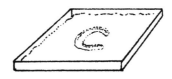

4. Choose the following activities that best meet the students' needs. Only one letter should be introduced and practiced at a time until the student has "overlearned" it.
   (Note: The following instructional sequence is recommended in order to establish a firm "learning base": teach letter name, teach letter sound, and teach how to write the letter. Students with very poor motor skills may not be able to learn to write the letter initially but may learn the letter name and sound. The teacher is responsible for ensuring that a student is not held back because of one extremely weak area, for example, handwriting due to poor motor skills.)

Activity 1: Writing in the Air

Write a letter on the board. With your back to the student, write the letter in the air. The student also writes in the air. The sound of the letter is said while the letter is being written. The hard *c* and *g* sounds should be taught first as most words on a preprimer level use the hard letter sound.

Activity 2: Gross-Motor Activities

You may want to provide a model of the letter being written. Continue sounding out the letter. Write a letter on the chalkboard and ask the students to come to the chalkboard and write the same letter.

    a. Write a letter in a box filled with sand or salt. Students may use their finger, a stick, or other writing instrument to copy it. Gently shake the sand to "erase" the letter.

b. Write a letter on a large piece of newsprint or paper with markers or crayons and allow the students to copy it. Finger paints and paint brushes may also be used.

c. Make sandpaper letters from sand, salt, or sugar sprinkled over wet white glue in the shape of letters. Letters may also be cut from sandpaper and glued to cardboard. Have the student use a finger to trace the sandpaper letter while saying the name or sound of that letter.

Activity 3: Stencils

For students who are having extreme difficulty with hand coordination, stencil writing may be helpful. If used, make a stencil of the letter using a meat tray or a piece of cardboard and an exacto knife. When using the stencil, place a green dot at the starting point and eventually fade it out. Continue saying the letter sound.

Activity 4: Dot-to-Dot

Provide a paper with dot-to-dot drawings of a letter. The first drawings should consist of many dots with the letters at the bottom of the page having fewer dots. The student is to trace over each of the dotted letters.

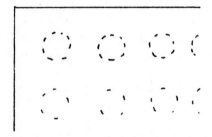

Activity 5: Tracing—Visual Closure

Write the letter to demonstrate the correct sequential stroke pattern. Have the student trace it. Then write the first part of the letter and have the student trace it and complete the remainder of the letter. Finally, reduce the cues.

Activity 6: Writing from Memory

Provide the student with a paper that has the letter on it. Let him/her look at it, trace it with a finger, and fold the paper over. Have the student write the letter from memory. Continue sounding the letter.

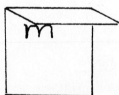

(Note: Similar letters should not be presented at the same time as they may cause confusion for the student. Example: *m n, p b d q, v w*. Do not present the letters in alphabetical order. Students need to learn the alphabet in sequence mainly for dictionary skills, which are usually not introduced until the later primary grades.)

Additional Suggestions:

1. It may be helpful to break a letter into its simplest parts and demonstrate how they fit together using an oral cue. For example, the letter *b* can be broken down into a | (line) and a ⊃ (half circle). Explain that the student merely has to draw a line and a half circle. A short phrase, "The bee buzzes down and then he goes around" (See *Reversal of b-d* activity) may help students having difficulty writing and/or confusing *d* and *b*.

2. Place a green dot at the starting point of the letter and a red dot at the termination point.
3. Introduce capital letters by means of familiar words such as student's name and city and state.
4. Using wooden or plastic letter forms, ask the student to identify the letter by tracing its shape with closed eyes. If wooden or plastic letters are unavailable, letters may be drawn with a finger on the back of a student's hand or on his/her back. Youngsters may work in pairs and tally points for each correct response. The activity may also be used as a group game.

manuscript handwriting guide

Descriptors: Readiness
Eye-Hand Coordination
Following Directions

Grade Levels: K–2

Rationale: Many youngsters find learning to write very difficult. Poor handwriting leads to frustration and incomplete and overdue written assignments due to slow student progress in school. This procedure[2] varies from others presented in this book by beginning with simple stroke patterns and graduating to pictorial representations. These strokes are represented in the way in which visually impaired youngsters might use them. Three similar letters (*l, i, t*) are introduced before teaching the students words containing the three letters. Thus, the students are taught a reason for learning letters in isolation. As each new letter is introduced, more words using the previously learned letters may be written. (Small letters are introduced before capital letters.) This is a more logical, meaningful way of teaching beginning handwriting skills than to teach isolated alphabet letters sequentially.

Objective: To present a sequential procedure for beginning manuscript handwriting.

Materials: Chalkboard and chalk
12″ × 20″ newsprint
Primary pencils or crayons
1-inch lined handwriting paper
Staff liner (for the chalkboard)

Procedure:
1. Verbalize and demonstrate the first symbol on the chalkboard.
2. The students repeat the verbalization and copy the symbol by writing it in the air.
3. Ask one or two student volunteers to come to the chalkboard to copy the model while verbalizing the stroke(s).
4. Distribute 12″ × 20″ newsprint to each student. Show the students how to fold the top of the paper to the bottom, crease, open, and fold one side to the other, crease-open. The student should now see four squares.
5. Ask the students to place one hand in each while counting the four squares aloud.
6. The students write with a crayon the symbol presented on the chalkboard in each of the four squares.
7. Depending on student age and skill level, you may ask them to fold the top to the bottom one more time to end up with eight sections.
8. Circulate among the students as they complete their papers. Ask the students to evaluate the best symbol and circle it. Encourage and reinforce each student's efforts.
9. Turn over the paper and introduce a second symbol (or provide more practice with the first one).

[2]P. Gallagher, "A Manuscript Handwriting Guide" (unpublished manuscript, University of Kansas, 1970).

SEQUENCE OF READINESS SYMBOLS:

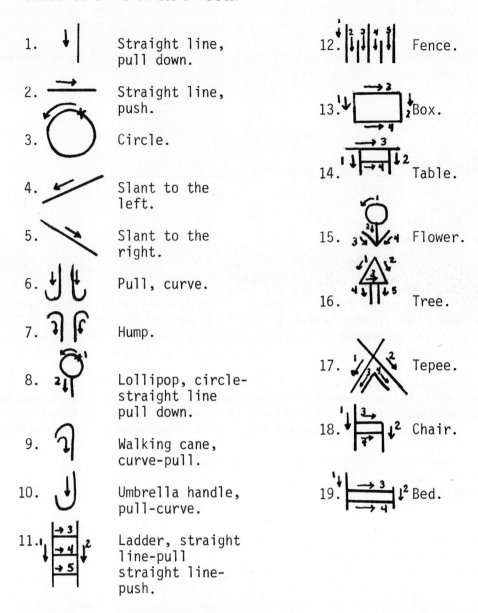

1. Straight line, pull down.
2. Straight line, push.
3. Circle.
4. Slant to the left.
5. Slant to the right.
6. Pull, curve.
7. Hump.
8. Lollipop, circle-straight line pull down.
9. Walking cane, curve-pull.
10. Umbrella handle, pull-curve.
11. Ladder, straight line-pull straight line-push.
12. Fence.
13. Box.
14. Table.
15. Flower.
16. Tree.
17. Tepee.
18. Chair.
19. Bed.

(Note: For students who encounter difficulty with the readiness instructions, repeat the procedures in the readiness section. Substitute ruled writing paper for the newsprint.)

10. Follow the preceding procedure when introducing the small manuscript letters, except that the students use ruled paper and pencils instead of newsprint and crayons. Use a staff liner on the chalkboard to demonstrate the correct spatial orientation of each letter.

11. Students should hold the pencil with three fingers at the level where the point of the pencil begins.
    (Note: You may want to place a small piece of colored tape on the pencil to remind students to put their fingers "on the line.")

12. Verbalize the strokes as you demonstrate each letter on the chalkboard. Ask for students to volunteer to write the letter on the chalkboard.

13. Circulate among the students as they write the newly introduced letter on their lined handwriting paper. Encourage good efforts and reinforce the students' efforts.

14. Introduce one letter a day with words to accompany the letter practice. Each word should contain only those letters previously taught.

SEQUENCE OF LOWERCASE LETTER FORMS:

1. Straight line, pull down.　　　　　　　　**l**

2. Short straight line, pull down.　　　　　**i**

3. Straight line, pull down.　　　　　**t**　　it, till, tilt
   Straight line, push.

4. Circle, short straight line.　　　　**a**　　at, all, tall, tail

5. Circle, tall straight line.　　　　　**b**　　bat, ball, bill, bait
   (on the left)

6. Circle but stop.　　　　　　　　　**c**　　call, cab, cat

7. Circle, tall straight line—　　　　**d**　　dad, lad, add, lid
   (on the right)

8. Beginning at this point each daily lesson can be a review of the previous lessons by having the students write the alphabet letters previously learned. The first line of the students' paper would be the review. All students seem to enjoy this as they can see their own progress.

   At this point, some children can begin writing sentences on the last line of the paper, for example, call a cab.

9. Straight line, push.　　　　　　　**e**　　bee, beet, bell
   Circle stop.

10. Hump-straight line pull down—　　**f**　　fall, fill, fell, feet, if
    straight line push.

11. Circle, pull-curve.　　　　　　　**g**　　bag, get, dig, tag, gate

12. Straight line, pull, back up　　　**h**　　hall, hide, hat, heat
    and hump pull down.

13. Pull, curve, dot.　　　　　　　　**j**　　jet, jab, jail

14. Straight line, pull.　　　　　　　**k**　　Bake, cake, kit, kite, hick
    Slant to the left.
    Slant to the right.

15. Short straight line, pull.
    Back up, hump over and down,
    back up, hump over and down.　　**m**　　make, made, milk, jam, beam

Directions for the remaining letters of the alphabet follow the pattern suggested in the above steps.

16.   n   an, name, can, hand, man

17.   O   noon, moon, no, of, off, top, not

18.   p   paint, pan, pop, apple, tape

19.   q   and   U   queen, quiet, quilt, quit, quack

20.   r   run, read, art, race, four

21.   S   sun, see, has, fast, ask, sail. This is the only letter that does not have previous instruction.

22.   V   vase, van, vast, vent, vest, vote

23.   W   wow, we, want, work, wind, water

24.   X   box, fox, tax, exit

25.   Y   yes, yellow, yarn, toy, boy

26.   Z   zoom, zoo, zero, zip, zone, zebra

27. Student's name. This lesson precedes the capital-letter sequence although the student has not encountered the formal instruction to capitals.
28. Dictate the letters of the alphabet in random selection and have the students write them on lined paper. Some students may go to the chalkboard and write five letters at a time before exchanging with five more students, and so on. This procedure turns practice into a game.

SEQUENCE OF CAPITAL LETTERS:

1. A letter a day is suggested.
2. Daily lesson consists of a single line of the capital letter of the day.
3. Simple sentences may be substituted for the single-word practice. Compile sentences appropriate for the student.
4. Names of the students in the classroom and days of the week can be used in the sentences, for example, Ann is here, or today is Tuesday.
5. Begin with the letter *I* and follow the alphabetical sequence. All students, and especially those students lacking in self-confidence, enjoy writing sentences beginning with *I*.

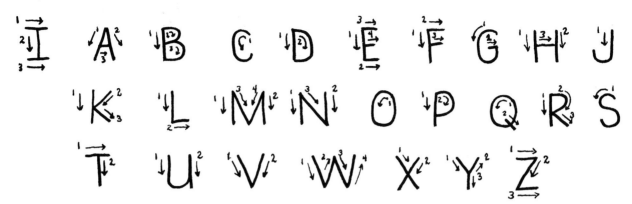

Additional Suggestions:

1. Minimize task requirements, for example, one line a lesson.
2. Cut ruled paper in half.
3. Write one sample letter per line on student's daily paper.
4. Draw red vertical lines for spacing problems.
5. Outline horizontal lines of the ruled paper with a black marking pen for the student with figure-ground disabilities.

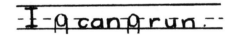

6. For word spacing the student can place index finger on paper after each written word.

7. Put rubber band on student's pencil near the paint line.

8. Substitute regular pencil for primary pencil.
9. Use ruled paper with narrow spacing.

eye-hand coordination activities

Descriptors:
Seatwork Activities
Fine-Motor Activities
Following Directions
Readiness

Grade Levels: K–3

Rationale: Young students need to develop good eye-hand coordination in preparation for writing letters, numbers, and words. It is fun to develop fine-motor ability using games and seatwork activities. Such activities serve to focus students' attention on better coordination. A transfer of these skills to writing letters, numbers, and words is the next step in preparing young students for academic success.

Objective: To provide the teacher with a variety of readiness, eye-hand coordination activities.

Materials: Chalkboard and chalk
Play Dough
Black marking pen
Ditto master
Duplicating paper
Colored beads of various shapes
Cookie sheets
Colored marking pens
Graduated sticks
Newsprint

Activity 1: Simple Mazes

Procedure: 1. Draw a simple maze on the chalkboard. A student volunteer completes the maze and draws a line through it.
2. A more complicated maze is drawn and the procedure is repeated.
3. Large sheets of paper with a maze are given to the students, who use a pencil to complete the maze.
4. An 8½″ × 11″ maze is duplicated for all students (Note: The maze gradually becomes more complicated while being placed on smaller sheets of paper.)

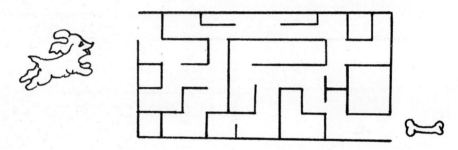

Activity 2: Dot-to-Dot Pictures

1. Construct simple dot-to-dot (or number-to-number) pictures on the chalkboard. Then graduate to paper.
2. The student is instructed to keep the pencil to the paper until the picture is completed.
3. Use commercial materials or design your own by tracing over a picture with numbers rather than an outline.

Activity 3: Placing and Pasting

1. Use simple geometric-shaped cookie cutters and draw around them with a black marking pen on a cookie sheet. Use squares, triangles, circles, hearts, diamonds, and so on.
2. Students are instructed to roll out Play Dough and cut play "cookies" out of the Play Dough.
3. Have the students match the "cookies" to the cookie sheet on which the same outlines have been drawn.

Activity 4: Bead Stringing

1. Tell the students which color and shape of bead you want each of them to put on a string.
2. Next, ask each student to string beads of given colors and shapes in sequences of two, then three, then four.
3. Begin with colors only.
4. Then use only shapes.
5. Finally, when the students are ready, you may mix colors and shapes.

Activity 5: Dot-and-Circle Game

1. Give each student a sheet of paper that has a green margin at the left and clusters of circles, squares, or other shapes of objects to the right of the margin.
2. Direct the students to start at the green margin and place a dot in each circle or square in the same row.
3. Various directions may be given; dots can be put in squares, crosses in rectangles, and so on. (Note: This activity prepares a student to read or work a paper from left to right, a necessary eye movement for reading.)

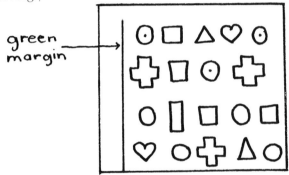

Activity 6: Coloring

1. Select coloring books or simple dittoed pictures.
2. Require the students to fill in the parts within the design. Do not choose too small a design if it is to be dittoed.
3. The design may be outlined with heavy wax crayons creating a slight ridge on the paper, which serves as a line not to be crossed when coloring.
4. Yarn may also be glued around the outline to provide a higher ridge for students with greater coordination difficulties.

Activity 7: Overhead Designs

1. Give students opportunities to reproduce designs, letters, and numerals projected for them on the overhead.
2. They may reproduce the designs in sand trays, on chalkboards, or on large pieces of paper.

Activity 8: Intermediate Eye-Hand Coordination Activities

Chalkboard activities can provide training and experience in a number of skills. Examples are eye-hand coordination, rhythm, perceptual-motor match, directionality, orientation, and form perception in preparation for cursive writing.

1. *Single continuous circles.* The student draws a large circle with the dominant hand, making several revolutions before stopping. The student repeats the task with the nondominant hand. If the student makes the circles moving toward the right, have him/her change and make continuous circle in the opposite direction.

2. *Double continuous circles* (to help coordinate both sides of the body). The student holds a piece of chalk in each hand. The student looks at an X drawn on the board opposite his/her nose. The student draws circles with both hands, using full arm movements.

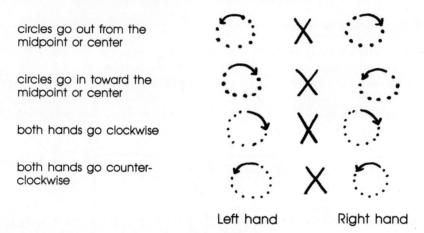

circles go out from the midpoint or center

circles go in toward the midpoint or center

both hands go clockwise

both hands go counter-clockwise

Left hand   Right hand

3. *Rythmic writing.* Introductory movements to cursive writing.

    a. This activity allows the student to practice a continuous reproductive task using rhythmic movements. The student stands next to the teacher at the chalkboard. Say to the student, "I am going to put some designs on the board. I will make one and then I want you to make one just like mine below it." The movements should be rhythmic and free flowing. Have the students stand at least 6 inches from the board. The following motifs may be used for this exercise.

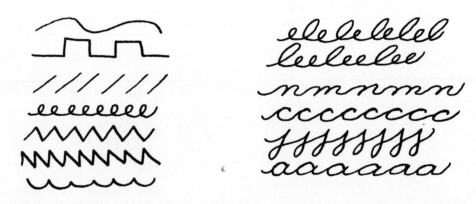

    b. If the student has difficulty performing the preceding tasks, the following may prove helpful. Discuss how the movement is made. For example: "First we go up and then we go down." Demonstrate on the board. Or, "We go away from our body and then toward our body."

    c. Introduce one or two movements a week. If a student has difficulty with any movements, allow additional practice as often as possible. Before introducing a new movement, review the previous ones.

    d. When the students are able to reproduce the motifs with accuracy, draw lines, approximately 3 or 4 inches wide, on the board and have them practice the motifs on the lines.

4. *Writing activities on paper.*

   a. The rhythmic writing activities used at the chalkboard should next be used with large sheets of paper and felt tip pens at a desk. Begin with an 18″ × 24″ paper, newsprint or old newspapers, and large felt pens. Initially, the student stands at his/her desk to perform the activities. When the student is able to complete the activities accurately, begin decreasing the size of the paper until reaching the standard 8½″ × 11″ size. The student should now sit at his/her desk.

   b. The cursive writing is introduced and practiced. Correct writing posture should be discussed and demonstrated. You may also line the paper with magic markers using three different colors on top, middle, and bottom line. This helps the student stay on and within the lines.

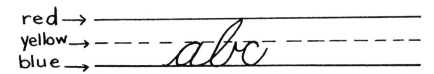

parent help with writing skills

Descriptors: Parent Tutoring   **Grade Levels:**   1–2
              Letter Practice

Rationale: Parents are excellent sources of tutorial help. By having parents reinforce skills introduced at school, students master new skills more quickly and thoroughly. In the present activity parents help their children with manuscript writing following a sequential practice technique.

Objective: To teach parents a sequential writing program to be used at home for tutorial practice with their child.

Materials: Lined writing paper (appropriate for the student's skill level)
Pencil
Chalkboard and chalk
Box of salt and baking pan 9″ × 13″ × 1½″
Ditto master
Duplicating paper

Procedure: 1. Demonstrate one sequential writing lesson for the parents.
2. Duplicate and distribute to participating parents copies of manuscript (or cursive) letters showing the exact sequential stroke pattern.
   Example:

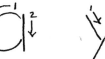

3. Identify which letter is to be taught to the student.
   Example:

M m

(Note: It is recommended that the alphabet not be taught in sequence at this time—because of *b-d* confusion, and so on. Rather, attention should be given to the most commonly used consonants in beginning sound/symbol learning, such as *s, m,* or *b.* The teacher may want to choose letters in a student's name.)
4. Demonstrate to the parents how capital and small letters (M m) are written. Use the chalkboard or salt tray to go over the letter (again and again) before writing it on paper. To assure consistency, it is important to provide the parents with a sequential stroke pattern chart as many adults use alternative strokes.

5. Design a beginning writing-practice paper that requires the student to practice capital and small letters, a single word beginning with a particular letter, and a simple sentence using the letter. (Note: Do not use words including letters the student has not yet practiced to avoid reinforcing wrong responses. Start by designing single-capital and small-letter practice, adding one word, and eventually progressing to a simple sentence.)

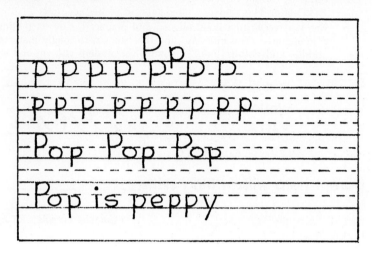

Additional Suggestions:

1. Parents may play a game with their youngsters to practice and reinforce letter writing. Parents call out a letter that has previously been practiced and the student writes it from memory on a chalkboard (in a salt tray or on a magic slate). If the correct sequential stroke pattern is used, the youngster scores one point. The game continues at a fast pace with the score being computed at the end of the game. The same letter may be used several times. The parent may call out "capital T," "small m," and so on.
2. Stickers should be awarded for correctly completed writing papers. For example, all papers may be fastened together in a booklet for the student.
3. Keep a chart for each student identifying the letters correctly mastered.

reversal of b-d

Descriptors: Visual Perceptual Discrimination   **Grade Levels:** 1–2
Writing Practice
Letter Recognition

Rationale: The *b-d* reversal problem of many students is often explained as stemming from perceptual problems or neurological damage. In reality, however, the reversal is more likely due to poor sequential writing formation. Such students usually start both the *b* and the *d* with a vertical line and must then decide to go either to the right or to the left depending on which letter is being written. This constant decision-making process causes many students to reverse a *b* and *d* when they are in a hurry. Reteach the student one letter at a time, but not at the same time. Have the student go over the same sequential stroke patterns again and again until it has, in essence, been "overlearned."

Objective: To teach a student automatically to write *b* or *d* correctly without reversals.

Materials: Paper
Chalkboard and chalk
Sand or salt tray
Crayons
Pencils

Procedure: Demonstrate the correct, sequential strokes for the *b* using any of the materials listed above. It is useful for children to recite a little "rhyme" relating to the process when learning these strokes. The *b* must always be formed by making a line first and then the ball.

"The bee buzzes down."   "And then he goes around."

Continue to practice the correct *b* formation using different materials until the student has consistently learned it by rote. At any time ask the student to write quickly a *b* for you. Students usually consider this a game and are anxious to show you they can do it. Be sure to reinforce all correct responses. Example: "That's great, Bob. I didn't catch you, did I?"

Only when the student can form a correct *b* consistently, should you go on to learning how to write a *d*.

The *d* should always be formed by making a circle (or *c*) first, then adding the stick. The following rhyme may be improved but it has worked for many students.

"Dog starts with d. Let's say this rhyme when we write a d."

"The dog goes around." "He jumps up." "And then he falls down!"

Go over the *d* again and again saying the rhyme while using the various materials until the *d* is also overlearned. Ask the student at various times during the day to write a *d* for you. S/he may not need the rhyme, but many do.

Additional Suggestions: The following may serve as helpful mnemonic devices:
1. You need a bat before you can hit the ball.

2. *B* begins the word *bed* and *d* ends the word *bed*.

_____more b-d reversal strategies_____

Descriptors: Visual Discrimination
Eye-Hand Coordination

Grade Levels: 1–2

Rationale: Reversals of *b-d* are not uncommon at the beginning of first grade but if students persist in reversing these letters, educators tend to become concerned. In most cases, however, the difficulty appears to stem from a sequential writing problem rather than a neurological impairment as some professionals have suggested. This activity offers some alternatives to *b-d* reversal ideas found elsewhere in this book.

Objective: To teach students consistently to identify and write the letters *b* and *d*.

Materials:

Black marking pen
Chalkboard and chalk
Sections of the newspaper
Ditto master
Duplicating paper
Pencil

Procedure:

1. Demonstrate the correct formation of the letter *b* on the chalkboard showing the students the correct sequential stroke pattern of using a down stroke then a circular movement to the right.
2. The students write the same pattern in the air saying "b" each time they form the letter.
3. Design a dittoed paper with a pictorial drawing of a *b*. Say, "*Bob* wanted to play *baseball* so he got his *bat* and *ball*. *Bob*, *baseball*, *bat*, and *ball*, each starts with a *b*."
4. The students repeat the saying and practice writing more *b*'s on the page.

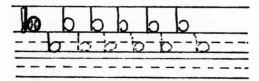

5. The students continue to practice the letter *b* until they are proficient at writing it consistently from memory for three days.
6. Introduce other letters during the next two to three weeks before introducing the letter *d*.
7. When introducing *d* follow the same procedure but present the *d* on the chalkboard in this manner: "*David* liked to play his *drum*. First he got his *drum* and then he found one of his *drumsticks*. *David*, *drum*, and *drumstick* all start with the letter "*d*.""

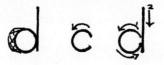

8. Distribute dittoed writing paper with the letter *d*.
9. The students continue to practice the letter *d* for three days. Later introduce both letters at the same time to determine whether or not the students can consistently identify and write each of them.

Additional Suggestions:

1. Put a sticker at the right-hand top corner of the students' desks for the *b*all on the *b*, to go toward the right and toward the sticker. Be certain that all students can tell you which is the right side of their desk, using their body for orientation if necessary. Ask them which side the sticker is on. A letter *b* can be taped at the upper right-hand side of the desks. Have the pupils show you daily which is their right hand. Ignore the word left, and the letter *d* at the present time. It will be taught later after the *b* is learned. Teach one concept at a time.
2. Cut circles and other shapes from the news portion of the newspaper or from magazine articles (use large print for younger students). Have the students circle *b*'s with a blue crayon or marker and *d*'s with a red marker. At first, the students should circle only one letter per shape, but after mastery of this skill, have the students circle both *b*'s and *d*'s in the appropriate colors on the given shapes.

   (Note: This activity may be too difficult for young children or students with poor visual discrimination.)

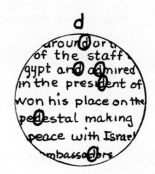

3. Some teachers like students to form a *b* with their right thumb in a vertical position and the rest of their fingers in a fist. Reverse the procedure by using the left thumb, for a *d*. The students must be able to differentiate between their right and left hands and correctly associate them with the proper letters.

left-handed writers

Descriptors: Fine-Motor Coordination   **Grade Level:**   1–3

Rationale: Left-handed writers are frequently frustrated by right-handed models or by being urged to use their right hands for writing. Left-handed students often develop inappropriate handwriting skills because their papers are not angled correctly. Some right-handed teachers feel that they cannot teach handwriting to left-handed students. However, it should be remembered that as a general rule, left-handed students perform many or all tasks the reverse of right-handed peers.

Objective: To present suggestions for classroom teachers to use with left-handed writers.

Materials: Paper
Masking tape
Pencil

Procedure: A student with a left-hand preference should not be forced to write with his/her right hand.
1. To help a left-handed writer, the writing paper should be positioned at a right angle parallel with the student's left arm and attach the paper to the desk with masking tape.

2. The student continues writing the assigned lesson (such as single-letter practice, sentence copying, creative stories) in this manner until s/he has formed the habit of slanting the writing paper to the right.
3. When masking tape is no longer needed, the student is shown how to move the paper up and away from the body as the writing progresses toward the bottom.
4. It may be explained to a left-handed student that his/her paper is not slanted in the same direction as the right-handed students by using the analogy of the paper being an airport runway and the student's hand an airplane. "It is important for the airplane's runway to be at such an angle that the plane can take off smoothly. Right-handed and left-handed students have different runways."

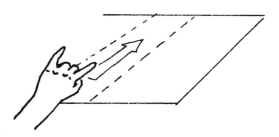

Additional Suggestions:

1. The incorrect hooked-wrist position observed in many left-handed writers may be helped by practicing with paint brushes, crayons, or chalk. Constant reinforcement of correctly holding the writing instruments will help many left-handed children hold pencils correctly.

2. In cursive writing, left-handed students' writing should be sloped slightly to the left. These students should be given appropriate sloping examples to follow. Examples may be obtained from other left-handed writers who exhibit good writing patterns.

> *tree house*

3. Special equipment, such as left-handed scissors and left-handed desk chairs, should be provided whenever possible.

beginning creative writing

Descriptors: Language Arts
Self-Concept
Written Expression

Grade Levels: 1.5–3

Rationale: Teacher fears and insecurities about creative writing prevent many instructors from actively trying such activities in the classroom. There is nothing more satisfying than writing and later listening to one's own original stories. However, stimulating creative writing is not an easy process. Following the guidelines presented in this teaching idea, everyone will feel successful about his/her creative writing product.

Objective: To present guidelines for teachers to use when introducing creative writing activities.

Materials: List of high-frequency words
Picture dictionaries
Regular dictionaries
Paper and pencil
Picture stimuli (if appropriate)

Procedure: 1. Decide on the motivational method to be used with your class.

    a. Picture starters: pictures are used to stimulate original stories.
    b. Story starters: either the beginning or the ending of a story is provided.
    c. Word starters: use of pictures and words spelled out to be used in a story. Example: Write a story using all the spelling words for the week.
    d. Stories about self: fears, feelings, special occasions such as birthdays and holidays, and so on.

2. Choose only one motivational method for each creative writing period.
3. Make the activity as exciting as possible. Your excitement will be contagious to the students.
4. Provide enough time to prevent the students from feeling rushed.
5. Brainstorm with the students about words they may need in order to write their stories. Write the words on the chalkboard for reference if needed.
6. Keep the classroom atmosphere relaxed to achieve spontaneity and self-expression. Creativity will not survive subject to criticism and pressure.
7. The teacher serves as the facilitator of the creative process. Move about the room assisting with spelling and offering suggestions, when asked. Do not attempt to impose your own ideas on the students' stories. Key questions may be asked to stimulate thinking without interjection of own ideas. Example: "What happened next?"
8. Proofread the finished products and make the necessary improvements in punctuation and spelling *after* the story is finished and turned in. Do not stress these corrections during the actual writing process.
9. Have students copy their products on "good" paper and illustrate if desired. Story paper with lines at the bottom and space at the top is recommended for the finished product.

10. Provide an opportunity for the students to share their illustrated stories with the rest of the class.

Additional Suggestions:
1. Keep a creative writing notebook for each student. As the school year progresses, add to the notebook. The students will be able to see improvements in their own writing abilities.
2. Display creative writing products on a bulletin board or in paperbound books. It is very satisfying to see one's own work being displayed.
3. Music is another means of motivating students creatively. Choose an appropriate recording and have the students write about the feelings and reactions it generated in them.

sequential copying skills

Descriptors: Eye-Hand Coordination   **Grade Levels:**   1–4

Rationale: Some students have difficulty copying words, sentences, and paragraphs, written on the chalkboard. Consequently, assignments may be incomplete or wrong due to poor copying skills rather than a lack of the academic skill needed to finish such tasks.

Objective: To teach the student how to copy words from a word on the page; from a parallel and slightly vertical plane, that is, desk, book, or easel, to the page; and from a vertical (chalkboard) plane.

Materials: Lined paper and pencil
Desk
Reading book in primary type
Small easel
Chalkboard and chalk
Black marking pen
1½″ × 5″ tagboard marker

Procedure:

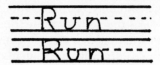

1. Write the word to be copied on a sheet of paper. Draw heavy black lines below the model on the paper. The student is to copy the word beneath the model.

   This technique can be used with two- or three-word phrases and simple sentences until the student can successfully copy and match the teacher's model word-for-word.

2. To teach the student to copy from one paper to another at the desk, place the word or group of words to be copied next to the student's blank writing paper. Ask the student to copy the words or sentence on the blank paper.

3. Have the student copy words or sentences from a reading book so as to provide different types of material and print sizes from which to copy.

   (Note: Some students with poor visual discrimination may need to use a marker or tachistoscope—see *Tachistoscopes* activity—to help isolate elements of what is being copied.)

4. Have the student copy the word or sentence from an easel that is placed on his/her desk. This prepares the student to begin copying from a slightly vertical rather than only a horizontal plane. (Note: The easel may be moved to another desk so that the student becomes familiar with copying words or sentences at a distance. The print must be large enough to enable the student to see it easily.)

5. The final goal is to teach the student to copy words or sentences from the chalkboard to paper. By using sequential steps the student is taught the transition of copying from one plane (horizontal) to another (vertical).

Additional Suggestions: See *Copying Skills* activity for visual memory practice.

instructional adaptations for
students with poor motor skills

Descriptors: Fine-Motor Skills   **Grade Levels:**   1–6
Writing
Spelling

Rationale: When a student is unable to use motor output (writing or printing) efficiently, frustration and a feeling of failure multiply. Adaptive techniques can be used in the classroom to prevent such feelings and help students succeed and complete tasks on time.

Objective: To present some adaptive techniques for students with poor motor skills.

Materials: Chalkboard and chalk
Paper and pencil
Tape recorder
Typewriter

Procedure:
1. Assess a student's academic difficulties and decide whether the student is programmed at the appropriate skill level. If the student is capable of completing assignments (that is, possesses the prerequisite skills), the difficulty in completing assignments may stem from a motor problem.
2. Decide what adaptations are possible for the student in the areas of test taking, spelling, math, note taking, and written assignments.
3. Use the following suggestions when applicable to that student:

TESTS

Instead of requiring the student to write laboriously long answers, use multiple choice, completion, matching, tape recorder (student records answers and teacher listens later when convenient), true or false, or oral tests.

SPELLING

1. Have student spell orally to teacher.
2. Have student spell orally to another student.
3. Have student use a typewriter.
4. Have student spell word into a tape recorder.
5. List four spellings of a word and have student underline the correct word.

smil	<u>smile</u>	smille	smele

MATH

1. Give student a smaller amount of written work assignments. (Example: copying fewer math problems from the board or book).
2. Give student paper on which problems are written down. The student supplies the answer.

2	8	2	3
x4	x4	x9	x9

3. Have student fold paper underneath problems in a book and write only answers.

DIRECTIONS AND NOTE TAKING

1. Hand student a written list of directions at student's reading level.
2. Provide a written outline of the material for the student to use when reading an assignment.

WRITTEN ASSIGNMENTS

1. Allow student to use tape recorder instead of writing all the answers.
2. Allow student time to take assignment home or to use extra school time for lengthy written assignments.
3. Allow student to tell the teacher about material s/he has learned.
4. Write some of the assignment and have the student write some. The student needs writing practice but it should not become a frustrating experience.

```
Dear Parents,
Our class is having a program on
_____  ____  _____.
```

Student finishes time, date and so on and signs the invitation.

5. Have student use a typewriter for composition.

copying skills

Descriptors:	Eye-Hand Coordination	**Grade Levels:** 1–6

Descriptors: Eye-Hand Coordination
Writing
Independent Seatwork

Grade Levels: 1–6

Rationale: Many students have difficulty completing seatwork assignments requiring them to copy from the chalkboard or from one section of a workbook page to another. If the youngster has any visual perceptual difficulties, the task becomes even more laborious and difficult. Poor copiers often copy down one number or letter at a time. Each time they look back to the original, they may choose a number or letter from a different problem or word, never monitoring the entire stimulus model. This copying method emphasizes the importance of looking at an entire problem (or word) and being able to reproduce it from memory. Accurate and quick copying skills allow a student more time to complete tasks.

Objective: To use a visual-memory technique to teach efficient copying skills.

Materials: Chalkboard and chalk
Paper and pencil
8½″ × 11″ tagboard (for cover sheet)

Procedure:
1. Write a math problem (or a word) on the chalkboard and ask the student to look closely at the whole problem (or word).
2. When the student says that s/he has looked at the original long enough, cover the problem and the student is to reproduce the problem (or word) from memory.
3. The student checks his/her written work against the original on the chalkboard when the original model is uncovered.
4. Continue to practice copying whole problems or words following this procedure until the student becomes a proficient and accurate copier.

(Note: The student is *not* required to work the math problems while participating in this activity. The objective is to learn how to copy entire problems or words from the chalkboard rather than being able to solve them.)

Additional Suggestions:
1. Use this method to teach reading and spelling words.
2. Use the same technique to practice copying from workbooks or other materials on a horizontal plane (desk) rather than the vertical plane (chalkboard).

(Note: Many students who are required to copy words from a workbook page to "fill in the blank" questions make copying errors. Such students may be considered to be giving an incorrect answer due to lack of knowledge of a subject or concept, whereas in reality the incorrect answer may stem from poor copying skills.)

expanding written language

Descriptors: Vocabulary Words
Written Expression
Spelling

Grade Levels: 3–6

Rationale: Many students have difficulty writing complex sentences and thus revert to using simple sentences requiring less complicated writing and spelling skills. This activity is designed to improve students' creative writing skills by helping them progress from simple to complex sentences.

Objective: To teach students how to write complete sentences by choosing words (or phrases) from word lists of nouns, adverbs, prepositional phrases, and so on.

Materials: Chalkboard, chalk, and writing paper (or ditto master of unfinished sentences)
Duplicating paper
Graded word lists or basal reader vocabulary lists
Pencil
Optional: envelopes, glue, tape, black marking pen

Procedure:
1. Write three or more kernel sentences on the chalkboard or on a ditto master to be duplicated for distribution to students. Kernel sentences have a subject-predicate relationship.

    Examples: The boy walked _____.
    Mother sat in the _____.
    Bill fell _____.

2. Using a graded word list or vocabulary list of a basal reader, write a list of appropriate words to complete each sentence. Include picture clues for ▓▓▓r readers.

Where
home
down
chair

The boy walked _____.
Mom sat in the _____.
Bill fell _____.

The student picks words from the word lists to fill in the sentence blanks. Check the answers or ask students to grade their own papers as answers are read aloud.

3. If students have handwriting difficulty, write each word indicating "where" on a separate slip of paper. Put the slips into an envelope labeled "where" (see #7).
4. Ask the student to read each sentence aloud to be certain the student can read all the words and understands their meanings.
5. Give the student the corresponding word list or envelope containing word slips. Ask the student to read each word aloud.
6. Ask the student to choose one word to complete each sentence.
7. Depending on writing skills, ask the student to write the word to complete each sentence, or glue the correct word card on the paper, or tape it on the chalkboard.
8. Give the student many opportunities to expand sentences using words that tell "where." Gradually increase the number of sentences presented.
9. Later, include distractors that do not tell "where" to teach the child to discriminate words that indicate "where" from other adverbs or prepositional phrases. Remind the student that some words do not tell "where." It is up to the student to find the words that *do* tell "where."

Additional Suggestions:

1. After the student has had plenty of practice selecting one word to complete each sentence, write phrases to be selected from a list.

Example:

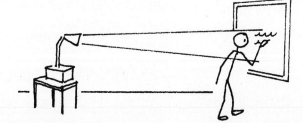

Where
in the backyard
at the fire station
over the fence

2. The same procedure may be used to teach words indicating "when," "why," and "how." Words in these categories require more language skills and involve more advanced concepts of inference and cause and effect.

cursive writing exercises

Descriptors: Eye-Hand Coordination
Motor Control

Grade Levels: 3–6

Rationale: By tracing letters, students get kinesthetic practice that strengthens motor skills and reinforces a left-to-right sequence. The following method allows the teacher to introduce beginning handwriting exercises on the chalkboard. The teacher puts a writing exercise on a clear transparency and projects it onto a chalkboard using an overhead projector. The student then traces the visual pattern. These exercises form a sequential visual image for the student to copy. When the students begin to trace, the teacher must show them where to start and stop to prevent them from practicing erroneous responses. It may be necessary to repeat the name of each letter for beginning cursive writers as it is practiced.

Objective: To teach students cursive w̶ ... an overhead projector and chalkboard.

Materials: Chalkboard and chal ...
Overhead projector ...
Clear transparencie ...
Marking pens for ...

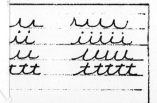

Procedure:

1. Write a large circle on a transparency and place it on the overhead projector to be projected onto the chalkboard.
2. The student first traces the circle with a finger and then with chalk on the chalkboard using outward movements.
3. Demonstrate a reverse procedure and have the student trace the circle using inward movements.
4. Make a racetrack on the transparency. The student stands in the center of the racetrack so that s/he crosses the midpoint as s/he traces.

5. Make transparencies containing rows of *is* and *us*, which are swing up letters. The transparency is placed on the overhead projector and projected onto the chalkboard. The student is asked to make a row of *is* and *us* on the chalkboard under the teacher's row model.

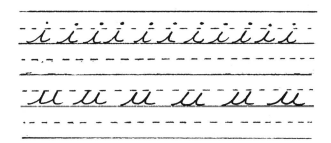

Dubrow[3] suggested that cursive letters be presented in the following order:

 a. The swing up letters: *i, u, w, t, r, s*
 b. The swing up and over letters: *n, m, v, x*
 c. The swing up and turn back letters: *e, l, b, h, k, f*
 d. The swing over and turn back letters: *c, a, g, d, q*
 e. More swing up letters: *o, p, j*
 f. More swing up and over letters: *y, z*

6. The projector is turned off when the student is finished. The handwriting may be examined to determine how uniformly and neatly the tracing was carried out and to give the student immediate feedback on the work.
7. The projector is moved away from the board to make the visuals larger or moved closer to reduce their size. If the student has difficulty tracing the exercises, large letters should be used. In turn, the visuals should be made smaller as the pupil's writing improves.
8. Since students will progress at different rates, this method should be individualized. Separate transparencies can be made for each letter or the level your students are working on. Transparencies are filed in an easily retrievable location.

Additional Suggestions:

When the student masters the chalkboard exercises, the student should proceed to writing on paper. Make simple dittos of each letter. The top half should contain three to four examples of the letter the student is to trace. On the bottom half of the ditto paper, the student practices writing the letter.

---

[3] H.C. Dubrow, *Learning to Write.* (Cambridge, Mass.: Educators' Publishing Service, 1968.)

Descriptors: Vocabulary Improvement **Grade Levels:** 3–6
Creative Writing
Spelling

Rationale: Students need to learn synonyms and antonyms in order to explain their oral and written language skills. Individualized activities and game formats make learning new concepts fun and challenge the student to collect new words.

Objective: To provide practice in correct use of synonyms and antonyms.

Materials: Ditto master
Duplicator paper
Notebook paper
3½″ × 5″ blank index cards
Chalkboard and chalk (games 3, 4, and 6)

Procedure:
1. The teacher defines *synonyms* and *antonyms* for the students and provides examples of each. The class is encouraged to contribute other examples of both types of vocabulary words.
   Synonym: A word that means the same, or nearly the same, as another word in the same language. Example: nice—pleasant
   Antonym: A word that means the opposite of another word in the same language. Example: sharp—dull
2. As part of vocabulary expansion, the teacher should plan one of the following games each day to provide further practice using synonyms and antonyms.

Synonyms:

Game 1: Overtired Words

Prepare a ditto master of sentences that contain many underlined overworked words. Students are to supply as many synonyms as possible for the underlined words. Copies of the worksheet should be for each member of the class.

Example: 1. He was a good boy. (Pupils might write: polite, kind, well-behaved)

2. It was a nice day. (Pupils might write: sunny, pleasant, clear)

The teacher may correct the papers individually or have the class orally check their papers together.

Game 2: Another Way to Say

The teacher composes a group of defining phrases and places each on an index card. The students are instructed to select a card and write as many synonyms as possible fitting the definition. The teacher checks the students' papers or provides answer cards in the back of the file for self-correction. Example:

cannot be found
not new
boys and girls
hope to get
where cows live
fair play

what person
mother's sister
glad rags
that man
give food
baby dog

student's Paper

lost
misplaced
disappear
vanish
mislaid
missing
astray
gone

The teacher may design individual records of the word cards completed by each student. The records are to be used until each student has used all word cards.

Game 3: Synonym Score-Up

The teacher prepares a list of words having many synonyms. The class is divided into two teams. The teacher or a student pronounces a word and asks the first player of the team to write a synonym for it on the chalkboard. A correct response receives one point. Then the first player of the other team writes another synonym for the same word and, if correct, scores two points. Now follows the second player of the first team who may score three points by giving a correct answer. The teams alternate their attempts to add other synonyms until a member fails. Points are now totaled up and the winning team is announced. A new word is then given and the game proceeds as previously described.

Game 4: Password Relay

The teacher prepares a group of cards for words that have many synonyms. The class is divided into teams and each student is given one card to be placed face down on his/her desk. At the signal, the first member of each team shows his/her card to the student seated behind him/her. That student goes to the board and writes "passwords," that is, the stimulus word and a synonym. If correct, two points are scored for the team. If the student does not know a synonym, a dictionary may be consulted and one point received for the correct answer. When the student has written the "password," the word card on his/her desk is shown to the next student and the game continues until all students have a turn. The points are tallied by a scorekeeper, with the team receiving the most points being declared the winning team. This game may be adapted for antonyms study.

Game 5: Word Matching

The teacher prepares a dittoed worksheet by listing a numbered series of words in Column I and an unnumbered series of synonyms in Column II. The students are to write the synonyms in the correct numerical order to agree with Column I and are then to use each synonym in a written sentence. The teacher may ask the students to read their sentences aloud while the rest of the class checks that both the original word and the synonym correctly fit the sentence. This activity may be adapted to practice using antonyms.

Game 6: Synonym Basketball

The teacher prepares cards for words that have many synonyms and gives an equal number of cards to the captains of two teams. The captain of Team A gives the first card to the first player, who pronounces the word and writes a synonym on the board. If the student is correct, a 1-point "basket" is scored and the "ball" is passed on to the other team captain who proceeds in the same manner. If Team A's answer is incorrect, the Team B captain calls on any Team B member to write a synonym on the board. If that word is correct, two points are scored and Team B retains "possession of the ball." The Team B captain then gives his/her first word card to the first player on that team. Continue the game until all players have had one turn. The team with the most points wins the game. The activity may be adapted to antonym word study.

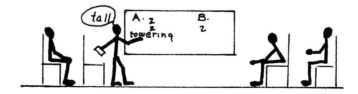

Antonyms: ### Game 1: Words and Opposites

The teacher lists several words having antonyms and asks the students to write the words in pairs on paper with the antonym (opposite word) next to each word on the list.

Example:

take	give
stop	go
their	(etc.)
yes	
down	
slow	
out	

Game 2: Opposite Sentences

The teacher prepares sentences on a ditto master or on the chalkboard. The students are to rewrite the sentences using the antonyms of the underlined words.

Example: He was a tall boy.
The horse walked slowly.
She was a short girl.
The horse walked quickly.
The night was very cold.
The day was very hot.

Game 3: Where's My Opposite

The teacher prepares pairs of word cards, each of which contains an antonym. One card is given to each student. The first student pronounces his/her word and writes it on the chalkboard. The person holding the antonym card then pronounces his/her word and writes it beside the first one. The second student in the row pronounces his/her word and the game progresses around the classroom in this manner. The game should continue at a fast pace until each student has had a turn to pronounce his/her word card.

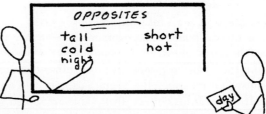

Game 4: Pairs of Sentences

The teacher lists pairs of antonyms on a dittoed worksheet or on the chalkboard and instructs the students to write sentences that include each pair of words.

Example: happy—unhappy
tall—short
weak—strong
The short boy was standing beside the tall tree.
The little girl was happy until her ice cream cone fell on the ground making her unhappy.

Additional
Suggestions: 1. The teacher may construct crossword puzzles as worksheets using synonyms and antonyms.
2. Students may be encouraged to create their own games using synonyms and antonyms.

Descriptors: Creative Writing   **Grade Levels:**   4–6
Reading Vocabulary
Dictionary Skills

Rationale: Word-collecting activities lead to more creative writing by motivating students to use everyday experiences to expand their vocabularies and to search for new and exciting words. Students who are required to write themes on personal experiences such as "My summer vacation" or "The biggest surprise of my life was . . ." often have difficulty getting started. Such students are sometimes described by teachers as being lazy or nonattentive. However, many students may want to write stories or themes, but lack word power and thus resort to dull descriptions, overused adjectives, and easily spelled words.

Objective: To teach students how to compile their own word lists and to organize the words into categories.

Materials: Notebook or student-made booklet
Pencil or pen
Commercial tabs
Dictionary
Thesaurus (optional)
Synonym and antonym lists

Procedure: 1. The students are asked to compile personal notebooks of vocabulary words divided into categories and separated by commercial tabs. The tabs are staggered from top to bottom of the edge of the pages. Categories might include: Taste, Sound, Description, Size, Transportation, Feelings, Smell, and Motion.

  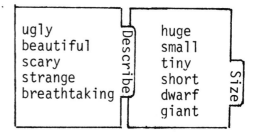

The tabs can be added to the pages of a commercial notebook or booklets constructed from notebook paper and construction paper covers entitled "Word File."

2. Students should be instructed to become alert to new words seen in books or newspaper articles, or heard on television and during conversations. The students compile individual notebooks consisting of these new words by writing them under the appropriate category or starting a new category when needed.

3. The teacher may plan one period during the week when students can orally share their new word acquisitions with classmates thus allowing other students to add more words to their own booklets if desired.

4. The teacher should encourage the students to refer to their word files when writing creative compositions. It is important to discuss with the students the use of "overworked" words such as *nice*. Other choices for that overworked word might include thoughtful, charming, helpful, or cooperative.

5. It may be necessary for the teacher to offer extra encouragement and guidance to students who do not appear confident about using their word files to assist them in creative writing. The personal word file dictionaries should also prove helpful in improving spelling skills.

Additional Suggestions:

1. The teacher may suggest a category that is to be included in all students' notebooks. The students are allowed 10 to 15 minutes to add words under the new category before sharing them with other students. For example, *Descriptive Sky Words*—cloudy, overcast, ominous, billowy, airy, fleecy, dark.

2. Students may be asked to write five descriptive sentences using their notebooks as references. Example: Sally ate several crispy, sour, green, bumpy pickles at the picnic.

singular and plural possessives' ladder

Descriptors: Grammar
Writing Skills
Language Arts

Grade Levels: 4–6

Rationale: Picture clues often reinforce new concepts. It is necessary for students to understand the use of singular and plural possessives as they write. This activity provides practice using the grammatical concept of possessives. Self-correction allows the students to work independently by checking answer cards.

Objective: The student will be able to form singular and plural possessives correctly on completion of four packets of activity cards.

Materials: 1½′ × 3′ tagboard
Clear vinyl contact paper
Grease pencil
54 5″ × 7″ note cards
Flair pens (black or blue)
Thumbtacks

Procedure:

1. Using tagboard, construct a large ladder on a bulletin board with the caption, "Can you make it to the top?"

2. Cover the steps with clear contact paper so that written words may be wiped off. Use a grease pencil or flair marker.

3. Prepare six packets, each consisting of eight pictures. Make two packets with singular possessives, two with plural possessives, and two with mixed possessives. Provide an answer card for the picture cards in each packet.

9. Answers
1. boy's ladder.
2. boys' ladder.
3. mouse's tail.
4. cats' whiskers.
5. oysters' pearls.
6. teacher's room.
7. apple's worm.
8. teachers' room.

4. Post the rules for forming plurals near the ladder.

    a. One person or thing *owns* or *has* an object ('s). Example: girl's dress, fox's tail, and fish's fin.

    b. Two or more people or things *own* or *have* objects (s'). Example: boys' boots, snails' shells, or monkeys' tails.

5. The student writes the possessive for each picture in a packet on the ladder rungs using flair pens or grease pencils. If the student misses a possessive, the student looks at the correct answer on the answer card and starts that packet over again.
6. When the student has reached the top, the student may proceed to a more difficult group of picture cards.

Additional Suggestions:

1. The ladder concept may be used to promote learning in other areas: vocabulary enrichment, word identification, word definition, and math problems.
2. The teacher may ditto individual consumable ladders and have the students work individually on the packets, which can be shared among them. After completing a packet, the students check their own work by obtaining the answer cards. The number correct for each packet is recorded on individual worksheets.

handwriting "demons"

Descriptors: Visual Discrimination
Eye-Hand Coordination
Legibility

Grade Levels: 4–6

Rationale: Early handwriters often have trouble with some of the connecting letters in cursive writing. Because of closure problems, the *a*, *u*, and *v* are sometimes mistaken for other letters. Such students may be considered to have missed spelling words on a test because of a writing rather than a spelling problem. It is often difficult to read their written essays. Consequently, they receive lower grades.

Objective: To direct students' attention to similar cursive letters and to provide practice using word pairs and sentences containing these letters.

Materials: Chalkboard and chalk
Writing paper and pencil (for each student)

Procedure:

1. Write the following letters on the chalkboard.

2. Explain to the students that it is very important to write cursive letters correctly because several of them look alike.
3. Say, "Look at the first letter. Is it supposed to be an *a* or an *o*? How can you make certain that the reader knows which letter you have written?" Ask a student to come to the chalkboard and demonstrate a correct cursive *a* and an *o*.
4. Ask the students to write five cursive *a*'s and five cursive *o*'s on their sheet of writing paper.
5. Continue the same procedure as the other figures (as illustrated) are presented.

6. Write the following word pairs on the chalkboard. Ask the students to practice writing the word pairs on their sheets of writing paper. Circulate among the students and look at the writing papers to determine whether or not the students are writing the words correctly.

    cat, cot   cent, ant   put, pot

    fun, fiend   sum, seem   use, vise

7. Write the following sentences on the chalkboard. Ask student volunteers to read each one aloud. Have the students write the sentence and hand them to the teacher for evaluation.

Put the cat on the cot. Use the valuable vise.
Pat the cat for fun.
The happy monster is a friendly fiend.

Additional Suggestions:

1. Use an overhead projector to demonstrate the handwriting "demons."
2. Use magic slates for further practice of cursive word and sentence writing.

creative word ladders

Descriptors: Language Arts   **Grade Levels:** 4–6
                 Creative Writing

Rationale: The introduction of stimulus word activities often encourages students to become creative writers and stimulates them to venture away from the routine, common written expressions. This teaching idea[4] suggests activities that prepare students to use a thesaurus.

Objective: To present activities designed to help students expand their vocabulary and thus provide an incentive to write more creative sentences, paragraphs, and stories.

Materials: Colored construction paper
Black marking pen
White shelf paper
Writing paper and pencil
Thumbtacks

Procedure: **Word Ladders**

1. Make a word ladder using color words. Ask, "What is white?" or "What is yellow?"
2. Record the class suggestions on construction paper ladders in matching colors.
3. Hang the ladders in the classroom to be used by students in their creative writing attempts during the year. For instance, after discussing the use of simile and metaphor in writing, a student may refer to the ladders for suggestions. Example: "The clouds were white and fluffy as whipped cream," or "The lemon-bright sun sat high in the sky."

---

[4] J. Schaff, *The Language Arts Idea Book.* (Pacific Palisades, Calif.: Goodyear Publishing Co., Inc., 1976).

Action Words Lists

1. Create action word lists using shelf paper.
2. Hang the lists in the classroom and allow students to add words during the year using a marking pen.
3. These lists then become a "thesaurus" of words that can be used in class for individual writing activities.

(Note: Brainstorm with the class to get lists started. For instance, ask the class, "What can blow?" "The wind." "How does the wind blow?" "It whistles," "it howls." Continue this line of questioning for whatever words you want to make lists for.

Deter-miners	Color Words	Size Words	Things People	Action Words	How Words	Where Words	When Words
the	silvery	gigantic	fish	fell	swiftly	on the road	yesterday
many	glowing	huge	bride	smiled	softly	in church	tomorrow
a	shiny	tiny	lemon	cried	loudly	at the store	last week
an	bright	enormous	car	swam	carefully	in the air	years ago
hundreds	dark		panda	roared	eagerly	overhead	some day
several	beautiful		basket	tiptoed	angrily		
some			doctor	crashed			

Word Category Sentences

1. Develop sentences from word categories by using a long sheet of shelf paper and divide it into categories.
2. Have the students think of words to write under each category.
3. When finished let students have fun putting words from each category into both meaningful and nonsense sentences.

Example: a. Numerous silvery, tiny fish swam swiftly at the beach yesterday.

b. Hundreds of puckery, enormous lemons laughed loudly at the store last week.

Definitions

1. Have the class contribute to a book of definitions by talking about the word to be defined.
2. Post the definitions, keep a class book, or have the students find pictures that illustrate each word so that they can create their own booklets of definitions.

Example:
Loneliness is . . . .
Sadness is . . . .
Delight is . . . .
Discomfort is . . . .
Mystery is . . . .
Imagination is . . . .
Mischief is . . . .
Worry is . . . .

Groups of sentence answers might be:
. . . . wearing shoes that do not fit.
. . . . sitting in a hot room.
. . . . listening to a boring talk.
. . . . sleeping on a lumpy mattress.

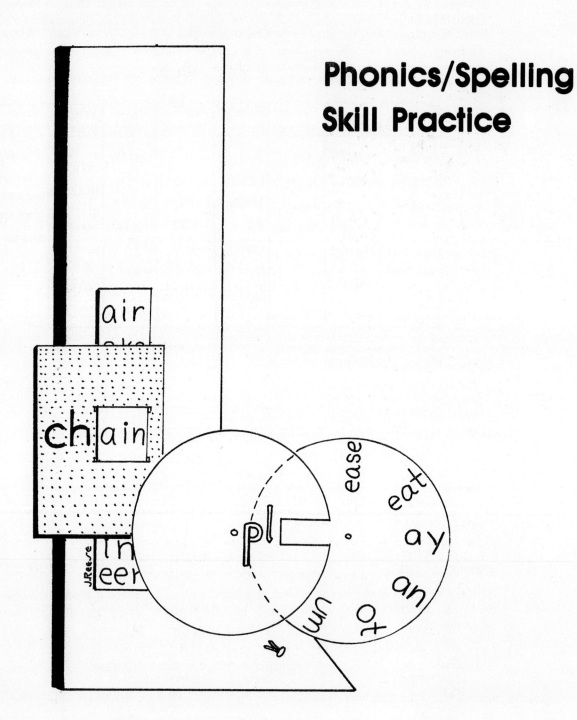

Phonics/Spelling Skill Practice

Descriptors: Phonics   **Grade Levels:** K–2
Reading Readiness

Rationale: Students who are learning to read need to establish a strong sound/symbol relationship. Often too many letters and their corresponding sounds are introduced at one time without allowing students much opportunity to practice identification of the newly learned letters and their symbols.

Objective: To provide the teacher with sound/symbol activities to strengthen students' consonant/sound association.

Activity 1: Picture Flash Cards

Materials: 5″ × 9″ index cards
Black marking pen
Crayons
Pencil and paper

Directions: For this activity the sound of the letter should be stressed, not the letter name. A combination of visual, auditory, and tactile processes should be used. The consonant letters must be presented one at a time with consistent reviewing of the letter. Begin with the common initial consonant sounds: *b, m, f, h, p, k, j, r, l, s, t, n, d, z, v,* and *w.* With letters that have two sounds (*c* and *g*), only the hard sound should be taught at this time. Since *x* and *q* are more difficult and rarely included as initial consonants for beginning readers they should be taught at a later time. Finally, the sound of *y* may be taught as a "laughing y." For example: "yuh, yuh, yuh, yuh." Students who experience difficulty in learning sound/symbol often put a *w* sound with a *y.* By using the example of the "laughing" sound this confusion is soon eliminated.

Procedure: 1. Present a card with a printed lowercase letter and a picture or drawing of a common word beginning with that sound.

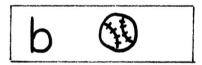

2. Say the letter sound, then the picture word, emphasizing the initial consonant. Example: bbb ball
3. Ask the student to repeat the letter sound and corresponding picture word. If the student fails, repeat steps 2 and 3 until a correct answer is obtained.
4. Ask the student to trace the letter with a finger, saying its sound while tracing. Show the student the correct sequential strokes for tracing the letter.
5. Ask the student to write the letter, saying its sound as it is written.

   a. If the student's motor skills are sufficient, have the student use a pencil or crayon.
   b. If the student's motor skills are substandard, have the student trace the letter in a pan of salt or sand.

Begin and end each session with a review of the earlier learned initial consonant sounds, completing steps 1 through 3.

**Additional
Suggestions:** 1. Taperecord steps 1 through 3 with the student. For independent work, ask the student to play back the tape for reinforcement and further practice. When the student knows two or more initial consonant sounds, the following activities are appropriate.

2. Use a set of simple picture word cards and ask the student to sort through them, setting aside those that begin with the initial consonant being learned. The teacher or aide checks the sorted cards for accuracy.

3. Use white glue to outline the letter on the flash card. As the glue dries, it becomes raised and transparent, thus allowing the student to feel the letter outline when tracing it.

Activity 2: Puzzle Cards

Materials: 3″ × 5″ tagboard cards
Paste
Scissors
Black marking pen
Crayons

Procedure: 1. Print the initial consonant on the left side of a 3″ × 5″ card or tagboard.
2. Draw or paste an appropriate picture on the right side and color it if needed.
3. Cut the cards on irregular lines to form a puzzle.

4. The student spreads the cards on a table and matches the letter to the picture, saying the initial sound and then the name of the picture.
5. Self-correction is provided by checking to see if the puzzle "fits."

Additional Suggestions: Pass out the letter sides of the puzzle to some students and the picture side to others. Ask one student to stand up and call out a sound. The student with the correct picture stands up and says the picture name. If the puzzle fits together the responses are correct.

Activity 3: Spin and Say

Materials: Tagboard
Cardboard pizza plate (optional)
Brad
Scissors
Black marking pen

Procedure: 1. Cut a circle out of tagboard or use a cardboard pizza plate.
2. Print any series of numbers on it and attach a spinner with a brad.
3. Using a tagboard card, print a corresponding number of initial consonants.

1. b
2. f
3. h
4. j
5. k
6. l
7. n
8. p

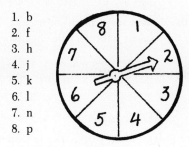

4. Ask a student to twirl the spinner.
5. The student reads the number and says the corresponding initial consonant from the card. If the student is ready, ask him/her to say a word that begins with the same sound.
6. The game is continued until all students have had a turn.

Additional Suggestions:
This game can be simplified by covering the pizza cardboard with clear contact paper. Using a grease pencil, write consonant letters within the sections and play the game by spinning the dial and saying the sound or giving a word beginning with that sound. The grease pencil may be wiped off and new letters added.

happy-sad faces

Descriptors:
Phonics Practice
Group Participation

Grade Levels: K–2

Rationale:
When students first learn beginning letter sounds they need opportunities to practice their newly acquired skill. Group games are a fun way to learn and an easy way for the teacher to assess students' skills.

Objective:
To provide group practice in beginning sound/symbol association. (Note: Since the game is designed to provide practice, the letters chosen for the game must have been introduced to the students previously).

Materials:
2½-inch circle, cut out of white poster board (2 for each student)
8-inch stick, cut from a tablet back or popsicle sticks (1 for each student)
Crayons
Glue

Front

Back

Procedure:
1. Have each student draw a happy and a sad face on the 2½-inch circles with bright crayons.
2. Paste the two circles together back-to-back with the end of the stick between them. The sad face is exposed on one side and the happy face on the other.
3. Students are seated in a small group of six to ten students so that they cannot see the other students' happy-sad faces when they are asked to hold these up.
4. The teacher (or group leader) makes a statement such as, "The first letter sound in the word *boy* is *b*."
5. The students show their "happy face" if the statement is correct or the "sad face" if the statement is incorrect. Example: "The first letter sound in the word *boy* is *d*."
6. The game continues in like manner at a fast pace. It can quickly be noted if some students do not understand the letter/sound concept and thus further individual help can be provided when necessary. The statement may be repeated and one of the students may be called on to show his/her puppet face to the others when immediate correction is needed.

Additional Suggestions:
Use the game to practice rhyming words (sad/mad; sad/sat), math concepts, and ending consonants.

Descriptors: Phonics Practice
Group Game

Grade Levels: 1–3

Rationale: Especially in the early learning-to-read stages, it is important that students learn to listen carefully in order to understand oral directions better or to learn phonics. Games provide a good format for reinforcing newly acquired skills.

Objective: To practice newly introduced phonics skills.

Materials: 5 12″ × 18″ oaktag sheets
Paper clips
Black marking pen
Scissors

Procedure:
1. Draw large, comical ears on the tagboard sheets using the black marking pen. A band, large enough to fit around the heads of the students, is drawn between and on each side of the ears.

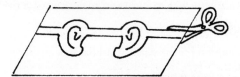 

2. The five sets of ears are cut out of the tagboard.
3. Choose five students to wear "listening ears" while they stand in front of the class. Paper clips are used to fasten the bands around the students' heads.
4. To practice phonics skills, the initial consonant *d* is chosen.
5. One student from the class is asked to pronounce a word of his/her choice. Example: "*doghouse*."
6. The same student chooses one of the five students wearing "listening ears" and asks him/her to verify whether the word is correct or incorrect as an example of a word beginning with *d*.
7. If the student answers correctly, s/he may keep the ears, whereupon the student who pronounced the word chooses another student to call out a new word.
8. If the student answers incorrectly, the two youngsters trade places and another student is chosen as the caller for the next round.
9. The game continues until all students have had a chance to wear the "listening ears." If a student has answered correctly twice, s/he may choose another student to take his/her place. This allows other students to get a turn.

Additional Suggestions:
1. Use the game to play "Following Directions." Example: "Go to the door, turn around three times, and hop backwards to your desk." One of the "listening ears" students is called on to carry out the directions. If the student completes the directions correctly, that student is allowed to keep the "listening ears." Otherwise, another student gets a turn.
2. Use the game for further phonics practice. Example: Blends, rhyming words, or consonant endings.

Descriptors: Consonant Blends/Digraphs   **Grade Levels:**   1–3
Word Drill
Individualized Practice

Rationale: Many students have difficulty learning blends and digraphs. This activity helps to improve reading and spelling skills when only one new concept is introduced and practiced at a time.

Objective: To enable the student to pronounce specific consonant blends/digraphs and give word examples for each of them.

Materials: Stapler
Colored construction paper for pages of the booklets
Black and red felt marking pens
Catalogues or magazines
Scissors
Paste
Folder

Procedure:
1. The teacher or students prepare construction paper for pages by printing one blend/digraph at the top of each page (on one side only).
2. During a time specifically set aside for this purpose, the students look for picture examples of one blend/digraph in catalogues or magazines.
3. The students will cut out pictures, checking with the teacher to make certain that they are correct, before pasting the pictures on the proper page.
4. The teacher or student writes the correct word under each corresponding picture.
5. The words may be color-coded by writing the blends or digraphs in red and the remainder of the word in black.
6. The pages are collected in a folder until the teacher or student is ready to assemble them into a booklet by stapling the pages to a cover constructed by the student.
7. The booklets may be taken home or kept in the student's desk as reference material.

Additional Suggestions:
1. A commercial scrapbook can be substituted for the construction paper pages. Parents may help their children make a booklet of this type at home.
2. Pictures may be drawn by the student or adult if catalogues are not available.
3. A similar booklet may be designed for beginning consonants, as a prerequisite to the blend book.

Descriptors: Decoding Skills
Short Vowels
Remedial Reading

Grade Levels: 1–3

Rationale: Vowels are a vital part of our word recognition process, yet many students have difficulty recognizing short and long vowels. This may partially be due to teaching techniques attempting to teach all vowels as a group rather than in isolation. By concentrating on one vowel at a time and teaching it until it is "overlearned," the student will acquire a better understanding of each vowel and the sound it represents. The magic box is a fun way for students to obtain vowel practice.

Materials: Masking tape
Pencil or crayons
9″ × 12″ drawing paper
Magic box (shoebox)
Scissors
16 3″ × 5″ index cards
Black marking pen

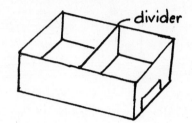
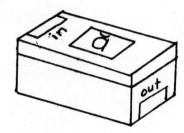

Directions: Construct a "magic box" from a shoebox. Tape a piece of tagboard inside the box to divide it into two sections (see illustration). Cover the box with colorful contact paper or decorate as desired. Put the lid on the box and cut holes in the box at one end of the lid and one end of the narrow part of the box as shown. Label them "out" and "in" with a black marking pen. Label the box with the vowel you are currently studying. Construct eight short *a* vowel word cards and eight corresponding picture word cards (see illustration).

   picture word cards

  word cards

Divide the 9″ × 12″ blank drawing paper into eight sections and number them as shown in the illustration. Give each student one sheet.

Procedure: 1. The instructor places the right picture word cards in the "out" section of the box.
2. The eight word cards are placed on the table next to the box.
3. The student selects a word card and reads it.
4. The student illustrates the word in the first section of the paper and writes the appropriate word under the picture.

5. The student puts the card in the "in" part of the box to prevent confusion with the other words yet to be illustrated.
6. This procedure is repeated until all eight words are written, illustrated on the worksheet, and the word cards are placed in the box.
7. The pupil next pulls a picture word card from the "out" slot of the box and matches it with his/her response for self-correction.
   Example:

8. If the student's repsonse matches the word on the card, the student marks that box with a " + " or some other appropriate notation decided on by the instructor and the student.
9. This procedure is repeated until all student responses have been checked.
(Note: This procedure is self-correcting because the students can quickly check their own responses and get immediate feedback. However, the instructor should check the students' work to note their progress or error patterns. While checking the words with the instructor, the student should read each word to the teacher underlining each word with a finger. This procedure helps the student focus on the whole word, not just the picture.)

Additional Suggestions:
1. The magic box is very versatile. It can be used for other vowel sounds as well as other skills, such as math problems.
   Example:

   $$\begin{array}{r} 2 \\ +\,4 \\ \hline \end{array} \qquad \begin{array}{r} 2 \\ +\,4 \\ \hline 6 \end{array}$$

2. Cover the label on the top of the box with acetate or clear contact so that the label may be easily changed with a marking pen to fit the appropriate lesson.
3. Make certain that only one vowel sound is taught at a time. Provide other activities using the same vowel until it is "overlearned." Do not introduce another vowel until the student has mastered the current one.

short vowels

Descriptors: Reading
Phonics
Games

Grade Levels: 1–3

Rationale: Young students beginning to read need to learn short and long vowel sounds for efficient decoding. Long vowel sounds are usually easy to master as they are represented by letter name. Visual letter recognition precedes practice with vowels. Short vowel sounds are more difficult for some readers as they sound very similar (Example: short *e* and short *i*) and are not identified by the letter name. It is important to introduce one short vowel sound at a time followed by various activities involving the use of that sound over a period of four or five days. The teacher should make certain that the students have mastered a particular short vowel letter-sound association before a second short vowel is introduced. (Note: Most students usually learn short vowels very quickly. The following activities are designed for the slower learner who often "picks up" splinter skills without actually establishing a learning "base" for basic skills.)

Objective: To teach the students the short vowel sound *a*.

Materials:

8″ × 10″ and 20″ × 20″ tagboard
5″ × 7″ blank index cards
Black marking pen
Drawing paper
Glue
Scissors
Crayons
A die

Chalkboard and chalk
Commercial short vowel materials
Newsprint
Ditto master
Duplicating paper
Pencil

Procedure:

1. Draw and Color an apple with a short *a* under it on the 8″ × 10″ tagboard.
2. Show the apple poster to the students and stress the short *a* sound in apple. Explain that the letter *a* has two main sounds—the long *a* as in cake and the short *a* as in apple, can, and bat. Put the short *a* poster in a prominent place in the classroom in view of all students.
3. Write the short *a* on the chalkboard. Ask the students to think of and list orally other words that contain a short *a* sound. Write the dictated words on the chalkboard under the *a*.
   Example:

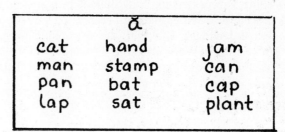

ă

cat	hand	jam
man	stamp	can
pan	bat	cap
lap	sat	plant

   Copy these words on a large piece of newsprint for later reference.
4. Give each student a piece of drawing paper and ask them to draw pictures of words with the short *a* sound. The teacher or aide helps the students write the word underneath each picture. Ask the students to tell you the names of the short *a* in their picture dictionary.
   (Note: Students with poor motor control tend to be less frustrated by cutting out pictures and gluing them on the paper than by drawing and writing. Others might prefer to dictate words while another student draws the picture. The papers may be taken home and "read" to parents; however, they should be returned to the classroom to be compiled into vowel booklets for each student.)

ă

cat   pan   can

5. The following day reintroduce the short *a* sound and reread the short *a* words on the newsprint chart. Provide the students with fifteen short *a* pictures (commercial or teacher-made) plus five distractors. Show one picture at a time to the students and ask them to identify it. If the students determine that it contains the short *a* sound, the picture card is placed on the chalkboard tray. If not, the picture is placed face down on a desk.

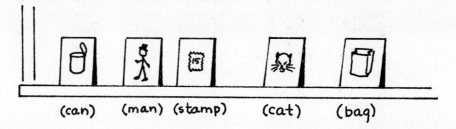

(can)   (man) (stamp)   (cat)   (bag)

6. Use a commercial (or teacher-made) ditto of short *a* picture words. Ask the students to color only the short *a* picture and to cross out all other pictures.

7. The following day give the students a dittoed worksheet of short *a* words with the letter *a* missing. The students are to write in the missing letter and draw a line connecting it to the corresponding picture.

8. Review all short *a* picture words and short *a* word charts each day. Have the students complete a third short *a* worksheet (commercial or teacher-made).

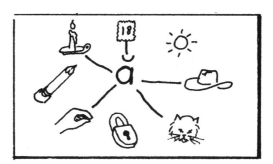

9. Construct a simple tachistoscope by cutting 2½-inch slots 1½ inches from the narrow sides of a 5″ × 7″ index card. Write six short *a* words on 2″ × 12″ strips of tagboard leaving 2 inches for each word. Insert the word strip through the slots and pull it across while the student reads the six words. Six other words may be written on the back of the strip, which may be removed, turned over, and reinserted. Several word strips may be designed and color coded if desired. Example: All short *a* words are written in red or written in black on colored red tagboard. Each vowel sound is assigned a different color. Caution: If a color-coding system is used you cannot be certain that students are making the sound/symbol (or letter) association—they may, in fact, be associating color/sound. Obviously, this would not be practical as most printed matter does not provide a color code. Initially it may be helpful to teach students to attend to the task using color cues; however, these should be faded out as soon as possible.

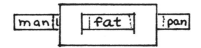

10. When certain that the students can correctly identify short *a* pictures, word cards, and worksheets, and can correctly discriminate these from distractors, the next short vowel sound should be introduced, such as short *o*. The above procedure is followed for the short *o* sound over four or five days.
11. Next, the students should be given some worksheets requiring them to discriminate between the short *a* and the short *o* words or pictures. Two to three days may be spent on such activities until the students demonstrate an understanding of the short *a* and short *o* sounds.

Example:
  Shuffle twenty **a** and **o** word pictures in one pile. Ask the students to sort them into two piles separating **a** from **o** sounds.

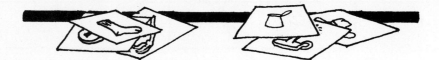

  Provide picture clues and ask the students to write in the missing vowel (only using **a** and **o** at this stage).

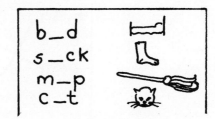

12. Introduce short *i* (Indian). Follow steps 1 through 9. Design games and worksheets using *a, o,* and *i* and follow step 11. Caution: Do not introduce a fourth short vowel sound until the students are proficient at identifying the first three. Allow consistent daily review over all previously presented picture and word cards or charts.
13. Introduce the short *u* sound and follow steps 1 through 12.
14. Introduce the short *e* sound and follow steps 1 through 13.
   (Note: Do not introduce short *i* and short *e* next to each other as they sound so similar.)
  Although this procedure may seem very time-consuming and slow, it usually pays big dividends in the long run because the students end up having completely mastered the five short vowel sounds. A common mistake is to introduce all five sounds at one time or over a period of only five days. Unless students are provided enough practice over each sound, the result is likely to be inconsistent learning.

Additional Suggestions:

1. After all short vowels have been carefully and slowly introduced, games using all five short sounds may be used (teacher-made or commercial). Dice games are fun. Ask the students to paste or draw 2″ × 2″ short vowel pictures on a large piece of tagboard (20″ × 20″) drawing one connecting line around the board (see illustration). The student throws a die and moves a token the corresponding number of spaces. The student says the picture name, recites the vowel sound, and says another word with the same vowel sound. If correct, the marker stays on that picture until the next turn. If incorrect, the student must go back to his/her previous place on the board. Example: Student rolls 4—moves four spaces—says, "sun = short *u* = umbrella."

2. Scramble picture cards for all short vowels and ask the students to separate them on the floor into five separate piles under the correct short-vowel letter.

3. Use commercial records or tape recordings of a specific vowel sound lesson.

digraph practice

Descriptors: Phonics
Sound/Symbol Review

Grade Levels: 1–3

Rationale: Beginning readers need to learn the sound/symbol for digraphs as well as initial consonants as these make up part of the words in many preprimer readers (Example: *she, the, this, what*, etc.). Because digraphs consist of two letters with one sound these are often difficult for some young readers to master. Consequently, additional practice using specific digraphs after these have been introduced is necessary before students are able to incorporate them into their cognitive structure. This activity suggests several methods of digraph practice.

Objective: To teach students the sound/symbol for the digraphs sh, th, wh, and ch.

Materials: Tagboard (for 20″ × 36″ wall charts)
3″ × 5″ flash cards
Black marking pen
Ditto master
Duplicating paper
Pencil

Pictures to represent words
    with digraphs (optional)
Scissors
Paste
Red marking pen
Chalkboard and chalk

Procedure: 1. The teacher writes the digraph on the tagboard flash card in large black lower case letters.

2. The teacher says the sound of the digraph and asks the student to repeat the sound while looking at the printed symbol on the flash card.
3. The students print the digraph on a piece of blank paper or on the chalkboard.
4. The teacher asks the students to dictate words that begin with the digraph being presented. Initially, the teacher may need to suggest some words.
5. The teacher writes the dictated words on a large tagboard chart leaving a space for an illustration by each word.
6. The students illustrate the words by a) taking turns at drawing on the chart, or b) drawing the illustration on blank paper, coloring it, cutting it out, and pasting it by the appropriate chart word. The latter method allows the students to work concurrently rather than having to wait for a turn to draw on the actual chart. Pictures may also be cut out of magazines or commercial catalogues if desired. (Note: Sometimes it takes a great deal of time to find an appropriate commercial picture for a particular word. Thus, informal illustrations may be more expedient.)

7. The students pronounce the words on the digraph chart daily to reinforce the phonics skill. By viewing the written word next to the picture the students learn many new sight words.

8. Other activities to reinforce the newly learned digraph should be presented to the students for additional practice (See Additional Suggestions). However, no new digraph should be introduced until the students have mastered the previous one.

Additional Suggestions:

1. Use a ditto to create the following worksheets:

   a. The student is asked to draw lines from the digraph to all pictures beginning with that digraph. Distractor pictures are included for sound discrimination practice.

   b. The student is to underline (or circle) only the words beginning with the digraph at the top of the paper. Add distractor words for visual discrimination practice.

   c. Student is asked to draw lines from stimulus words to pictures representing the words. (Note: Only words that have previously been presented on picture charts should be used. Add some distractor words or pictures.)

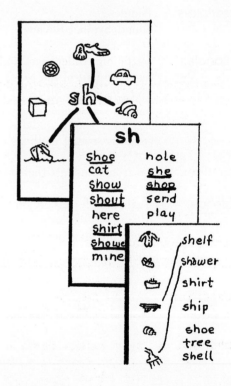

2. Construct a railroad track out of tagboard and write digraph words along the track. Students may use a toy train or truck to move along the track saying each word they pass. The teacher or aide must be present to check the accuracy of the responses.

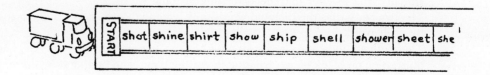

3. Make tagboard digraph charts with cardboard "pockets" to hold pictures representing the digraph. Shuffle many pictures (from magazines or commercial picture cards) beginning with digraphs and allow the student to sort the pictures into the correct chart pocket.

Check the cards in each pocket saying the picture names aloud for additional practice.

4. Word wheels provide good practice opportunities. Students may construct their own using two 6-inch tagboard circles and a brass fastener.

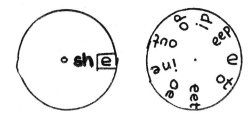

5. Ask the student to write a list of digraph words using two colors. To accentuate the digraph being studied, the digraph may be written in red with the rest of the word written in black.

> sh oe
> sh ip
> sh eet
> sh

_____phonics practice with word wheels_____

Descriptors: Phonics Practice   **Grade Levels:**   1–4
             Linguistic Word Families

Rationale: Many students need a great deal of practice to continue being able permanently to retrieve new concepts. Practice can be fun when students construct word wheels and practice consistently at home or at school.

Objective: To provide phonetic blending practice with consonant/vowel/consonant word families.

Materials: 9″ × 12″ oaktag (makes 2 wheels)
             Black marking pen
             Scissors

Procedure: 1. Cut 5-inch diameter circles out of oaktag.
             2. Cut a rectangle 2″ × 5″ and attach to the center of the back of the circle using a brad fastener.
             3. Write beginning consonants on the parameter of the circle.
             4. Select and write the appropriate word endings on the oaktag strip (see word lists).
             5. Ask students to pronounce the correct words as the tagboard strip is rotated around the circle.
             6. Students may share the word wheel with other students and may take it home for further practice.

Word Family Lists

Consonant/vowel/consonant

top	cat	fun
stop	fat	run
mop	flat	pun
hop	pat	bun
pop	mat	gun
crop	hat	sun
shop		spun
cop	tap	pick
flop	lap	nick
drop	sap	sick
	nap	lick
tip	rap	tick
lip	cap	click
sip	map	slick
rip	yap	
dip	trap	luck
zip	flap	duck
trip	clap	buck
drip		tuck
whip		muck

Consonant/vowel/consonant

men	man	tack
pen	fan	rack
den	pan	sack
hen	can	back
ten	ran	
then	tan	
when	bran	
	plan	
get		
pet	pin	
met	fin	
let	win	
net	tin	
jet	sin	
bet	spin	
set	thin	
yet		

Examples of Circle Types

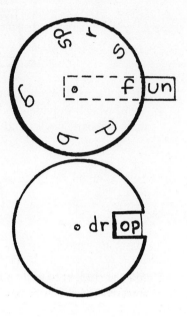

Additional Suggestions:

1. Write beginning two- and three-letter blends on the strip and word endings on the word wheel (see illustrations).
2. Write endings such as "-ing" on a tagboard strip with a 1″ × 2″ section cut out of it.

Example:

Attach this type of strip to the front of a word wheel with words ending in **e** written around the parameter.

scat   spread
scan   sprain
scum   spring
scotch   spray
scope   sprint
          sprinkle
          sprawl
          sprang
          spree

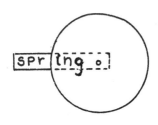 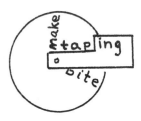

_____more blend games_____

Descriptors: Blends   **Grade Levels:**   1–4+
                     Phonics
                     Individual Practice

Rationale: Most students benefit from consistent practice of newly acquired skills. These games present many blends thus they should be used even after the student has mastered them. Originally the blends should be taught one at a time.

Objective: To practice further recognizing words that begin with two-letter blends (games 1 and 3) and to pronounce orally a word beginning with a particular blend (game 2).

Materials: 2 to 4 markers
                  Tagboard
                  Brad
                  Black marking pen
                  Crayons or colored marking pens

Game 1: Touchdown

1. Construct a tagboard football to desired size (younger students may prefer larger footballs) and cut out four 1½-inch slits about the center of the football with 1 inch between the slits (see illustration). Add black markings and color the football if desired.
2. Cut out four to six strips 1¼ inches wide and 8 inches long (depending on the size of the football).
3. Write blends on one strip. Place a second strip next to it and write down words at the appropriate grade level beginning with each of the blends.
4. This game may be played individually, or with a partner to check the answers. The blend strips are pulled through the tagboard football. As each blend forms a new word, the player reads the word aloud.
5. Scores can be kept by giving a "touchdown" for each five correct words.
6. A second strip of word endings can be added and moved to make different words using the same beginning blend.

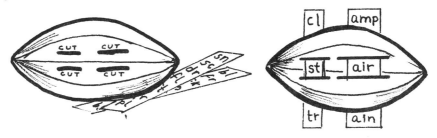

Game 2: <u>Blends</u> <u>Clock</u>

1. Construct a large clock from tagboard poster paper and attach a tagboard "hand" in the center with a brad. Make sure the hand will turn freely.
2. Print some two-letter blends that have previously been introduced to the student around the outside edges of the clock.
3. Each student is given one turn to spin the hand and say a word beginning or ending with the sound on which the hand lands. A point is given for each correct word.

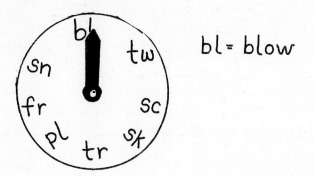

Game 3: <u>Blends</u> <u>Sail</u>

1. Cut a piece of tagboard 18" × 24" and draw two sets of racing spaces containing an equal number of spaces.
2. Cut forty-eight cards in the shape of racing pennants and write a word on each starting with blends, such as train or stop.
3. Cut six cards in the shape of racing pennant—three marked with penalties such as "Go back 2 spaces" and three pennants with rewards such as "Windy, move ahead two spaces."

4. Make markers for each of the two players.
5. The first player draws a card and if s/he can read the word printed on it, s/he moves a marker one space. If s/he cannot read the word, s/he stays put.
6. The next player proceeds in the same way. When drawing a pennant telling the player to move backward or forward, the player follows the directions given.
7. The winner is the first player reaching the end of the course marked "You Win."

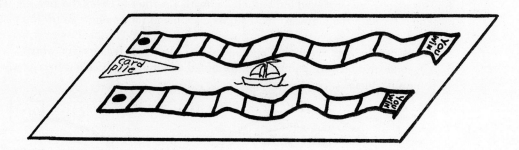

Additional Suggestions: Instead of having cards containing words, cards with blend combinations, such as *bl* and *tr* may be used. The student must say a word beginning or ending with the blend.

Descriptors: Phonics
Spelling
Word Recognition

Grade Levels: 2–6

Rationale: Children with good phonetic skills often pay the closest attention to the beginning and/or ending portions of words, ignoring the significant medial sections. This deficit should be attacked only when the reader has mastered the phonic skills appropriate to the words used.

Objective: To teach a student to attend to the medial portion of words after noting the beginning and ending of the word.

Materials: Blank index cards
Red and black marking pens
Blank Language Master cards (if appropriate)
Metal ring fastener (if desired)

Procedure: Make a list of ten words with frequently mispronounced medial segments. Print them on flashcards or Language Master cards as shown by the illustration. The middle letters should be enlarged, two to three times larger than the initial and final letters and they should be in a heavy, bright, contrasting color, for example, *ch* and *en* are black and *ildr* is red.

   Flash the cards to the child and remind the child to pay close attention to the middle group of letters. Each correct response can be marked with a star in the corner of the card. When s/he has successfully read a word on three consecutive occasions, proceed to a similar card without enlarged letters, but color cued.

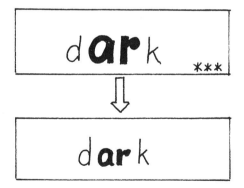

   When the child can correctly read the word printed this way three times, drop the color cue and move to the word printed plainly on a card. Allow the child to keep his new sight words in a notebook or on a ring. Introduce a new word as one is learned.

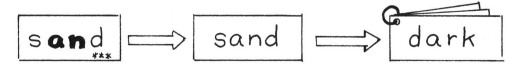

Additional Suggestions: This technique can also be applied to vowel digraphs and blends as well as initial or final letters in words.

window pocket blends

Descriptors: Two-Letter Blends
Three-Letter Blends
Phonograms (parts of words)

Grade Levels: 2–6

Rationale: To draw attention to specific phonetic elements within words it is often useful to devise drill activities that are fun for students. The tachistoscope used in this activity is easily made from a blank envelope.

Objective: Given a series of phonograms, the student will combine a specific blend with individual phonograms to make real words.

Materials: 3½″ × 6½″ plain white envelopes
3″ × 5″ blank index cards
Black and red marking pens
Scissors or hobby knife

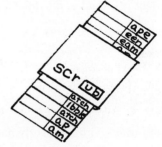

Procedure:
1. Cut the narrow ends off the envelope so that it measures 4¾ inches in length. The width remains the same. Seal the flap.
2. Exactly ½ inch from the bottom, draw a line across the bottom of the envelope. The window will be cut out on this line beginning ½ inch from the right side of the envelope and measuring ⅜ inch wide (measure up from the line) and 1¼ inches long (see example).
3. Write a blend in red ink on the line in front of the window.
4. Draw lines ½ inch apart across the width of the index card. Draw another line along the length in the middle of the card 3 inches wide, thus making it 1½ inches from either side of the card. Draw a parallel line ½ inch from the long right side of the card. The phonograms are written on the lines between the two long parallel lines.

 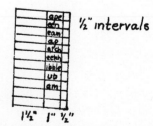

Write the blends in red ink and the phonograms in black ink. Slide the cards inside the pocket from the top until the first word appears in the window. As the student pronounces each word, slide the card down until the next word appears. Each blend will have a separate envelope and a phonogram card.

Additional Suggestions:
1. Practice reading vocabulary words on the tachistoscope. Let each student make his/her own envelope tachistoscopes.
2. Practice math problems (5 + 3 =, 8 × 3 =, 30 ÷ 5 =, and so on). The above exercises can be individualized to fit the needs of each student.

Descriptors: Spelling
Visual Discrimination

Grade Levels: 2–6

Rationale: Interest in spelling may be stimulated by the following activity in which students are asked to create their own words from a longer stimulus word. This activity may be designed for individual students, small groups, an entire class, or relay teams. Points are awarded for correct and unique words. The student with the highest score wins the game.
(Note: Slower students may find this a frustrating activity and may need modeling by the teacher or other students. Perhaps such students need to be paired with students—each would count the total number of words generated as the score for each.)

Objective: To encourage students to write as many words as possible using the letters in a stimulus word provided by the teacher.

Materials: Chalkboard and chalk
Writing paper and pencil
Dictionary (to check words)

Procedure:
1. The teacher writes one stimulus word on the chalkboard. Student volunteers are asked to take turns coming to the chalkboard and writing small words using the letters in the stimulus word. Explain that only the letters in the stimulus word may be used. If the stimulus word contains the same letter more than once, the student may use words containing the same number of specific letters.

   Example: "Please"

   A student may write see, sea, plea, ease, pea, and so on.
2. The teacher introduces a new stimulus word. This time, students are asked to write as many words as possible on writing paper based on the word.

   treasure

are	eat	set
as	err	stare
at	rare	star
ate	sat	sure
ease	seat	tense
see	sea	reset

3. The students count the number of words generated and write that number at the top of each paper.
4. The students take turns orally reading and spelling one word at a time from their papers. Other students who also wrote the word read aloud put a check mark next to the word on their papers. Each check mark earns one point; all check marks are added at the end of the game. Each word written by a student must be correctly spelled or no points are awarded.

5. Students having unchecked words on their papers are asked to pronounce and spell them aloud to the class. If only one student has a particular word, s/he circles the word. If other students want to challenge the spelling, they may do so, and the dictionary is consulted to check the correct spelling. If the circled word is unique and spelled correctly, the student earns 5 points. Thus, the total score for each student is the number of check marks plus 5 times the number of circled words.

Additional Suggestions:

1. Teams may be formed. Using the previously described scoring procedure, the team who has the most points within a given length of time wins the game.
2. During the year, appropriate holiday words may be chosen as the stimulus words. Example: Christmas, Santa Claus, Valentine, Halloween, Easter.

spelling bingo

Descriptors: Reading
Writing

Grade Levels: 1–6

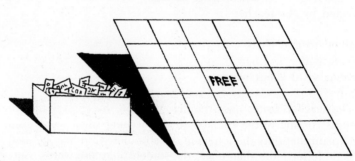

Rationale: Students in each grade are expected to master a specific number of spelling words. It is more fun to practice these words in a game format. If spelling practice is divided into ability levels it is important that each group play the game using words on their level only.

Objective: To teach a student to recognize visually a word when hearing it pronounced and orally spelled aloud. Writing spelling words is further enhanced by each student preparing a bingo card.

Materials: Ditto master of blank bingo card
5″ × 5″ colored construction paper (1 for each student)
Light construction paper for 1½″ × 1″ word cards
1-inch square colored construction paper markers (25 for each student)
Pencil or pen
Black marking pen

Procedure: As the teacher dictates the spelling words, the students are directed to write them on any of the squares marked on the 5″ × 5″ grid. The center square can be marked "Free." The teacher may ask the children to copy the words from a list or to write the words from memory. There should be more words than squares. The child may choose twenty-four words from the list of words. First-grade students may use a smaller number of words (twelve squares).

After all the spelling words are written on the grid, the papers are exchanged. The spelling word cards are placed in a box or a paper bag. One student draws a card, says the word, and spells it aloud. Any student who has the given word on a grid covers it with a marker. Then, the next student draws a word, reads it to the class, and spells it. This continues until someone has "word bingo."

The winning sequence of markers should be predetermined and could include the following variations: one row horizontally, vertically or diagonally; both diagonals, the four corners; or all the borders.

Additional Suggestions:

1. Use the bingo format for social studies (such as presidents and states) or science words.
2. Use for phonics practice (such as prefixes and suffixes).

Descriptors: Auditory-Visual Approach   **Grade Levels:** 1–6
Individualized Spelling

Rationale: Poor spellers often do not make satisfactory progress when only exposed to traditional methods of learning to spell, such as writing multiple copies or filling in blanks. These students can have an individualized spelling program on reading vocabulary words that need to be reinforced or common words needed for creative writing exercises. The tape recorder allows the student to hear as well as to see the words to be studied and repetition is readily available when necessary. A cassette tape recording allows the teacher to plan such individualized lessons. In this activity the students are provided with multisensory stimuli as they hear, see, and write the spelling words.

Objective: To provide multisensory practice lessons of individualized spelling words for students using a tape recorder.

Materials: Cassette tape recorder(s)
Blank cassette tapes
Paper and pencil
Ditto master
Duplicating paper

Procedure: 1. The teacher assigns a specific list of spelling words for each student in the class. Some of the lists may be duplicates; however, it is important for the teacher to have a written record of each student's program.

Example:

	Oct. 5-9	Oct. 12-16
Sue	List 1 ✓	List 2
John	List 3 ✓	List 4

2. The teacher, aide, student, or volunteer uses the following procedure for recording word lists on tape. Each tape is labeled, numbered, and placed in folders.
3. Worksheets (if appropriate) are labeled and placed in folders or large envelopes with the corresponding cassette tape. Blank writing paper may also be included in some of the folders. Directions for each lesson are added to each labeled folder with the worksheet or blank writing paper.

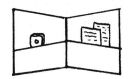

4. Each student selects the assigned spelling list folder and uses the tape recorder and earphones during a specific time period. (Note: Students will be working on this activity during various periods of the day since most classrooms do not have a tape recorder per student.)

5. The student uses self-correction or teacher feedback to determine the percent correct on the spelling lesson. If more practice is needed, additional activities are designed (such as practice flash cards, writing from memory, spelling games) using the exact words on the assigned spelling list.
6. The teacher or aide administers a spelling test to the student using the appropriate spelling word list. If the student scores at least 90 percent correct, the student may proceed to the next list of spelling words after the previous list has been checked in the teacher's progress record book.

Activity 1

The teacher has previously presented and pronounced all new spelling words to the student, thus, the student has already seen and heard each word on the list before beginning this activity.
1. The teacher records each word from the list on a cassette tape at 10 to 15 second intervals and repeats the word list by pronouncing and spelling it. Example: "Simple s-i-m-p-l-e simple"
2. The student listens to the tape and writes the word on blank writing paper during the silent interval on the tape.
3. If the silent interval is not long enough for the student's writing ability, the student stops the recorder until ready for the next pronounced word.
4. The student then corrects the list of written words by listening to the teacher's spelling during the last part of the tape.
5. Missed words are circled, corrected, rewritten, and finally pronounced and spelled by the student on the blank tape at the end of the lesson.
(Note: A written answer list of correctly spelled words may be used for self-correction if desired. However, the auditory feedback may be more valuable for the student at this time.)

Activity 2

Students with poor handwriting skills often find lengthy written spelling lessons extremely frustrating. This activity requires the students to fill in missing letters rather than writing the entire word. It stimulates students with poor fine-motor skills as the goal of correctly spelled words is met without excessive motoric demands.
1. The teacher prepares a ditto master and duplicates copies of the word list with missing letters to accompany the tape recording of the spelling word list.
2. The student listens to the tape while looking at the dittoed worksheet.
3. That student writes in the missing letter sounds during the timed silent interval between each word.

> Example: The teacher records: "ship, fresh, shrimp, fish" on a tape providing a lesson on the **sh** sound.
> 1. _ _ ip
> 2. fr _ _ _
> 3. _ _ rimp
> 4. fi _ _

4. The student may listen to the correct answers or use a written answer sheet to check his/her work as described in Activity 1.

Activity 3

This activity is designed to increase the students' ability to spell new words and to increase their vocabulary.
1. The teacher records the definitions of words on tape with a silent interval between each word.
2. The students listen to the definition and then write the word on a word list.

3. The teacher may record the correct answers on the tape or put a list on the bulletin board to allow students to correct their own work. One point is earned for the correct word matching the definition; another point is earned if the word is spelled correctly.
   Example: The recorded message: "A small animal that often lives on farms, and gives us eggs." Students write: "chicken."

Activity 4

To increase students' ability to spell new vocabulary words.
1. Give the students a spelling word list, a blank cassette tape, and a sheet of paper.
2. The students record the words on the list using the following procedure:

FIRST WORD

1. Say it into the tape—Example: cat
2. Use it in a sentence—Example: The cat can run down the street.
3. Say it into the tape—Example: cat
4. Write it on paper.
5. Cover the word and write it again.
6. Say it into the tape—Example: cat
7. Spell the word—Example: c-a-t
8. Say it into the tape.

SECOND WORD

Repeat the previous sequence for each word on the list. At a later time, the students may listen to their tape and write each word once on a new sheet of paper during the silent interval on the tape (4 and 5 above).
(Note: This is, in essence, a self-administered spelling test.)

Additional Suggestions: The teacher designs and duplicates a blank crossword puzzle with a few letters included as extra clues. The definitions are recorded on a cassette tape. The students listen to the tape, stop the recorder, and write the correct spelling word in the appropriate spaces.

Example: Tape recording: #1 Down—"A green insect that hops and eats leaves."
        Answer: Grasshopper

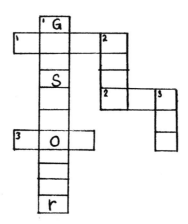

multisensory spelling approach

Descriptors: Multisensory Approach
Spelling
Reading
Writing

Grade Levels: 1–6

Rationale: Intellectual processes are at the heart of learning to spell. Learners must commit to memory the forms of irregular words for which no generalization can be formulated as well as the spelling generalizations judged to have the greatest utility. Before the sensori-motor processes can be employed to translate the word heard to its graphic representation, students must either recall the exact form of the word from their visual memory, or recall and apply a phoneme-grapheme correspondence generalization that fits the particular word they want to write.

Objective: To describe how a teacher might use a multisensory approach to teach a spelling word to the students.

Materials: Chalkboard and chalk
Paper and pencil (1 for each student)

Procedure:
1. Read the word in a sentence to the students. Example: "The *store* is open."
2. Write the sentence on the chalkboard.

> The store is open.

3. Read the sentence orally again and underline the word as it is read.

> The <u>store</u> is open.

4. Point to the word and ask the students to pronounce it aloud. "store"

> Store

5. Write the word in isolation.
6. Ask the students to write the word in the air and to pronounce the name of each letter as they form it. "s-t-o-r-e"
7. Ask each student to write the word on paper.

> Store

8. Erase the chalkboard and ask the students to fold down their paper to cover the word. Ask them to write the word from memory.

> Store

9. Ask each student to write one sentence containing the new spelling word. Call on three or four students to read their sentences aloud. (Note: This step may be very difficult for students who cannot write well. The teacher may ask such students to dictate a sentence, which another student writes for them.)

Additional Suggestions:
1. Ask for one student volunteer to write the new word on the chalkboard after several sentences have been read aloud. Have the students check the word with their individual papers.
2. Test the students at the end of the lesson to determine whether or not they have remembered the word studied in this lesson.
3. Review the words on another class day. If the students cannot remember them, reteach them. Do not introduce a new list of words until the students have mastered the previous one.

word bingo

Descriptors: Spelling
Skills Practice
Following Directions

Grade Levels: 1–6

Rationale: Many students need repeated practice if they are to learn spelling words. *Hearing* the word spelled aloud while *looking* at it and subsequently *writing* it provides a multisensory approach for practice sessions. Bingo has long been a favorite with elementary youngsters. It can be used to reinforce spelling as well as reading sight word practice.

Objective: To practice chosen spelling words by playing bingo.

		without		
people				
		free		
	sleeping			

Materials: Ditto master of a 5″ × 5″ grid
5″ × 5″ dittoed tagboard squares (1 for each student)
1″ × 1″ colored construction paper squares (25 for each student)
Duplicated spelling word list of 30 words for the student's grade level (1 for each student plus 1 extra)
School box or cigar box
Sack (optional)

Procedure:
1. The teacher gives each student a tagboard bingo grid with the center square marked "free" and a dittoed list of spelling words. (Note: Within one class there might be three different bingo groups using three different word lists to meet the students' needs, for example, easier words for slower learning youngsters or more difficult words for other students.)
2. Each student is given twenty-five colored 1″ × 1″ squares of paper. The students place one on the "free" square .
3. The students randomly pick words from their spelling list and write them in any square on the bingo card they choose. As it is written on the card, the word is crossed off the list. Since only twenty-four of the thirty words remaining are needed for the game, six will be left over. By starting with a larger pool of words all students' cards will be different.
4. The extra dittoed word list is cut into individual word strips and placed in a box or sack.

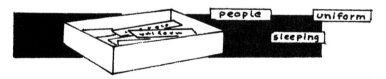

5. One student draws a word out of the box (or sack), pronounces it, and spells it aloud to the class. Example: "without" "w-i-t-h-o-u-t"
6. Each student who has the pronounced word on his/her grid covers it with a colored paper marker (1″ × 1″).
7. A second student draws another word following the same procedure. By allowing each student a turn in spelling a word aloud to the class, more students have a chance to practice their spelling words.
8. The game continues until one student calls bingo because s/he has one row of words covered vertically, horizontally, or diagonally.
9. Several rounds of bingo may be played. The students should exchange their cards each time.

Additional Suggestions:

1. The caller first spells the word letter-by-letter and then pronounces the whole word.
2. Play "blackout," that is, the entire board must be covered before calling out "bingo." In this manner the game will take longer.
3. Keep the word card grids, markers, and extra words in 9″ × 12″ brown envelopes marked with the grade level and list of words. The envelopes may be kept on the materials shelf and used with different groups of students at various times during the school year.

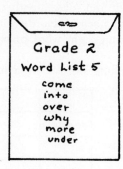

find the hidden word

Descriptors: Spelling
Visual Discrimination
Figure-Ground Discrimination
Word Jumble

Grade Levels: 2–6

Rationale: Students with poor spelling skills are often found not to attend to tasks. By being shown how to pay more attention to details such as the sequence of letters in a word, such students may find that spelling ability is one of their best areas. Beginning with a left-to-right sequence using a tachistoscope the student is gradually introduced to a more complicated format with words written vertically and diagonally as well as horizontally. Often students are initially presented with a difficult format, which makes the task particularly difficult for pupils with poor visual perceptual skills. The following activity will aid the student in accurate visual discrimination of words.

Objective: Students will correctly circle a spelling word among a background of letter distractors.

Materials: Ditto master
Duplicating paper
8½″ × 11″ tagboard (1 for each student if needed)
Scissors or hobby knife
Pencil

Procedure: 1. Write the appropriate spelling word list on the left side of a ditto master. A horizontal line of jumbled letters including the spelling word is written next to each word (see illustration).

am	a r e c **a m** i n e	am
and	b **a n d** o m d p n	and
big	d i p i b i g e d	___
come	c a n e c o m e n	___
four	f o d f o u r f o	___
have	l o n h a v e y n	___

2. Duplicate copies of the word list for each student in the class.
3. Cut a window in the 8½ × 11″ tagboard to expose one row of letters at one time. (Note: The window size will vary according to grade level, size of the print, and student ability. The tachistoscope eliminates extraneous stimuli and allows the student to concentrate on one row of letters at one time.)
4. The student is asked to find the spelling word imbedded in each row of letters and circle it. This activity draws specific attention to the sequential order of letters in a word.
5. The student writes the word on the line following the row of letters to provide practice in writing the spelling word.

Additional Suggestions:

1. As students develop the skill to find words imbedded in horizontal rows of letters quickly, design a new grid where the words are written vertically as well as horizontally. The tagboard tachistoscope may be used again to find the hidden words.

am	l a m d b g a
and	o b r n i f n
big	f u o d g o d
come	h a v e a u e
four	a n r g v r c
have	r c o m e d b

2. Design a more difficult grid where the spelling words are written horizontally, vertically, and diagonally and have the students follow the above procedure.
3. As the students progress to a higher level of spelling ability, ask them to write a sentence using the spelling word identified in the puzzle grid.

"vowel vans"

Descriptors:
Visual Discrimination
Spelling
Puzzle Format

Grade Levels: 3–6

Rationale: Students with poor spelling ability often reverse vowels in words containing more than one vowel. This activity is recommended for use with students who have previously studied the spelling words presented and, thus, have already seen the words written correctly. The activity challenges those students who need to focus on specific deficit areas such as vowel reversals.

Objective: To provide students with worksheets containing spelling words with scrambled vowels that must be correctly rewritten.

Materials:
Ditto master
Duplicating paper
Pencil

Procedure:

1. The teacher introduces the activity by writing a well-known spelling word with reversed vowels on the chalkboard.

Example: fruit: vegetable:
          eppla   paes
          (apple)   (peas)

2. A student volunteer writes the correct word underneath the word with the scrambled vowels in view of the students in the class.
3. When all students understand the procedure, the teacher distributes a dittoed worksheet of "vowel vans" with food words and says, "The food vans are to deliver food to the grocer, but the driver cannot read the labels. Rewrite the words so that both the driver and the grocer will know where to place the foods."
4. Students write the correct word underneath each scrambled word on the dittoed worksheet.
5. The students correct their papers together orally or use an answer sheet provided by the teacher.

Additional Suggestions:
1. Use vans with other types of words such as furniture, flowers, or trees.
2. Provide students with dittoed worksheets containing blank vans. Write the scrambled words on the chalkboard and ask the students to write correctly one word on each blank van on their worksheet.

how do you look up a word when you can't spell it?

Descriptors: Dictionary Skills
                     Spelling
                     Language

Grade Levels: 4–6

Rationale: Intermediate students often need to look up a word that they have heard but do not understand. It is difficult for them to find the word in a dictionary if they do not know how to spell it. The teacher says the new word and asks the student to try to write it down the way it sounds, rather than first reading the word.

Objective: To teach students a strategy for finding a dictionary definition of a word whose spelling is unknown.

Materials: Ditto master
                   Duplicating paper
                   Chalkboard and chalk
                   Pencil (1 for each student)
                   Dictionary (1 for each student or group of students)

gemnasium   jimnasam

gymnesom ? gimnaseom

Procedure:

1. The teacher designs a worksheet with three columns—first letter | second letter | third letter—and writes the same three column headings on the chalkboard.
2. The teacher pronounces a word that the students understand but probably cannot spell. Example: "gymnasium." The teacher uses the word in a sentence. Example: "Tim liked to run in the gymnasium."
3. Using the chalkboard the teacher asks the students what the first letter, the second letter, and the third letter of "gymnasium" might be.
4. The students suggest letters, which the teacher writes under each column.

   Example: first letter   second letter   third letter
                 g or j   i or y   m

5. The students write the different letter combinations on their worksheet and start to look up each word beginning in the dictionary until they find the complete word and its definition.

   jim _____   gim _____

   jym _____   gym _____

6. It is important that the teacher not dictate more than three words during one class session. The activity is time consuming and becomes frustrating if too many words are assigned at one time.

Additional Suggestions:

1. Compile a list of words that can be used for this activity. Only use three at one time.

   Example: pageant   campaign
             battalion   hysteria
             burrow   mechanical
             caliber   mutilate
             phantom   photograph

2. Assign the students to two teams. Students that correctly write each dictated word earn one point per word for their team. The team with the highest score wins.

Language:
Readiness
Listening Skill Practice
Language Concepts

_____how to teach matching skills_____

Descriptors: Following Directions   **Grade Levels:**   Preschool
                   Eye-Hand Coordination   Kindergarten
                                                                          Special Education

Rationale: During readiness activities young students are often asked to discriminate objects or drawn symbols by matching them. To help youngsters who may not understand the matching concept, this may be taught sequentially using task analysis. This teaching idea simplifies the matching task and includes a color-matching activity to reinforce further newly acquired matching skills.

Objective: To teach students to match concrete objects and color squares, and how to put together two-parts of a simple puzzle by matching them.

Activity 1: Matching Concrete Objects

Materials: 2 identical dolls
                 2 identical trucks
                 2 identical toy dogs

Procedure: 1. Place one doll and one truck on the table. Hold up the other doll and say, "Find this one." If the student answers correctly, reinforce the behavior. Repeat the doll matching three times. If the response is incorrect, say, "No, this one," pointing to the doll. Help the student select the doll and reinforce in order to shape the behavior. Repeat the activity until the child responds correctly.
2. Hold up the truck and say, "Find this one." If the student answers correctly, reinforce the behavior. Repeat the truck matching at least three times. If the response is incorrect, say, "No, this one," pointing to the truck. Help the student select the truck and reinforce the correct response in order to shape the behavior. Repeat until correct.
3. Place doll, truck, and dog on the table. Repeat this activity for each item as above.
4. Continue until the student can correctly match all three items.
5. Add the name to each item to expand language concepts, such as "Find two dolls."

Activity 2: Matching Colors with Puzzle Cues

Materials: Scissors
                 Red, yellow, blue, green construction paper
                 White poster board
                 Glue

Procedure: 1. Cut eight 8-inch squares from each color and four white squares from the poster board.
2. Glue or laminate colored squares to poster board to strenghten them.
3. Cut colored squares into simple puzzles.

4. Place two pieces of one color on a desk 2 inches apart. Demonstrate how they go together. Say to student, "You do." If the student completes the task correctly, reinforce the response and repeat three times. If the student completes the task incorrectly, demonstrate again. If necessary, help the student move the puzzle pieces.
5. Repeat for all four colors. Do one color at a time.
6. Place two pieces of one color on a desk 5 inches apart. Say to the student, "You do." Repeat for each color.
7. Repeat the same procedure but place the two pieces far apart at diagonal corners.

8. Expand the procedure by placing four pieces, two colors, randomly on a desk. Demonstrate and then say to the student, "You do."
(Note: Unless you think the student is ready for more, do not put more than two puzzles on the desk at a time to prevent distraction.)

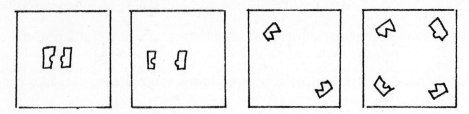

Activity 3: Matching Colors with Matchboxes

Materials:

4 small matchboxes
red, blue, yellow, white spray paint
20 poker chips

Procedure:

Spray paint closed, empty matchboxes and five chips each—red, blue, yellow, and white.

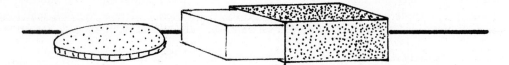

1. Place the red box and one red chip on the table and demonstrate putting the red chip in the box. Say, "Now you do." Give remaining chips to the student one at a time. Remove materials from desk.
2. Repeat the above procedure separately with other colors.
3. Place the red box and the yellow box, one yellow and one red chip on the table. Demonstrate how to put the correct color into each box. Say to student, "You do." Introduce remaining chips paired two at a time.
4. Repeat Step 3 using the blue and white boxes.
5. Place all four boxes on the desk. Use only four chips at a time, one for each color. Demonstrate first and say to student, "You do."
6. Continue until the student becomes proficient at the matching activity.

Additional Suggestions:

1. Teach the correct color name when the student has learned how to match. Example: "Find the two yellow puzzle pieces and put them together." Teach only one color name before adding a new word.
2. Use dittoed worksheets and ask the student to match pictures (rather than concrete objects) by drawing lines between two identical drawings.

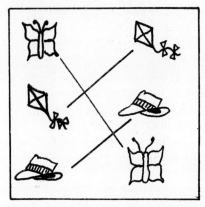

Descriptors: Language Skills
Visual Discrimination
Fine-Motor Skills Practice

Grade Levels: K–1
Educable Mentally
Retarded
Trainable Mentally
Retarded
Preschool

Rationale: Good visual discrimination is an important reading readiness skill. New language concepts that correspond to visual-discrimination activities are vital for achievement of optimum learning.

Objective: To use a variety of learning activities to teach students how to discriminate sizes and shapes and to learn the language concept for each.

Activity 1: Boxes

Materials: Ditto master
Duplicating paper
Boxes in a variety of sizes and shapes

Procedure:
1. Send a dittoed note to parents asking them for boxes in different sizes and shapes.
2. The students place the boxes on a large table (or on the floor) in the classroom.
3. Pointing to the various boxes, ask the following questions:

   a. "What shape is this box?" (round, square, rectangle)
   b. "What size is this box?" (large, small, big, little)
   c. "What colors do you see on the box?"
   d. "What came in the box? How do you know?" (picture clues, shape)

Activity 2: Body Size

Materials: Black and red marking pens
Masking tape
Yardstick
3' × 3' tagboard chart

Procedure:
1. Attach a 3' × 3' tagboard chart to the wall with masking tape. Write the date at the top of the chart in black.
2. Ask the students to take off their shoes and stand with their backs and heads up against the tagboard wall chart.
3. After measuring each student with the yardstick, mark the students' names and exact heights on the chart with the black marking pen.
4. Use the same procedure to measure the students at the end of the school year, but this time mark the lines, names, and heights in red next to the students' earlier marks.

5. The chart provides a dated, permanent record of each student's growth during the school year and gives the teacher an opportunity to talk about such language concepts as taller, tallest, shorter, shortest, and so on. (Note: The teacher can also discuss length of hair, "Jane has long hair, Sue has short hair.")

Activity 3: Bulletin Board Shape Centers

Materials:
Bulletin board
Colored construction paper
Scissors
Thumbtacks
Ditto master
Duplicating paper
Pencil
3½″ × 5″ blank index cards

Procedure:
1. Cut out a shape and pin it to the bulletin board with the word beneath it.

    During class discussion, ask the students to talk about objects that are shaped like a circle (sun, full moon, ball, pizza, dinner plate, and so on).
2. The students draw a circle in the air with you showing them where to start and stop.
3. Five or more students take turns going to the chalkboard and drawing a circle. This group activity enables you to note any students who are having difficulty with the task.
4. The students are given dittoed worksheets containing a circle with directional arrows drawn on it. The students are to trace the circle with only their fingers, saying the word "circle" each time they have traced it. After tracing the circle in this manner for five to ten times, the students may trace the circle using a pencil. They repeat this procedure five to ten times.
    (Note: Students with poor motor control may need further practice using a salt or sand tray before drawing with a paper and pen. Gently shake the tray to erase the shape each time. The teacher may need to demonstrate the starting and stopping points to help the student with motor planning.)
5. The students are given blank pieces of paper and asked to draw a circle. They may look at the circle on the bulletin board when necessary.
6. Additional worksheets of the circle shape should be provided for further practice.

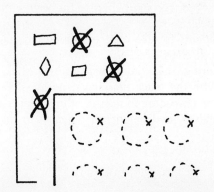

218

"Cross out the circles on the paper." You must first demonstrate how to mark the paper with X's. "Begin at each X and draw circles on this paper."

7. Use construction paper shapes or commercial materials (such as plastic, cardboard, wooden) to practice sorting shapes. "Put all the circles in this pile." Continue practicing with the circle shape until all students have mastered the concept before introducing another shape.
8. Introduce a second shape and follow steps 1 through 7. Example: Square.
9. As each shape has been taught, add it to a permanent bulletin board for reference when needed. Add the written words beneath each shape as many youngsters learn new sight words by labeling.

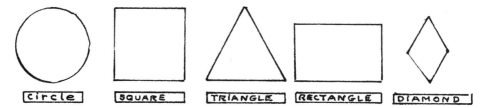

Additional Suggestions: Combine shape practice with color words and direct students to follow oral directions using teacher-made dittoed worksheets.

"Find the circle. Color it red."
"Find the square. Color it yellow."
"Find the triangle. Color it green."

As students become more independent and can recognize color words, expand the worksheet by using rebus pictures.

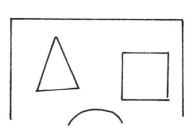

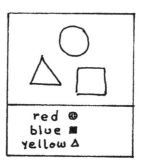

_____ **spatial—temporal awareness**_____

Descriptors: A Sense of Time   **Grade Levels:**   K–1
                  Readiness

Rationale: Many beginning students have not yet developed an awareness of time and the passage of time. They may ask at lunch, "Is it time to go home?" or confuse yesterday with tomorrow. Some students may ask if it is time for a birthday party when they first arrive at school and see that a student has brought a treat for the end of the day. This activity is designed to help students reference the passage of time with known activities or events.

Objective: To help young students develop an awareness of time.

Materials: Kitchen timer
                Metronome
                Stopwatch

Procedure:

1. Ask the students to tap their feet, nod their heads, or snap their fingers in time to a metronome, which provides both auditory and visual cues.
2. Use a stopwatch to record three minutes, then stop the metronome and the tapping, nodding, or snapping.
3. Ask the students to guess how many minutes they have been keeping time with the metronome. Their responses will indicate to the teacher how well the students perceive the passage of time.
4. Continue the activity but have the students stop at varying times, such as one, two, or four minutes. Note whether or not the students are becoming more proficient at measuring time.
5. Set a kitchen timer with a bell. Ask the students to walk around the room and stop when they hear the bell.
6. Again, ask the students to guess how long they were walking around the room. Continue using the timer with a bell while students perform familiar activities such as putting on coats, lining up for recess, or coloring a paper. At the completion of each activity tell the student how many minutes have elapsed; compare one activity to another. Example: "It takes you much longer to color a paper than it does to line up for recess."
7. Keep a simple record of how closely the students have guessed the actual length of time when playing the timed activities.
8. Compare time span to activities that are familiar to the students. Examples: "Tomorrow is when you wake up in the morning." "A whole day is from when you go to bed tonight until you go to bed tomorrow night." "The lunch period is as long as two morning recesses."

Additional Suggestions:

1. Ask two students to walk to the lunchroom, turn around, and come back. The rest of the class are to time the students during this activity. Continue the game by sending pairs of students to the principal's office, nurse's office, gym, playground, and so on.
2. Time a reading group and note how many seatwork papers were completed during the same length of time (this will vary by student ability; figure a mean score). Announce the time spent to the class. Example: "It took fifteen minutes for the rocket reading group to read their story with the teacher. Most students finish three seatwork papers during the fifteen minutes."
3. Ask the students to have their parents help them keep a time record of various home activities, such as eating breakfast, dressing, eating dinner, playing outside with friends. The records may be shared with other class members and comparisons of time spent on similar activities may be discussed.

John Harper - Monday	
Breakfast	10 minutes
Dressing	20 minutes
T.V.	1 hours
Playing	1½ hours
Dinner	15 minutes

sequential color concept program

Descriptors: Readiness
Language Concepts
Following Directions

Grade Levels: K–1
Special Education

Rationale: Young students need to learn color concepts as prerequisites for reading, writing, and following directions. Some youngsters find such concepts difficult to learn. The teacher first needs to analyze what the student understands and then plan an appropriate sequence of learning activities. This simple color program proceeds from matching through recognition to oral identification of colors.

Objective: To present a sequential program for introducing to young students the color concepts red, blue, yellow, and green.

Materials: 3″ × 3″ colored squares (2 each for the colors red, blue, yellow, and green)
Optional: colored objects such as toys, mittens, crayons, blocks, in the colors red, yellow, blue, and green (see Additional Suggestions)

Procedure: MATCHING

1. Place the four colored squares on the table in front of the student and keep the matching four squares.
2. Hold up one color (red) and say, "Find another one just like this one." The student may move your square next to each of the squares on the table if necessary to determine which one matches the model. The student holds up the matching color.
3. Continue the matching activity using the other colors, but mix up the four colors on the table each time so that the student does not learn to associate a color with a position on the table.
4. Follow the same procedure as step 1 but add the color name to the model card. Example: "Find a red card like mine." Continue this procedure with the other three colors mixing the order of the four cards each time.

RECOGNITION

5. Place the four colored squares on the table in front of the student and say, "Show me blue." "Show me yellow."
6. The student points to the color named. Repeat this procedure with all four colors until the student is proficient at correctly picking the named colors.

IDENTIFICATION

7. Place the four colored squares on the table in front of the student and point to one of the colors saying, "What color is this?"
8. The student says the color name. Continue the activity using all four colors until the student is proficient.

Additional Suggestions:

1. Add more colors and follow the same procedure.
2. Use colored objects (see Materials) and say, "Show me the orange car. Show me the purple block." Continue by asking the student to tell the color of an object you have chosen. "What color is this block?"

3. Teach language concepts by asking the student to say: a red car, a purple block.
4. Teach beginning number concepts by saying, "Give me 2 blue blocks and 1 red block. How many do I have now?"

before

Descriptors: Readiness
Language Skills
Following Directions

Grade Levels: K–1

"What comes before the kite?"

Rationale: Many readiness and primary educational activities require young students to follow directions such as, "Mark the picture that comes before the dog," or "Write the number that comes before 4." Some youngsters may miss the point of the directions because they do not understand the language concept *before*. This activity was designed to sequentially teach the concept *before*.

Objective: To teach a student the concept of *before* by four sequential activities.

Materials: 12 4″ × 6″ tagboard cards
Black marking pen
Drawing paper
Pencil

Assumptions: The student can correctly identify and match the nouns: flower, kite, tree, train, ball, and house.

Activity 1:

1. On 4″ × 6″ tagboard draw two identical pictures of the nouns: flower, kite, tree, train, ball, and house.

2. Give the student six picture cards while keeping an identical set.
3. Sit with the student side-by-side facing the same direction.
4. Place two picture cards (the flower and kite) in front of the student and say, "What picture comes *before* the kite?"
5. The student replies, "The flower comes before the kite." (Note: If the student misses the answer, show the correct answer and repeat the original question.)
6. If the student answers correctly repeat, "Yes, the flower comes before the kite."
7. The student now matches the picture of the flower in his/her hand with the picture of the flower on the table. S/he then collects the pair of pictures and places it in a separate pile to the left.
8. Continue playing the game in the same manner using the remaining four pictures by changing the pictures next to the kite, which thereby remains as a constant. (Note: By keeping the kite as a constant the student's eye is trained consistently to look to the left of the kite picture as the concept *before* is learned.
9. When all five pairs are collected, count them and write the total number next to the student's name on the drawing paper.

Change the kite picture by choosing another constant and continue another round of the game following steps 4 through 9 as previously described. If the student has mastered the *before* concept using two stimulus cards continue with Activity 2.

Activity 2

1. Place three picture cards on the table, again with the kite on the right side.
2. Say, "I'll bet I can catch you now. I've added another picture. What comes *before* the kite?"

3. The student answers, "The ball comes before the kite."
4. If the student answers correctly, allow the student to match the picture of the ball in his/her hand with the ball picture on the table. The student collects the pair and places it on the left for later computation.
   (Note: If the student's answer is incorrect refer to step 5 under Activity 1. Do not award the pair of cards until the student can spontaneously answer the question correctly.)
5. Continue through the set changing the first and second pictures, but keeping the kite as a constant, at the end of the picture sequence.
6. When all pairs are collected, count the number of pairs and add to the tally chart as previously described. When the student has completed two or more sets with 100 percent accuracy proceed with Activity 3.

Activity 3

1. Place three picture cards in front of the student, but this time the kite is in the middle of the sequence.

   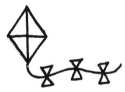

2. Say, "What picture comes *before* the kite."
3. The student says, "The train comes before the kite." If the student is incorrect, refer to step 5 under Activity 1.
4. If the student answers correctly, the train picture in his/her hand is matched to the train picture on the table and the student earns another pair.
5. Continue through the set changing the first and third pictures but keeping the kite in the middle as a constant.
6. When all pairs are collected, count the number of pairs and add the score to the tally sheet. Change the kite to another picture and continue the game as described. When two or more sets have been completed with 100 percent accuracy, continue with Activity 4.

Activity 4

1. Place any two picture cards in front of the student. Ask the student which picture comes before the second picture chosen (use no constant such as the kite). Repeat this step five times using any combination of picture pairs.
2. Place any three cards in front of the student and continue the game.
3. Place any four cards in front of the student and continue as before.

**Additional
Suggestions:**
1. Increase the number of pairs of picture cards for Activity 4.
2. Use the same sequential procedure to teach the concept *after*.
3. Use the same procedure with numbers.
   "What number comes *before* 3?
   Eventually eliminate the number and ask the student to tell what number comes before 3.
   "What number comes before 10 in this sequence?"
4. Follow the same number procedure to teach the concept *after*. "What number comes after 8?"

effective listening

Descriptors: Attending   **Grade Levels:**   K–2
                    Readiness

Rationale: Listening is an important readiness skill for young students because most instruction is presented orally during the primary years. Students with poor auditory skills have difficulty following directions. The following activities teach attending, discrimination, and listening-comprehension skills.

Objective: To increase students' awareness and identification of environmental sounds.

Materials: Chalkboard
                  Celery, apple, carrot
                  Plastic container with lid
                  Rice, sand, macaroni
                  Common household objects (spoons, flour sifter)
                  Tape recorder

Procedure:
1. Stress the importance of listening by introducing one of the activities. Say, "You would not know where to go during a fire drill if you didn't listen to directions. That could be very dangerous."
2. Implement one of the described activities.
3. Hold class discussions to talk about the importance of good listening skills.

Activity 1: Listening for Sounds

Ask the students to close their eyes and become auditorily sensitive to environmental sounds around them. Ask them to notice the sounds of a person walking down the street, a fire engine, a buzzing light, a car, even breathing. The students identify these sounds as a group.

Activity 2: Teacher-Made Sounds

Ask the students to close their eyes. Make some sounds such as dropping a pencil, tearing a piece of paper, opening a window, snapping the lights, cutting with scissors, or writing on the chalkboard. The students try to identify each sound after it has been made.

Activity 3: Food Sounds

Ask the students to "listen to the kind of food that is being eaten, cut, or sliced without peeking!" Use celery, an apple, a carrot, and similar foods.

Activity 4: Shaking Sounds

Small items can be placed in a variety of lidded containers—plastic, glass, ceramic, metal. Put a different item in each—rice, sand, chalk, macaroni. Shake the container and ask the students to tell what makes the sound.

Activity 5: Find the Sound

Hide a ticking clock or a music box somewhere in the classroom. Play "Find the Sound" by locating the noisy object. Students take turns hiding the item.

Activity 6: Household Objects

Bring some ordinary household objects to class. Ask the students to turn their backs toward the objects while you make a sound. See if anyone can guess what they are. Let a student take a turn making the sound, asking you to guess. Suggestions: Roll an egg in a stainless steel bowl, strike a tub of water, tap a pan lid, work a flour sifter, hit spoons together, rub sandpaper together, pull plastic containers apart. Let your imagination run wild!

You will be amazed to find how quiet your students can be. Do not allow them to shout out the answers.

Additional Suggestions: Recorded sounds can be purchased or made. Sounds of typewriters, animals, trains, and vacuum cleaners can be recorded on tape and played for the class. Ask the students to volunteer answers or ask them to write their answers on paper. Check the papers as a group.

_____days of the week_____

Descriptors: Time Sequencing
Language Skills

Grade Levels: K–2

Rationale: Reciting the days of the week in sequential order is a confusing and difficult task for some youngsters. By means of a simple worksheet and flash cards this task can be simplified.

Objective: To help students remember the days of the week in sequence.

Materials: 3½″ × 5″ blank index cards
Black marking pen
Crayons
Pencil (1 for each student)
Ditto master
Duplicating paper

Procedure:

1. The teacher constructs flash cards, each listing one day of the week. On the reverse of the card the same day is lettered along with the appropriate symbol for the day.

2. Using basic sight vocabulary activities (see *Sight Vocabulary Word Practice*), the teacher presents one to three flash cards to teach the students to recognize the words for each day of the week. The symbol for each day is also explained at this time. Eventually, all the words are presented to the student, but not at one time.

SUNDAY—For the Teutonic peoples, the day was sacred to the SUN.

MONDAY—From the Anglo Saxon word "monandaeg" meaning the MOON'S DAY.

TUESDAY—From *Tyr*, the Anglo Saxon word for the Norse god of war. FOX was chosen because he is a crafty animal noted for his evasion tactics.

WEDNESDAY—From WODEN, the chief god in Norse mythology.

THURSDAY—This day was considered sacred to Thor, the Teutonic god of THUNDER.

FRIDAY—Named after Freyja, a goddess who had a beautiful chariot drawn by CATS.

SATURDAY—Named after the Roman god Saturn, the god of harvest. COW is the farm animal.

3. The teacher prepares a dittoed worksheet (see illustration) of the sequential order of the days of the week. Copies are duplicated and handed out to students.
4. The teacher explains to the students that the road in the worksheet activity will be taking them through all the days of the week. The teacher says, "The road may only be traveled in one direction. The arrows show you the way to travel through each day."
5. The students begin traveling at "Start" and follow the road to the first day of the week, Sunday.
6. The students should be able to recognize the word as a result of the previous flash card activities. The students may color the figure representing Sunday—the sun.
7. The group activity is continued until the symbols for all the days of the week have been colored.

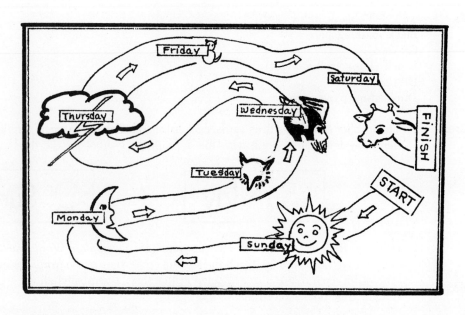

Additional Suggestions:

1. Design, cut, and paste a dittoed worksheet that requires students to cut out the symbols and paste them next to the correct day on the "road" worksheet.
2. Present the seven flash cards in scrambled order to the students and ask them to rearrange them in correct sequential order.
3. After the students have learned to read the words and have the motor skills to write them, present a blank dittoed worksheet of the road with seven stops and ask the students to write in the appropriate word at each stop.

basic language concepts

Descriptors: Language
Following Directions
Readiness

Grade Levels: K–2

Rationale: Many students have problems following oral or written directions because they lack mastery of key concept words or phrases such as *in a row*, *separated*, or *almost*.

Objective: To teach students basic language concepts frequently used in auditory directions.

Materials: Blank index cards
Black marking pen
Ditto master
Duplicating paper
Pencil
Boehm Test of Basic Concepts[1]
Chalkboard and chalk
Blocks

Procedure:

1. Administer the *Boehm Test of Basic Concepts* and determine which students need to learn particular concepts used in the classroom.
2. The words listed below are taken from the *Boehm Test of Basic Concepts*. These directional concepts need to be taught to students as they are expected to follow auditory directions during school activities, especially when taking tests.

top	corner	matches
through	several	always
away from	behind	medium sized
next to	in a row	right
inside	different	forward
some, not many	after	zero
middle	almost	above
few	half	every
farthest	center	separated
around	as many	left
over	side	pair
widest	beginning	skip
most	other	equal
between	alike	in order
whole	not first, or last	third
nearest	never	least
second	below	

[1]Ann E. Boehm, *Boehm Test of Basic Concepts* (New York: The Psychological Corporation, 1971).

3. Pick one concept and design activities requiring the students to practice the concept using index cards, dittoed worksheets, and the chalkboard. For example, to teach the concept of "not the first or last, intermediate position," the following procedure is used:

   a. Introduce the word or phrase and its meaning. Draw three squares on the chalkboard. Point to the middle one and say, "This square is not the first or last."

   b. Demonstrate. Show a picture of three blocks and say, "This block is not first or last." Do the same using pictures in a row, desks in a line, cars parked in the street, and so on. Ask the students to identify the concept using various examples: Teacher shows letters and asks, "Is this letter the first or the last?"

   Student responds, "This letter is not the first or the last."

   c. Give directions. Ask the students to follow specific directions using the newly learned concept. Teacher says, "See the smiling face, the triangle, and the number two. Which picture is not first or last?"

   d. Present a worksheet (as illustrated) and orally give directions for each item.

NOT FIRST OR LAST

Look at the bug and his legs. Mark the leg that is not first or last.

Look at the string and the beads. Mark a bead that is not first or last.

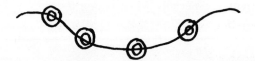

Look at the balloons. Mark a balloon that is not first or last.

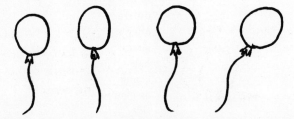

Look at the hole and the mice. Mark the mouse that is not first or last.

Look at the carrots and the ball. Mark the carrot that is not first or last.

e. Ask the student to practice the new concept. Teacher says, "Tell me about this picture of the baseball."

Student responds, "It is not first or last."

Additional Suggestions: Provide similar worksheets to determine whether or not the students have retained the newly learned concept.

learning body parts

Descriptors: Spatial Orientation
Identification of Body Parts
Music for Fun

Grade Levels: K–2

Rationale: Young students love to sing songs and move their bodies accordingly. Use a familiar song to teach body parts.

Objective: To teach or reinforce a child's discovery of body parts.

Materials: Piano or xylophone

Procedure: 1. Use the tune to "Mary Had a Little Lamb." Sing and point to or touch body part mentioned:

Put your finger on your foot
On your foot, On your foot
Put your finger on your foot
Show me where it is.

Beginning instruction should incude eyes, ears, nose, mouth. Add foot, arm, leg, chin, elbow, knee, ankle, and so on after the students have mastered the initial body parts.
2. Encourage the students to join in as you sing the song again. If they cannot sing, have them point to the body parts sung.
3. Say, "Put your finger on your foot." Encourage the students to point to their foot.
4. Use the above steps for other body parts.

Additional Suggestions: If this activity is used in a small group (three to five students), you may want to see if the concepts have generalized. Use the same tune substituting different students' names and body parts. (For example, put your finger on Tom's foot.)

_____same/different liquids_____

Descriptors: Visual Discrimination
Texture, Taste

Grade Levels: K–2

Rationale: Many readiness activities include visual-discrimination tasks that present students with a series of drawings and require them to mark the drawings that are the same or to mark out the drawing that is different. It may be useful to teach students the concepts same/different by using concrete materials such as glasses of liquids. This idea is a "change of pace" from most routine procedures.

Objective: To teach the concepts of *same* and *different* using various liquids.

Materials: 5 (or more) small clean plastic cups
Liquids (Note: Use similar colored liquids. For example, vegetable oil, vinegar, water with yellow cake coloring, perfume, yellow liquid household cleaners, lemonade, yellow soda pop, olive oil.)
20″ × 30″ tagboard chart
Black marking pen

Procedure:
1. Pour equal amounts of different liquids in each of the five glasses.
2. Place all the glasses in front of the students.
3. Ask the students if the liquids are the *same* or *different*.
   (Note: The colors are very similar.)
4. After the students reply that the five glasses are very similar, ask them to smell the contents of the five glasses and tell what differences they notice.
5. Guide the students to notice differences in smell, texture, and taste.
   Caution: Make certain that the students only taste safe liquids.
6. List the similarities and differences stated by the students on a large chart.

Similarities (Same)	Differences (Different)
All are liquids	Different smells
Same color	Different texture
Same amount	Different taste

Additional Suggestions:
1. Place three glasses of liquids in front of the students. Two of them are the same and one is different. Ask the students to tell which two are the same and which one is different. Ask them to explain why.
2. Introduce the drawings that illustrate the concepts of *same* and *different*. Relate the drawing to the glasses of liquids that have been identified by the students as *same* or *different*.

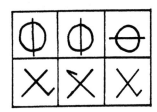

_____giving oral directions_____

Descriptors: Poor Auditory Memory   **Grade Levels:**   K–2
Understanding Directions

"Line up by two's to go to the auditorium for the play."

"Turn to page 47 in the math book. Get out your pencil and paper and finish all the problems on pages 48 and 49."

"Remember not to talk in the halls. We'll stop at the office to leave our lunch money."

Rationale: Some students literally "turn off" their hearing when the teacher gives too many oral directions at one time. Such students are usually the same who ask, "What did you say? What am I supposed to do now? What page are we supposed to do?" When it becomes necessary for the teacher to repeat the directions several times valuable time is lost.

Objective: To teach students to attend to and understand oral directions when they are first presented by the teacher.

Materials: Paper and pencil
Ditto master
Duplicating paper

Procedure: 1. Before giving directions the teacher must

    a. make sure the room is quiet
    b. tell the children to look at the teacher, "Let me see your eyes" (while pointing to own eyes)
    c. tell the children to listen, "Put your ears on and listen carefully"
    d. say, "There are $\times$ number of directions.
       #1 "_____ ____ __."
       #2 "_ ____ _____."

2. While giving the directions the teacher must

    a. speak clearly and distinctly
    b. hold up one finger when giving the first direction, second finger when giving the next direction, and so on.

3. To ensure that the students have listened and understood the directions, the teacher must ask various students whether they know what to do first, second, and so on. For example, "Susie, what are you supposed to do first?" "Kevin, what are you supposed to do next?"
4. Finally, the teacher should ask if there are any questions.

Additional Suggestions:

1. Some children may need to write directions down as they are said or draw pictures in a sequence to remind them of what to do.
2. The teacher may want to hand out a dittoed abbreviated outline for the students to follow as each direction is given.

creating musical compositions

Descriptors: Creativity
Rhythms and Music
Visual-Motor Practice
Self-Concept

Grade Levels: K–3

Rationale: Many professionals believe that the arts have therapeutic power. Students having difficulty with their sense of self-worth often lose sight of the fact that they are capable and creative human beings. This activity is designed to focus on each student's creative potential.

Objective: Students will help create a musical composition and will participate in its performance.

Materials: Magic marker
20″ × 36″ newsprint

Procedure:

1. Announce to the class that the students are going to look for objects in their environment that make sounds. (It is a good idea to follow this activity by having the students look for things at home that make noises or sounds and bring one object or idea to the classroom the following day.) (Note: Objects or ideas that might be mentioned in this sound exploration include doorbells, yelling, a slamming door, a meowing cat, a barking dog, and a fire siren.)
2. Ask one student for a sound, which s/he is to draw a picture of on the newsprint. (It is helpful to group the sounds in "fours" on the paper as four is a standard beat pattern.)

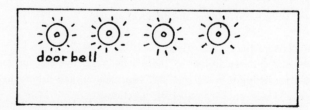

3. Continue soliciting student responses until you feel that the composition is completed. You might want to have a student present a sound several times on a line. This allows the student to play a sound for the group.
4. Have each student practice a sound once it is recorded.

John's sound—Bell

Teresa's sound—
Foot stomping

Joe's sound—Beating
on the desk

For example, when you point to each sound, the three students (John, Teresa, and Joe) play their composition for the class. Following their demonstration, the entire class may play it. The composition may be entitled "John, Teresa, and Joe" or the students may choose another appropriate title (such as "Sounds I hear," or "Noises").

DISCUSSION

The students feel a sense of accomplishment after creating the musical compositions. Individuals are singled out for their ideas; they experience a sense of pride in viewing their idea as worthwhile. All the students experience working together to create a musical environmental composition. This also represents a good visual/auditory sequence task when the children read the compositions.

Additional Suggestions:

1. Invite other classes to your room to hear and see the original compositions.
2. Ditto the compositions and ask each student to keep a notebook of all compositions.

creative dramatics

Descriptors: Self-Concept
Group Activities

Grade Levels: K–3

Rationale: Because of the needs of many handicapped students to work on a one-to-one basis with a teacher or aide in small groups, opportunities for peer interaction and the general principles of turn taking and socialization are sometimes limited. Creative drama techniques can be used in the classroom to foster personality growth and social interaction skills.

Objective: To present several creative drama techniques that can be used in a group setting. (Note: In creative drama, there are no right or wrong answers. As long as the students follow the rules set down by the teacher, every response is appropriate.)

Materials: Small empty box
Objects (ball, paper clip, eraser, pencil, book)

Activity 1: The Box

1. Place the students in a semicircle (on chairs or on the floor).
2. Explain to them that they are going to play a game, and that it is extremely important that they listen to each student's response.
3. Explain to the students that you are going to pass a box around the circle. The idea of this creative-thinking situation is to imagine and name an object that could fit into the box.
4. Lead the students by asking questions such as: "What do you think this is?" "A box." "Good.

What could be inside of it?" "I think that maybe a rubber band could fit in there." "We are going to pass the box around the room and each of us will name an object that could fit in the box. Listen carefully because you can't give me the same idea as your classmate."

5. Allow each student an opportunity to name only one object each time the box is passed.
6. Record each pupil's response on paper. It is very important to reinforce each student verbally for his/her response (for example, "That's a good idea! You're really thinking! What a good imagination!").
7. At first it may be necessary to remind the class members that you will not accept duplication of an answer. If a student repeats a previously expressed idea, explain that the particular idea was already suggested and that s/he needs to think of another one.
8. Stay with that student until a response is given. It is important for the student to realize that s/he has imagination and can contribute to the group activity.

(Note: Students usually enjoy this activity and are surprised at how many ideas they can come up with. The activity should be terminated while the students are still interested in it—(usually about four or five times around the circle.)

Additional Suggestions: Name a particular category for the students to think about (for example, fruits, toys, toy animals). Follow the same game rules.

Activity 2: An Object

1. Show an object to the students (such as paper clip, eraser, ball, or book).
2. Ask the students what the particular object is used for. "Does anyone know the name of this object?" "An eraser." "Good! What do you use it for?" "To clean chalk off of the board." "Good explanation."
3. Say, "Today we are going to play another imagination game. I am going to pass this eraser around the room and I want you to think of an object that is the same size and shape as this eraser but is used for something else. For example, I think this eraser could be a super, delicious ice cream sandwich. Now, think of something else this eraser could be. Don't tell your idea to anyone. I will pass the eraser around the circle. As it comes to you, you can share your idea with us."
4. Pass the eraser around the circle.
5. Record the students' responses. The students may suggest some very imaginative ideas.

(Note: The intent of this activity is to make the students aware of their ability to think creatively. Duplication of answers is not acceptable. This activity should be stopped while the students are still interested in it.)

following verbal directions

Descriptors: Listening Skills   **Grade Levels:**   K–3
Auditory Comprehension

Rationale: Students are expected to follow auditory directions as an integral part of classroom instruction. Sometimes students have had practice following directions involving gross-motor activities without transitional activities between this stage of following directions and the next level where they are expected to follow commands using paper-and-pencil responses. The teacher must bridge this gap by carefully planning exercises proceeding from auditory directions for motor activity to auditory directions for paper/pencil tasks. If a student is found not to be following directions, the teacher must consider the length of the directions, the conceptual level of the words, and the complexity of the sentence structure before deciding on a particular remediation program.

Objective: To teach students to follow auditory directions beginning with gross-motor activities and concluding with paper-and-pencil tasks.

Materials: Paper and regular yellow pencil
Book
Desk
Colored blocks
Box and paper bag
Red and blue crayons
Window and door
Shelf

Procedure: 1. Ask the students to listen carefully while they are given a direction that will only be stated once. The students are told that this is a "listening" game.
2. Begin with simple directions and proceed to more complex ones.

Example:

"Bring me a book."
"Bring me a pencil and some paper."
"Give the book to Sue."
"Walk to the door."
"Sit under the desk."
"Put the book on the desk."
"Put the red book on the desk."
"Put the yellow pencil under the chair."
"Put the blocks in the box."
"Put three green blocks in the bag."
"Put the blocks in the bag on the shelf."
"Give the pencil to me and give the book to Alice."
"Give the blue crayon to Jim and give the red crayon to me."
"Go to the window, get the red book from the shelf, and sit on the chair next to Jane."

3. Continue the game using body movements and positional prepositions.

Example:
"Clap your hands."
"Shut your eyes."
"Put your hands under your chin."
"Put your hands under the chair."
"Put your hands behind you."
"Put your hands behind your head."
"Put your hands on your knees."

4. Introduce paper-and-pencil tasks.
(Note: If students are asked to follow directions involving paper and pencil, they must first understand the language of the task. For example, if the student is to draw a circle around an apple and a square around an orange they must know the concepts of apple and orange, and must recognize and know how to draw a square and a circle. They must also understand the concept of *around*.

If the students understand the language concepts and can draw an X and a circle use the following directions involving a set of pictures on a worksheet. Note that the directions increase in length, complexity, and the number of concepts involved. Prerequisite knowledge of symbols, prepositions, and color is necessary as is auditory memory. The students must understand what each of the pictures represents.)

Example:
"Point to the wagon."
"Point to the ring."
"Point to the carrot."
"Point to the hat."

"Point to the airplane."
"Point to the dog and then the
    telephone."
"Point to the broom."
"Make an X on the carrot."
"Draw a line under the dog."
"Draw a circle around the airplane."
"Make an X beside the hat."
"Draw an X on the machine that has wings."
"Draw a circle around the animal that has
    fur."
"Draw a ring around the vegetable that
    grows in the ground."
"Draw a green X on the wagon wheels."
"Color the handle of the broom yellow."
"Underline the one we fly in."

5. Ask the students to exchange papers and, as the students check the accuracy of the response, repeat the directions.

Additional Suggestions:

1. Teach students to listen carefully by asking them to shut their eyes while you make a familiar sound. The students are to write down what they heard. Use five sounds. Have the students compare their answers scoring 1 point for each correct answer.

    Examples: Opening a can of pop
              Wadding paper
              Running a finger over comb teeth
              Stapling some papers
              Ticking kitchen timer

2. Ask four students to whisper, two to shuffle their feet, and two to wad some paper while you give the class some complicated paper/pencil directions.

    Example: Draw eight circles. Put a red dot in the second circle and cross out the first and seventh circles. Color the third circle blue and the fifth circle orange. Underline the first three circles.

Discuss with the students how difficult it is to follow directions in a noisy classroom.

Descriptors: Auditory Discrimination
Auditory Memory
Following Directions

Grade Levels: 1–3

Rationale: Students often misunderstand oral instructions due to a lack of attention. As a result, they may do poorly on assignments that they are otherwise capable of doing. Good listening techniques can be fun as well as rewarding. These activities[2] reward good listening while establishing early habits of paying attention.

Objective: To present class activities designed to encourage students to listen carefully.

Materials: Puppet
Chalkboard and chalk
Box (treasure chest)
Classroom items (books, games, toys, baseball bats, ruler)

Procedure:
1. Choose one of the following activities for the class depending on age level.
2. Evaluate the effectiveness of the activity by determining if better listening habits have transferred to other academic areas.
3. Periodically hold class discussions about the advantages of good listening habits and the disadvantages of poor listening habits.

Activity 1: Puppets as Attention Getters

Using a hand puppet is an effective way to get students to listen. Have the students decide on a name for the puppet. Each day the puppet visits the class to describe an exciting happening, to read a school announcement, or to bring pencils, games, new plants, toys, or equipment for class use. As soon as the puppet appears, the children are ready to listen. A puppet may also be used at the end of the day to summarize important events or happenings. The puppet can praise pupils for being good listeners or ask them what they learned or what they enjoyed most during the day.

Activity 2: Listening for the Magic Word

Choose an unusual word to be used some time during the day. Use words appropriate for your students' grade level. Write the word in a corner of the chalkboard for the children to see. Instruct the class to listen for the word and, as soon as anyone hears it, to say, "Magic word." The student who hears it first receives a special privilege for the day. A few interesting words to get you started might be *magpie, cucumber, eureka, antifreeze, quirk,* or *thud.*

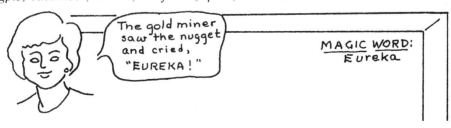

---

[2] J. Schaff, *The Language Arts Idea Book*. (Pacific Palisades, Calif: Goodyear Publishing Co., Inc., 1976).

Activity 3: Clapping Your Hands

Ask the class to listen for the two sounds at the beginning of *step*. Ask them to clap once if they hear this sound when you pronounce more words: *stem, some, bank, steep, sleep, stop, stir, skip, past, staple, steeple.*

Read a paragraph or a story to a group of students, asking them to clap their hands:

   a. when they hear the name of an animal.
   b. whenever they hear a word that describes something.
   c. every time they hear a word that names something.
   d. when they hear a word that begins (or ends) with a certain sound, as *b.*

Activity 4: Guessing the Secret Place

Play this listening game by having the students listen to the directions given by a teacher or a student to describe a certain spot in the room, school, or community. Let the individual who correctly guesses the secret place give directions to a new place.

Activity 5: Treasure Chest

Place many simple, familiar objects in a box labeled "Treasure Chest." Ask a student to be king or queen. The royal person says, "Bring my _____, _____, _____, _____ and _____," naming several things in the box. The king or queen chooses a student to bring the items from the chest. If the chosen student gets all the items mentioned, that student becomes king or queen.

Additional Suggestions: See *Listing Skills.*

_____months of the year_____

Descriptors: Sequencing Skills
Language Development

Grade Levels: 1.5–3

Rationale: The concepts of seasons, days of the weeks, and months of the year are taught in the primary grades. Some students experience difficulty in learning the names as well as the sequence of these time-related events. Based on the fact that visual cues are often helpful to many students, the months of the year are compared in this activity to a clock face.

Objective: To teach students to remember the months of the year in sequence.

Materials: 36″ × 36″ and 12″ × 1½″ tagboard
Black marking pen
Brass fastener
Blank index cards
Crayons or commercial pictures
Paste and scissors (optional)

Procedure:

1. Draw a circle with a 22-inch diameter in the center of the large piece of tagboard.
2. The numbers 1 to 12 are appropriately spaced around the circle with a marking pen to resemble a clock.
3. The 12″ × 1½″ tagboard strip is colored black and added to the center of the circle with a brass fastener, thus enabling it to move.
4. The months of the year are written outside the circle next to each appropriate number beginning with January by the number one.
5. Small pictures representing each month are added to the words to provide a visual cue for each month. For example, February—heart. The pictures may be drawn and colored by the student or may be cut out of magazines and catalogues.
6. The teacher and students read aloud the names of the months in sequential order beginning with January. One student moves the single pointer around the circle as each month is named.

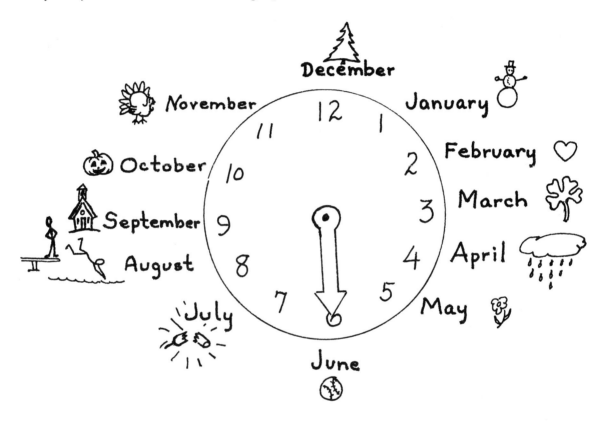

7. The teacher or students may take turns covering up the numbers, the words, or the visual cues with index cards before students are asked to recite the names of the months in sequence.

    Example: "What month is this?"

8. This activity should be practiced for a short time each day until the students have become proficient at naming all twelve months in sequence with little prompting and without visual cues.

Additional Suggestions:

1. Write the names of the twelve months on blank index cards. Shuffle the cards in random order and ask a student to arrange them in proper sequence. The teacher or a classmate checks for accuracy.
2. Draw a large circle with clock-like numbers on a ditto master and duplicate copies for all the students. The students add the months of the year and draw symbols by each to represent each month. The papers may be pinned to the bulletin board.
   (Note: A movable hand may be added to each clock. However, in this case sturdier material, such as tagboard, must be used.

_____"the terrible twos"_____

Descriptors: Language   **Grade Levels:**   3–6
Spelling
Reading Comprehension

Rationale: Learning homonyms can be difficult for young students with auditory or language problems but the following activity makes it fun. The homonyms *to, too, two,* should already have been introduced to the students before implementation of this activity.

Objective   To provide a practice worksheet for the homonyms *to, too, two.*

Materials: Ditto master
Duplicating paper
Pencil

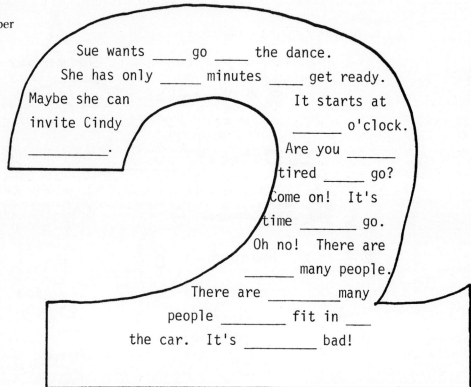

Sue wants ____ go ____ the dance.
She has only ____ minutes ____ get ready.
Maybe she can   It starts at
invite Cindy   _____ o'clock.
_____.   Are you _____
                                       tired ____ go?
                                       Come on! It's
                                       time _____ go.
                                       Oh no! There are
                                       _____ many people.
There are _____ many
people _____ fit in ___
the car. It's _____ bad!

Procedure: 1. Prepare a ditto with a large number 2 as shown in the illustration above.
2. Ask the students to practice the homonyms *to, too, two* by filling in the blanks.
3. Check the papers during class time to provide immediate feedback to the students.

**Additional
Suggestions:**   1. Use the same practice exercise to teach other homonyms such as *bear, bare* or *plain, plane.*
2. Ask students to design their own homonym papers and exchange them with classmates who subsequently complete the papers. (Note: This activity requires extra supervision and would be difficult for the slower students.)

_____science fantasy trip_____

Descriptors: Listening Skills   **Grade Levels:**   4–6
Relaxation
Visual Imagery

Rationale: It is important for students with poor reading or writing skills to be able to participate in classroom activities on the same level as their peers. These students are often not able to read science materials on their grade level. This fantasy idea allows students vicariously to experience a trip to the Grand Canyon. It develops good listening skills and promotes vivid visual imagery. The students also learn new information that can later be communicated to others.

Objective: To take the students on a "mental trip" to the Grand Canyon.

Materials: Paper and pencil
Tape recorder
Art materials (pictures, glue, scissors)
Crayons or colored marking pens

Procedure: 1. Ask the students to relax, shut their eyes, and imagine they are going on a trip. Ask them to feel the tension leave their necks, to let their arms become limp, their hands feel loose, and their feet feel light.
2. Relate the following story in a soft, calm voice.

Picture yourself in a van filled with hiking gear. You are dressed for a hike down the Grand Canyon.

Before you arrive at the entrance to the Canyon, you pass through an Indian village and see the mud pueblos of the Hopis. The Havasupai and Navajo also live near the Canyon.

Once you get to the parking lot at the edge of the Canyon, you all scramble out of the van and get ready for the descent. You begin to move in single file down the Canyon on the narrow trail. You see a group several yards ahead of you trekking down the trail on burros.

It is hot. You feel the heat of the sun's radiation from the Canyon walls as you continue hiking down the almost mile-long trail to the bottom of the Canyon.

You walk on and see several peculiar designs in the Canyon walls and stop to look at them for a while. You discover that the designs are fossils—imprints of plants and small animal bodies that lived and grew here thousands of years ago. As you progress down the trail you notice more and more fossils—each one different from those you had seen before.

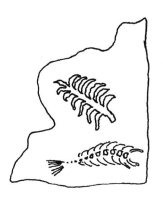 

You continue on down the Canyon and notice that the walls have changed colors. Erosion and the Colorado River have carved their way through various layers of sandstone, limestone, shale, and granite. After many hours, you reach the bottom, hot . . . thirsty . . . and hungry.

You take your backpack off and plunge into the cold water of the Colorado River. It feels so cool and refreshing.

You crawl out and the group moves over to a camp area and makes a fire.

The sun is going down and you all watch the color changes on the walls of the Canyon. It's so beautiful! Blues, purples, reds, oranges, and various shades of yellow become distinct, and they mix together softly, gradually disappearing one by one until all of the colors turn into darkness, and the only colors you see are the stars twinkling in the sky so far above you.

 You each had prepared "Camper's Stew" before your journey. Now you smell the hamburger, potatoes, and carrots cooking in the individually wrapped tin foil packages over the hot coals of the campfire. For dessert, you roast marshmallows, place them on a graham cracker with a square of chocolate. Food never tasted sooo good!

You all sit around the campfire and warm yourselves as the evening temperature drops. The Canyon becomes very cool at night and you snuggle your jacket around you for extra warmth.

You think about all the experiences you want to share with your family and friends when you return home.

Tell the students, "Slowly open your eyes and just keep calm for a few minutes."

3. Let the students pick one of the following options as a follow-up activity:

   a. Write a letter to your friends, describing your experiences.
   b. Make a collage of the sights, sounds, and experiences of your fantasy.
   c. Make a tape-recorded journal of your fantasy trip.
   d. Write a poem about one particular aspect of your experience.

Additional Suggestions:

1. Present an auditory trip to the desert, mountains, ocean, zoo, park, tropics, a volcano, or an expedition to observe some animal in its natural habitat.
2. Use slides or movies to augment the lesson.

—collage

rainbow rhymes

Descriptors: Sensory Impressions   **Grade Levels:**   4–6
                   Language Arts
                   Creative Writing

Rationale: It is often necessary to direct students' creative writing ability. Relating moods and feelings to colors helps them to express themselves better when writing compositions.

Objective: After completing this activity, the student will be able to relate feelings or emotions to a corresponding color.

Materials: Book or film, *Hailstones and Halibut Bones*[3]
                 Construction paper (red, white, blue, green, black, and brown)
                 Notebook paper/pencil
                 Bulletin board and thumbtacks
                 Scissors

Procedure: 1. Read with your students or share with them the film, *Hailstones and Halibut Bones*, to stimulate them to think about colors.
                 2. Ask students to choose a color and to list all the ideas that particular color brings to mind.

---

[3]N. O'Neill, *Hailstones and Halibut Bones* (Garden City, N.Y.: Doubleday and Company, 1961). Film: *Hailstones and Halibut Bones*. Parts I & II. Sterling Films, 241 East 34th Street, New York, N.Y. 10016.

Encourage them to include feelings, smells, and sounds as well as objects. (A piece of colored construction paper under their notebook paper will keep the color before the students while they are thinking.)

3. Students may write their ideas as poems that may or may not rhyme.
4. The students share their creative efforts with the rest of the class.

Additional Suggestions: The poems may be placed in a pot at the end of a colorful rainbow displayed on a bulletin board. Descriptors may also be written on each color of the rainbow.

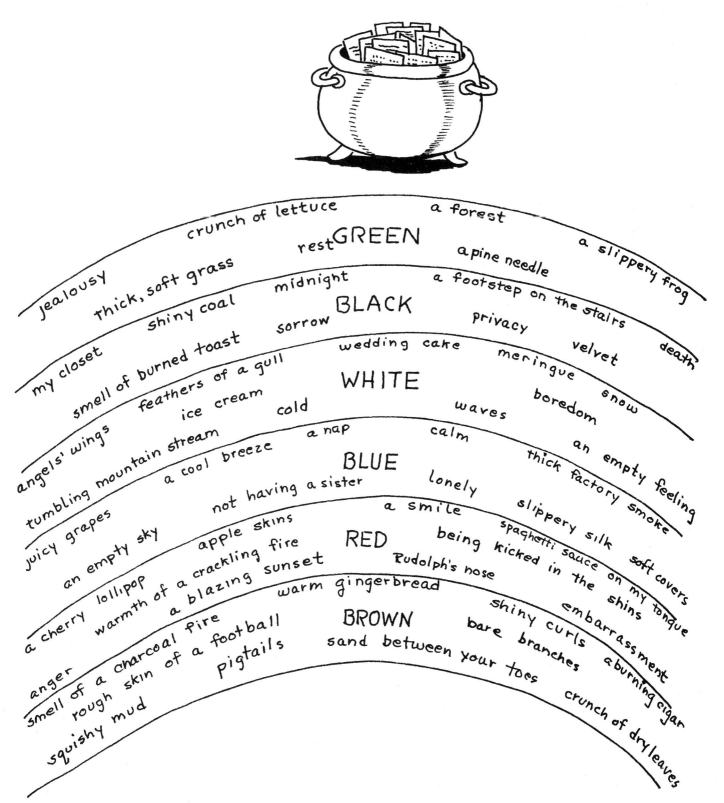

GREEN
crunch of lettuce   a forest   rest   a pine needle   a slippery frog
jealousy   thick, soft grass

BLACK
my closet   shiny coal   midnight   sorrow   a footstep on the stairs   death
smell of burned toast   privacy   velvet

WHITE
feathers of a gull   wedding cake   meringue   snow
angels' wings   ice cream   cold   boredom

BLUE
tumbling mountain stream   a nap   calm   waves   an empty feeling
a cool breeze   lonely   thick factory smoke

RED
juicy grapes   not having a sister   a smile   slippery silk   soft covers
an empty sky   apple skins   being kicked in the shins
a cherry lollipop   warmth of a crackling fire   spaghetti sauce on my tongue
a blazing sunset   Rudolph's nose   embarrassment

BROWN
anger   warm gingerbread   shiny curls   a burning cigar
smell of a charcoal fire   pigtails   bare branches
rough skin of a football   sand between your toes   crunch of dry leaves
squishy mud

Descriptors: Group Activities   **Grade Levels:** 4–6
                   Research Project

Rationale: Students retain important information by developing a method for organizing what they have learned. When studying a country, state, city, or region in social studies, for example, it is helpful to organize the basic information into a simple brochure for visitors. Creating the brochure is a valuable learning exercise.

Objective: To teach students how to organize descriptive material into a brochure format.

Materials: Research materials
                   Magazines
                   Colored construction paper
                   Scissors
                   Pen

Procedure:
1. The students are asked to research a country, state, city, or region as a small-group or individual project.
2. Students use social studies or history books, encyclopediae, and maps to research their specific assignments. They might want to look up the following information about a state: capital city (if appropriate), location, geographic features (rivers, mountains, ocean), population, average temperature (summer and winter), average rainfall, crops, industry, and recreational facilities.
3. As part of the brochure students should entice visitors to the location by describing: ideal areas to stay in (near lake, mountains), recreational activities, cultural activities, and type of clothing to wear when visiting (summer and winter).
4. Suggest that students search magazines and newspapers for words or pictures that illustrate the area. The students mount the gathered information on a piece of construction paper folded into thirds. All six sides can be used to display the information gathered about a particular country, state, city, or region. A map may also be included.

**Additional
Suggestions:**
1. Send the brochures to another class and ask the students to pick the three most popular locations to visit.
2. Ask the students to prepare a five-minute (individual or group) "Chamber of Commerce talk" about their area to present to the rest of the class. Large posters or charts may be designed and displayed on the bulletin board during the presentation.

_____informal calendar test_____

Descriptors: Calendar Assessment   **Grade Levels:** 4–6+
                   Criterion Reference   Special Education
                   Understanding Oral Directions   Prevocational
                                                                            Training

Rationale: The ability to understand information presented on a calendar is essential as a general life skill. It is also important as a prevocational training tool.

Objective: To assess the competency of a student to orally respond to questions involving information presented on a calendar.

Materials: Examiner checklist
Calendar test protocol

Procedure: 1. The examiner gives the student a copy of the calendar and asks the student to use it in answering the questions presented.
2. The examiner follows the checklist when asking the questions.

name _____   date _____

examiner _____   grade _____

                                                          Correct   Incorrect

Part I

Calendar Awareness

1. Why do you use a calendar?
2. What month does the calendar show? (October)
3. What month comes before? (September)
4. What month comes after? (November)
5. How many days are in this month? (31)
6. How many weeks are in this month? (4)
7. What holiday is in this month? (Halloween)
8. When is the holiday? (October 31)

Part II

Days of Week Given Date

What day of the week is _____ on?

    October 10?   (Friday)
    October 14?   (Tuesday)
    October 1?   (Wednesday)
    October 25?   (Saturday)
    October 12?   (Sunday)
    October 6?   (Monday)
    October 23?   (Thursday)

Date Given the Day/Position in the Month

What day of the month is _____ on?

    First Tuesday? (October 7)
    Fourth Thursday? (October 23)
    Third Sunday? (October 19)
    Last Friday? (October 31)
    Fifth Wednesday? (October 29)
    Second Monday? (October 13)

Part III

Application

If you work every Monday and Thursday night . . .
    1. How many nights do you work in this month?
        (9)
    2. Can you go to a party on October 9?
        (No, have to work that night.)

If you are paid on _____, when will you be paid this
month?

    Fourth Friday? (October 24)
    October 17? (Third Friday)
    First and third Wednesday? (October 1 and 15)
    Last of the month? (October 31)
    First of the month? (October 1)

a. Part I assesses basic calendar awareness including the purpose, name of month and position in sequence, holiday, and number of days/weeks.

b. Part II assesses the ability to state the day of the week given the date, and the date given the day/position in the month.

c. Part III assesses the application of the skills in Part II in career or vocational-related situations including work and pay schedules.

d. The correct answers are written in parentheses next to each of the questions.

e. The examiner records a plus (+) in the correct column if the student is correct, and a minus (−) in the incorrect column if the student misses the question. It is important for the examiner to write the student's actual response under the incorrect column in order to plan a remediation program better.

Additional Suggestions: Part III may also be adapted for intermediate students in regular classes who will not be in prevocational training.

Example:

1. If you were on a committee that meets every Monday and Thursday evening, how many evenings would you be meeting this month? (9)

2. Would you be free to attend a movie the evening of October 9? (No. The committee meets on that day.)

3. The pay schedule questions apply to all students who will be earning a living eventually. Any of the questions may be adapted to the needs of the learner.

OCTOBER						
SUNDAY	MONDAY	TUESDAY	WEDNESDAY	THURSDAY	FRIDAY	SATURDAY
			1	2	3	4
5	6	7	8	9	10	11
12	13	14	15	16	17	18
19	20	21	22	23	24	25
26	27	28	29	30	31	

Descriptors: Diagramming Skills   **Grade Levels:** 5–6
"Same As" and "Different From"
Item Sequencing
Dictionary Use
Visual Discrimination

Rationale: Some students have difficulty organizing their work, a problem that may extend into the areas of visual discrimination and seeing patterns. By using doodles and words, students can learn basic organizational skills in a novel way.

Objective: Given a doodle worksheet and a teacher-prepared answer sheet, the student will identify similarities in wavy, jagged, curved, circular, and angled shapes and arrange them in columns.

Materials: Paper and pencil
Diagram on blackboard or overhead projector for students to copy from

Procedure:

1. Say, "Detective Dorky found this mess on a paper in the trash. Can you figure out how to organize it into three groups? When you do, make three headings on your paper and join the detective force."

2. Use oral cues to help the students get started. Say, "Are any of the doodles almost the same? How are they the same? If you see any doodles that are almost the same, put them in the first column on your paper."
3. After the students are catching on, you may help individual students with more difficult doodles by saying, "Can you find an angled doodle? Are there any more doodles with angles? Put them all in the third column."
4. The completed diagram should resemble the one below, but individual students may label their columns differently. Some may find curved/jagged/straight columns, and some students may find curved straight or angled/combination of both.

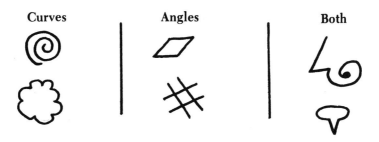

| Curves | Angles | Both |

247

After the students have grasped the concepts of sorting and organizing, the teacher might use the same principle with an assortment of words and have the students enlarge their diagram to four columns. The concept of headings and subheadings might also be introduced. The following are samples of a lesson using both columns and headings to organize a group of seemingly unrelated words.

Procedure:

1. Say, "Detective Dorky found this note next to the body of a murdered man. To find out what the victim was planning to do over the weekend, figure out how to organize this mess. After you figure it out, arrange your clues into four columns and think of a heading for each column. Good luck— you'll need it!"

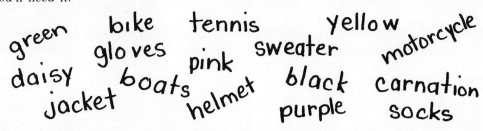

green   bike   tennis   yellow
daisy   gloves   pink   sweater   motorcycle
jacket   boats   helmet   black   carnation
purple   socks

2. For the heading/subheading idea, use the same information, but ask the students to fill in the blanks on the worksheet approximated below.

A. _____
   1.
   2.
   3.
   4. sweater
   5.
B. Colors _____
   1.
   2
   3.
   4.
   5.
C. _____
   1.
   2.
   3.
D. _____
   1.
   2.

**BEHAVIOR
MANAGEMENT/SELF
CONCEPT
STUDY SKILLS**

Descriptors: Following Directions
Providing Classroom Structure
Behavior Management

Grade Levels: K–2

Rationale: Distractible students who have difficulty staying on task usually experience problems learning basic academic skills. Such students are also very frustrating to teachers and to their peer group because they cause disruption of classroom activities. Not only are these distractible students missing academic skills, they are also establishing poor peer relationships and are earning the description of "behavior problems." Instead of blaming the youngster, the teacher needs to evaluate carefully the educational environment to determine what changes can be made to help the student succeed. The suggestion in this activity has been used successfully with distractible youngsters; however, since all students are unique, the same techniques may not work for all of them.

Objective: To provide the teacher with strategies for working with distractible students.

Materials: Masking tape
Tagboard
Black marking pen
Timer
Scissors
Paste, crayons
Chalkboard and chalk

Procedure:

1. Evaluate the student's current academic skill levels. If the assigned work is too difficult (or too easy) for the student, s/he finds it difficult to attend to the task. If the student cannot do the assigned work, provide worksheets at the correct skill level. Plan time to explain the directions and other guidelines to the student having difficulties to ensure that s/he knows exactly what is expected.

2. Directions should be clear, simple, and short. (Do not give more than two at one time to kindergarten students, for example). Pause after each direction.

    Example: "It is time for math. (pause)
    Get out your workbook. (pause)
    Get out a pencil. (pause)
    Turn to page 7." (pause)

3. Visual reminders (picture cards) paired with simple directions or class rules are helpful for many students who shout answers, talk to the student next to them, or do not attend to the teacher. Hold up the appropriate picture card as each direction is given.

Example: Be quiet   Listen

Watch the teacher   Raise your hand

Look at me

Again, use short directions. Make certain that the student understands the meaning of the directions.

4. Assign physical boundaries so the student knows exactly where to sit during story time and work time. Place an *X* with masking tape on the floor where the student is to sit.

It is helpful if the *X* is next to the teacher's chair. Thus, if the student becomes restless, you may quietly reach over and touch him/her on the arm or shoulder. If the student sits on the perimeter of the circle, it is easy for the student to get up abruptly and wander around the room, thus causing you to interrupt the story to call the student back.

5. Use a timer with a bell to help keep the student on task for gradually increasing lengths of time. Example: If the student can work four to five minutes, set the timer to ring at six minutes. Continue to seven or eight minutes. Reinforce the student for working until the bell rings. Keep a visual chart of the student's successes.

The student colors in one section each time until the bell rings. When all sections are colored, the student earns fifteen minutes of free time.

6. Reduce the stimuli on a worksheet by cutting it into strips and assigning one strip at a time. Cut some sections and paste on other papers, use a cover sheet to reduce the stimuli.

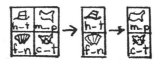

7. Since peer approval is usually very important to this type of student, allow the student to earn points for the class by staying on task. Set a timer on a varying schedule from three to seven minutes during group or individual activities. If the student is "on task" when the bell rings, hold up a smiling face and mark 1 point for the class on the chalkboard. Say, "Susan is earning points for you by working (or listening)." If the student is not following the rules, hold up a frowning face and quickly move back to the assignment without further comment. When 10 points are accumulated, the class is awarded a reinforcing activity (for example, favorite game during gym class, free time, extra art project, or class party). In essence, you are paying attention to the student for positive behaviors and allowing the student to earn special activities for the entire class.

8. When assigning seatwork to a distractible student:

   a. Have all materials needed for the task at the student's desk. This prevents the student from walking around the room to gather materials.

   b. Give simple oral directions using only key words. "Listen. Circle beginning *B* sound pictures. Do it now."

   c. Touch the student to let him/her know when you are pleased with the "on task" work. A touch paired with whispered secret praise makes the student feel unique.

9. Use visual motivation sheets (see *Visual Motivation* activity). Reward the student for completing tasks on time. A visual record of a student's accumulative success is very reinforcing by itself.

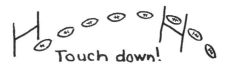

10. Allow the student to move around legitimately after s/he has been sitting at the desk and worked an appropriate length of time (Example: fifteen minutes). Send that student on an errand to another teacher's classroom, to the principal's office, or ask the student to pass out papers. It is not realistic to expect a distractible student to sit for long periods of time.

11. Allow the student to work in a box office (see *Box "Offices" to Reduce Distraction* activity) to shut out extraneous visual stimuli. Use of earphones allows students to shut out distracting auditory stimuli.

Additional Suggestions:

1. When the timer goes off at varying intervals while the student is still "on task," hold a thumb up and score a point under "thumbs up" on a chart. If the student is not on task, hold a thumb down and record similarly on a chart. The total is calculated at the end of the day. The number of down thumbs is subtracted from the total number of thumbs up. Set the criterion, but one "rule of thumb" (no pun intended!) is to allow a small reward for 5 points or more, a larger reward for 10 points, and so on.

Name _____	
Thumbs—up ☺	Thumbs-down ☹

2. Design a simple daily report card. Such a report card might look like this:

	Date _____
Nancy sat quietly today for:	
	YES NO
Story Time	☑ ☐
Reading Readiness	☐ ☑

The student takes the daily report card home. The parent provides a visual motivation chart for the student. Example: For each "yes" the student may add a sticker to the orange tree or may color an orange. The "no's" may be ignored. When the orange tree is full, the student earns something special at home such as baking cookies, staying up fifteen minutes later at night, or choosing a TV program. In this manner parents can provide reinforcement at home for successful school achievement.

reinforcement for withdrawn students

Descriptors: Self-Concept   **Grade Levels:** K–3

Rationale: Teachers are often concerned with the aggressive, disruptive type of student. However the anxious, withdrawn pupil also represents cause for concern. Several strategies can be used by the teacher to help the withdrawn student overcome an inability to associate with classmates, fear of math, test anxiety, and similar problems.

Objective: To improve the anxious-withdrawn student's personal and academic adjustment.

Materials: Stickers
Tagboard charts
Paper and pencil

Procedure:
1. Teacher praise is not always a reward for shy students, at least not initially. Because their self-concept is poor, teacher praise for such individuals may not correlate with what others have communicated to them and how they feel about themselves. Therefore, *tangible* or *activity-type rewards* may be more reinforcing in the beginning.

2. Use the *peer group* to draw the student out. Select one student with whom the shy pupil feels comfortable and have that student help the pupil become more assertive. For example, you might say, "Nancy, I think that Patty (withdrawn student) might like to play this spelling game with you," or "Nancy, I think Ms. Nelson could use Patty's and your help with correcting math papers."

3. To make academic responses simple and anxiety free, *programmed instruction* may be used. Such teaching techniques not only break complex tasks down to simple steps, but also ensure high rate of correct answers. Such successes aid in the development of greater self-assurance.

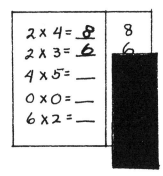

4. To build the self-confidence of anxious students, plan experiences that allow them to *overlearn* skills. This can be done by teaching a skill in a group format, assigning students a worksheet containing the skill, playing a trial game relating to the skill, and finally asking the student to help another student who may be having problems with the particular skill.

5. Provide a *predictable classroom environment*. For the anxious, withdrawn student novelty is threatening because learning new concepts or adjusting to new situations can be very upsetting.

Extra instructional attention and personal support will be necessary when moving from a mastered concept to a new concept. Gradually, the anxious student should be exposed to less structured tasks.

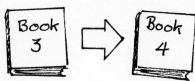

6. Give *disciplinary action in a nonoverwhelming way.* Anxious students do not need the "reality rub-in" that more aggressive students may require. A simple look at the student or a statement of what was done incorrectly would be sufficient.

_____ let's get rich! _____

Descriptors: Reinforcement   **Grade Levels:**   1–3
                     Self-Concept

Rationale: Students in our culture usually realize the value of money. To capitalize on this knowledge and to promote better self-concepts, a behavior management program using banknotes with each student's photograph may be implemented to reinforce positive behaviors. It is time-consuming to prepare the banknotes; a teacher aide, parent volunteer, or older student would be helpful.

Objective: To reinforce positive classroom behaviors and teach the value of money.

Materials: A small photograph of each child
                     Teacher-made banknotes (see illustration)
                     Glue
                     Scissors
                     Marking pen
                     Photocopy machine

Procedure: 1. The teacher dittoes banknotes following this design:

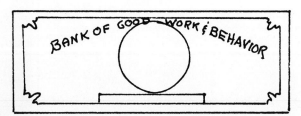

2. The teacher collects the students' photographs and makes several photocopies of them by placing eight to twelve on each sheet of paper.
Example:

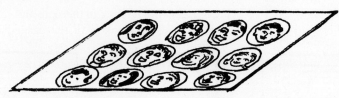

3. The students cut their photographs into oval shapes and save them to add to the blank banknotes when they are awarded to the student.
4. Whenever a student meets the criterion set by the teacher for a certain activity, s/he is awarded a banknote for a specified amount as shown on a price chart (see illustration). Students paste their photo on the banknote with their name written below it. The teacher writes the denomination of the note (ones, fives, and tens) in the corners.

5. Special privileges and rewards may be "bought" with earned banknotes. Disruptive behavior or poor work results in either "payment" by the pupil or in not getting paid by the teacher. (Note: It is imperative that work assignments be on each student's skill level.)
6. The teacher should devise a price chart with student input according to classroom priorities.

EARNS	
1. Finishes work on time	$5
2. Correct assignment	$2
3. Being quiet	$3
4. Coming in on time	$2
5. Helping others	$4

COSTS	
1. Quarreling	$8
2. Homework not completed	$5
3. Interrupting	$3
4. Being late	$4
5. Out-of-seat	$2

BUYS	
1. Extra free time for games, clay, and so on (fifteen minutes)	$5
2. Use arts and craft corner	$5
3. Choose a game for gym	$4
4. Time to read a library book	$4
5. Listening to records	$6

Additional Suggestions: The students may also collect their banknotes and keep them to buy a "big prize" at the end of the month.

_____ observing and recording student behaviors _____

Descriptors: Behavior Management Procedures
Charting
Identifying Behaviors

Grade Levels: K–6

Rationale: Many teachers think of behavior management as a system of rewarding youngsters with candy without much knowledge about the procedure or its rationale. All teachers would greatly benefit from understanding the techniques and learning how to record and change behaviors. Behavior modification has three central features. First, it focuses on *behavior*, that is, what people actually do, rather than on such private and subjective events as thoughts, feelings, and attitudes. Second, it studies the *consequences* of people's behaviors (the reinforcements and negative consequences of their behavior). Third, it *experiments* with different arrangements of these consequences to determine which are most effective in altering an individual's behavior.

Objective: To teach how to observe and record behavior by using procedures that are both practical and effective.

255

Materials: Ditto master
Duplicating paper
Pencil

Procedure:
1. The teacher chooses one of the following methods of recording behavior and duplicates copies of the record sheet.
2. The teacher records target behaviors to be improved.
3. The teacher implements certain environmental changes and records the behaviors on the same chart.
4. The teacher evaluates the effectiveness of the environmental changes.

Discussion: There are seven procedures for observing and measuring student behavior.
1. *Narrative Recording*
This type of recording is also know as *continuous* or *anecdotal* recording. The teacher or parent makes a running account of all the classes of behavior observed, either in a long-hand account or via a tape-recorder description of the student's behavior and the environment. All recorded observations can be organized into a three-column recording sheet, as in this sample:

Time	Antecedent Events: Exchange Initiations by Others	Behavior of Student	Consequent Events: Exchange Reciprocations by Others
9:20		1. Sits quietly at desk in classroom copying assignment from chalkboard.	2. Teacher ignores.
	2. Teacher ignores	3. Student leans toward peer (pupil seated at desk to student's left) and whispers something.	4. Teacher gets up from desk and walks toward the student's desk. Stands beside desk quietly with arms folded.
9:21	4. Teacher gets up from desk and walks toward the student's desk. Stands beside the desk quietly with arms folded.	5. Student stops whispering to classmate, picks up pencil, and resumes copying assignment from chalkboard.	6. Teacher says to student, "That's right. I want you to get back to work, Tommy."

Although impractical for extended observation and data collection, such narrative recording may be helpful in the later identification of student behavior that the teacher wishes to change or modify. However, narrative recording has the disadvantage that it requires a great deal of time on the part of the observer; also, while recording, the observer may miss observing certain other ongoing behaviors. Still, the teacher may wish to employ this method of observing and recording student behavior as a basis for later selection of those behaviors targeted for modification.

2. *Outcome Recording*
This type of recording is the direct measurement of the temporary or permanent products (results) of behavior, rather than of the behavior itself. In outcome recording the result is always observed after the behavior has taken place. Teachers have long been used to recording spelling scores, the number of problems worked correctly on math tests, and whether or not assignments have been completed and handed in. In all of these cases, a student's behavior results in a permanent product that can be observed and counted and lends itself very well to repeated measures of behavior over time.

	Math Test	Spelling
John	82%	60%
Susan	70%	95%
etc.		

3. *Event Recording*

Event recording is another useful tool for observing student behavior in the classroom or at home. The method is based on counting the number of times a discrete behavioral event occurs. For the most part, the behavioral event is of short duration, has a similar format each time it occurs, and has a definite beginning and ending. This observational and measurement procedure is easily administered and is particularly advantageous in the classroom setting as, in many instances, it does not interfere with ongoing teaching since it can be accomplished by simply tallying with a pencil on paper or by using a small hand or wrist counter. Thus, a teacher can count the number of times a given event (such as talk out, an argument, a fight, or pupils coming in late) occurs by tallying with a pencil or paper or by using the small hand or wrist counter: ⊞ |||

4. *Interval Recording*

Interval recording is yet another procedure for measuring behavior. The period of observation is divided into brief, continuous intervals and notations are made as to whether or not a given behavior occurs during these intervals. The duration of the intervals varies anywhere from ten seconds to three hours. (Generally speaking, however, the greater the frequency of the behavior being exhibited, the shorter the intervals should be.) Thus, in interval recording, the observation session is divided into equal time periods. A stopwatch is useful for this type of recording. The teacher records the occurrence or nonoccurrence of behavior during these intervals. In the illustration, the teacher has recorded whether or not a student attended appropriately to an assigned task during ten-second intervals of a two-minute observation period.

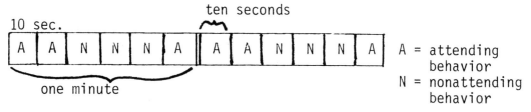

The teacher wrote A during six intervals and N in the other six. Thus, the student observed attended 50 percent of the time (twelve ten-second intervals or a total of two minutes).

The chief advantage of the interval recording method is that it indicates both the relative frequency and the duration of the behavior being observed. Also, by adding a second or third row of recording squares the observer can record a number of behaviors simultaneously. A disadvantage of the interval recording method is that it usually requires the observer's undivided attention. However, some behaviors such as yelling, fighting, or out-of-seat behavior in the classroom may not require the concentrated attention of the teacher or parent. In these situations this method of behavioral measurement may be used.

5. *Time Sample Recording*

The technique of time sample recording is similar in some respects to interval recording except that it does not require continuous observation. For this reason it is more convenient than interval recording in most cases. A teacher or parent records the student's behavior only at the end of a time interval. For example, a parent may want to estimate the percentage of time a child wears a hearing air during the day or a teacher might wish to record a student's study behavior during a given period in the classroom. In time sample recording, the time available for observation is divided into intervals. In the illustration below, a thirty-minute observation period was divided into ten three-minute intervals. The teacher recorded the behavior only at the end of the intervals, that is, once every three minutes. At the end of each three-minute period the teacher looked at the student and recorded whether the behavior was occurring at that instant.

	30 minutes										
Minute	3	6	9	12	15	18	21	24	27	30	A = attending
Behavior	A	A	N	N	N	N	N	N	A	A	B = nonattending

In the example above, the time sample record shows that the student was attending at the end of the first three-minute interval and again after six minutes. At the end of the next six three-minute intervals, however, the student was not attending although s/he was again attending at the end of the ninth and tenth intervals. Thus, the record shows that the student was attending four out of ten (or 40 percent) of the time observed.

6. *Duration Recording*

It is sometimes more important to know how long a behavior lasts than to know how often it occurs. For instance, a young student might suck a thumb only once a day, but the thumbsucking might last several hours. Duration recording is a measurement of behavior used to indicate the length of time a behavior occurs. Accordingly, it is used if the elapsed time of behavior is recorded during a specific observation period. A stopwatch is usually the most efficient tool for making duration recordings. Clocks and conventional watches can be used in situations where less precise measurements are sufficient. Behaviors such as thumbsucking, amount of time spent working on classroom assignments, and time spent engaged in cooperative play can all be measured by duration recording.

thumbsucking

9/3/76	9:00 - 11:30	40 minutes
Susan B.	11:30 - 1:00	20 minutes
	1:00 - 2:30	

7. *Planned Activity Checklist*

The planned Activity Checklist, more commonly known as "pla-check" is sometimes used to sample the behavior of groups. In fact, it is similar to the time sample technique except that at the sampling times the observer counts all the individuals engaged in the behavior bing measured. The pla-check technique requires that

a. The observer (teacher) scientifically defines the behavior (planned activity) s/he wishes to record in a group of students.
b. At given intervals (for example, each ten minutes) the observer counts as quickly as possible how many individuals are engaged in the behavior and records the total.
c. The observer then counts and records as quickly as possible how many individuals are present in the area of the activity.
d. The number of pupils present is then divided into the number of pupils engaged in the behavior. By multiplying the quotient by 100 the teacher finds the percent of those engaged in the behavior at a particular time.

Kindergarten Free Time

Time Intervals	Behavior Exhibited	# of Individuals Engaged in Behavior	# of Individuals in Activity Area	Total % Engaged in Behavior at Particular Time
9:10	playing with toys	6	8	75%
9:20	playing with toys	5	8	62%
9:40	playing with toys	3	8	37%

EXAMPLE OF APPLICATION OF THE "PLA-CHECK" TECHNIQUE:

An art teacher wants to determine what portion of the class is working on an assigned art project during a fifty-minute period. Each ten minutes the teacher quickly counts how many students are working on the project. The teacher than counts the number of students present. Example: During the first part of the period the teacher finds that 10/20 and 15/20 are working; during the second part of the period, ten boys who had been excused to work on another project return to class; the teacher now finds 15/30, 30/30, and 20/30 of those present to be working on the assigned project. Thus, according to these calculations, 50 percent, 75 percent, 50 percent, 100 percent, and 67 percent (a mean of 68 percent), worked on the assigned project during the class period.

A Planned Activity Checklist can be used to measure such activities as the percentage of kindergarteners playing with toys or sleeping during nap time or the percentage of school-age children attending appropriately to a given task.

Additional Suggestions: See *Taking Baseline Data* activity.

_____**visual motivation**_____

Descriptors: Reinforcement
Academic Success
Behavior Management

Grade Levels: K–6

Rationale: Students having difficulty in school are often not motivated to attend to the required task. They are sometimes described as hyperactive, lazy, daydreamers, or as having a poor attention span. This type of a student needs to experience success and to see progress (an accumulation) of these successes. The old adage, "Nothing succeeds like success," applies to this population as well as to normal learners. The following activity helps promote visual motivation.

Objective: To stimulate interest in completing academic, social, or behavioral tasks.

Materials: Colored construction paper
Glue
Tagboard
Paper
Black marking pen
Crayons
Scissors

Procedure:

1. Identify the exact behavior that you want to increase. Example: spelling words, math problems, completing assignments, vocabulary words, working independently, entering the room quietly.
2. Be certain that the behavior is appropriate for the student's ability and/or skill level. Example: A student with poor motor ability should not be expected to write as neatly as a student without handicaps; spelling words should not be too difficult for the reading ability of the student.
3. Decide the criterion for earning the reward. Example: 90 percent correct, attending to task for fifteen minutes, working quietly for ten minutes independently.
4. Select the award according to the student's desires, that is, something the student would enjoy. Example: Being a tutor for younger students, helping the janitor, choosing the recess game, extra free time, a field trip. Use extrinsic awards such as candy, food, and money only if no other awards prove effective. Substitute a more natural classroom award as quickly as possible.
5. Evaluate the activity. Since this activity is a visual record of successful performance the evaluation becomes more simplified. By comparing this information with the student's level of performance prior to the initiation of the activity you can decide whether or not it has been effective. If it is not working you need to reevaluate:

   a. the skill level (is it too difficult?)
   b. the award arrangement (is it realistic? all-day performance versus half-day?)
   c. the award itself (is it something the student really desires?)

Activity 1: Gumball Machine

1. Using a black marking pen, draw a large gumball machine with empty round circles representing gumballs.
2. The teacher and the student set the criterion for success (see 1 and 3).
3. The student colors in one gumball for each criterion reached. Example: ten words correctly spelled earn one gumball.
4. When all gumballs have been colored, the student's award might be a stick of sugarless gum.

Activity 2: Stamp Book

1. Fold one sheet of paper in half and draw blank squares on each page to represent a stamp book.
2. The student earns one sticker (or cancelled stamp) each time a criterion is reached. Example: Working independently for ten minutes, 90 percent correct on the math assignment.
3. When the stamp book is completed, a previously agreed on reward is earned. Example: acting as kindergarten tutor, a trip to a fast-food restaurant, extra free time.

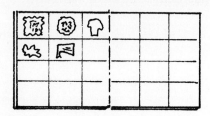

Activity 3: Puzzle

1. The student draws, colors, and cuts out a picture (magazine pictures may also be used).
2. Outline the picture with a heavy black line on a plain piece of paper.
3. Cut up the picture into ten to fifteen puzzle pieces and place in an envelope.
4. As each criterion is reached, glue one piece of the puzzle within the black line. Example: Reading ten basic sight words 100 percent correct earns one puzzle piece, cooperating in a group assignment earns one puzzle piece.
5. When the puzzle is completed, the reward is earned. Example: A field trip, principal's special helper, class leader for the day.

Activity 4: <u>Charts</u> <u>or</u> <u>Graphs</u>

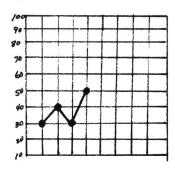 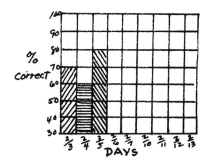

Older students can also benefit from visual motivation. Use activities that correspond with their interest level. Graphs—bar or connected line graphs—are useful for daily progress records. Use colored flair pens or colored pencils.

Activity 5: <u>Stars</u>

Stanley R. LIBRARY CARD	
☆	Cowboy Sam
★	Kites

Stars continue to be very effective reinforcers. Use a library card. List each extra book read by the student and add a star next to the title.

Activity 6: <u>Racetracks</u>

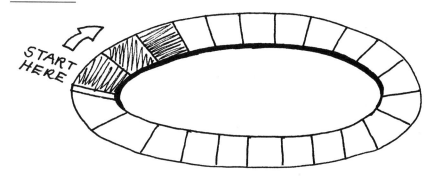

1. Draw a racetrack with a black marking pen and mark off equal sections from a starting point.
2. The student colors in one section each time the criterion is reached.
3. When all sections are filled in, the award is earned.

Additional Suggestions:

1. P. Glazzard and M. Regan, *Primary Bulletin Boards to Motivate Learners* (Denver, Col.: Love Publishing Co., 1978).
2. M. Regan and P. Glazzard, *Intermediate Bulletin Boards to Motivate Learners.* (Denver, Col.: Love Publishing Co., 1978).

classroom reinforcers

Descriptors: Behavior Management   **Grade Levels:**   K–6
                   Self-Concept
                   Rewards

Rationale: To reward students' good behaviors teachers often need a variety of readily available reinforcers. This list serves as a stimulus for the teacher to generate more ideas.

Objective: To present a list of possible classroom reinforcers.

Procedure: Read through the list and choose those reinforcers that would be most appropriate for your classroom.

tokens	chance to help other students	clean chalkboard
praise	no homework	rubber stamps on hand
free time	music pass	stars on a chart
extra recess	music teacher helper	read to younger children
self-graphing	principal's assistant	listen to records
daily good reports to parents	janitor's assistant	crosswalk patrol leader
extra art time	tutor for a younger student	flag raiser
building models	balloons	honor roll
field trips	treasure chest of tiny toys	grades
messenger boy/girl	longer lunch periods	first for show-and-tell
room party on Friday	magazine selection	sharpen pencil for class
nurse's helper	student grader	roll call leader
library time	choose a game	sit in front of classroom
extra reading (free reading)	points toward prize	sit in back of classroom
lunch counter	money	sit by windows
stars or stickers on paper	extra privileges	sit by door
paper on wall	extra physical education time	grade homework
sitting by friend	picnic	feed classroom pets
class leader to bathroom	teacher for the day	turn lights on and off
class leader to cafeteria	extra time to cook	clean erasers
teacher smile	teacher-assigned paycheck	certificates of achievement
pat on back by teacher	swimming privilege	food
happy faces on papers	bowling privilege	soda pop
name on board	game equipment manager	sugarless gum
library pass		

behavior reinforcement schedules

Descriptors: Behavior Management   **Grade Levels:**   1–6
                   Task Analysis

Rationale: A teacher may consider a student to present a behavior problem without being able to specify the problem or a sequential way of eliminating it. For example, it is not enough to label a student "hyperactive" since this label does not tell you what to do about the problem. This activity presents ways of identifying problem behaviors and appropriate reinforcement schedules for eliminating the undesirable behaviors by reinforcing desirable ones.

Objective: To describe methods of analyzing behaviors and to present sequential reinforcement schedules.

262

Materials:

Ditto master
Duplicating paper
Black marking pen
Library pocket card
Two 3″ × 5″ blank index cards (cut into three 1″ × 5″ tickets each)

Procedure:

1. Before an intervention technique is begun, observe the student throughout the day and make notes about his/her desirable and undesirable behavioral characteristics. Behaviors to look for are listed below:

Name: John Smith

Desirable	Undesirable
1. Likes to be a teacher's helper. 2. Likes animals. 3. Does well with gross-motor activities. 4. Has a sense of humor.	1. Does not complete paper/pencil tasks. 2. Has temper tantrum about once a day consisting of: swearing, hitting others, throwing objects, shouting. 3. Runs away from the group about once a week.

2. After carefully observing the student, choose ONE BEHAVIOR AT A TIME to be eliminated by reinforcing its positive counterpart. Make a list of possible reinforcers. For example, if a child talks out 25 times in one day, reinforce every 30 minutes of quiet behavior using check sheet #1.

3. Begin with this highly structured, frequently reinforced schedule for a student with considerable limitations and distractions. Every five to ten minutes throughout each thirty-minute period of the school day comment on the student's behavior and reinforce with a large *X* or a Happy Face placed in the square if the student has not talked out inappropriately. Be sure verbally to praise the student while checking off a square.

4. If all four squares are filled in at the end of the thirty-minute period, the student receives the appropriate reinforcement as shown by the illustration. (Note: The student plans the reinforcement activities with the teacher before beginning this activity.)

#1

DATE:				JOHN'S GOOD BEHAVIOR Reward
X	X	X	X	9:00 - 9:30 Take lunch ticket to office.
X	X			9:30 - 10:00 Go for a walk around school with aide.
X	X	X		10:00 - 10:30 Help aide get juice.
X	X	X	X	10:30 - 11:00 Recess
				11:00 - 11:30 water plants
				11:30 - 12:00 Eat lunch with friend of choice.
				12:00 - 12:30 Feed hamster
				12:30 - 1:00 Line leader to music, art or P.E.
				1:00 - 1:30 ERRAND BOY check mail in office

5. To reinforce work completion for a student who may only turn in four out of ten assignments use check sheet (#2) after first determining if the assignments are on the student's independent level.

6. Using check sheet #2, praise the student and check off the appropriate activity period if the student completes the assignment or other activity during that period. If all six morning activities are completed, the student may eat lunch with a friend; otherwise, the student eats in a teacher-designated seat.

7. If all afternoon activities are completed, following the same procedure, the student can water the plants.

8. As behavior improves, gradually extend the time between reinforcements. Using check sheet #3 the student who has stayed with the group for all twelve activities and has worked appropriately may choose a ticket from a reinforcement menu pocket chart.

9. Gradually increase the length of time and good behavior requirements to earn awards.

10. Check sheets #4, #5, and #6 are designed for rewards to be given on completion of the 25, 50, and 100 checks the student must earn. Multiple behaviors can be reinforced with multiple checks. If the student has stayed with the group for math and completed his independent work, the teacher may give a check for each skill. A bonus check might be given if the work was done correctly. Have a reinforcement menu (see *Reinforcement Menu* activity) available for the last three check sheets to allow the student a choice of reward.

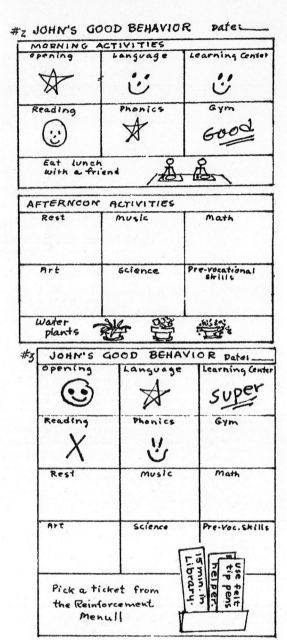

#4   NAME: _____

1	2	3	4	5
6	7	8	9	10
11	12	13	14	15
16	17	18	19	20
21	22	23	24	25
Date begun:	Date finished:	Special Goal:	Reward:	

REMINDERS:

1. Let the student help you choose the reward.
2. Alter rewards periodically to prevent satiation.
3. Begin the management program with one behavior at a time. When the student is thoroughly successful with this behavior, add one more.

Additional Suggestions:

1. See *Visual Motivation* activity.
2. See *Reinforcement Menu* activity.

#5   NAME: _____

1	2	3	4	5
6	7	8	9	10
11	12	13	14	15
16	17	18	19	20
21	22	23	24	25
26	27	28	29	30
31	32	33	34	35
36	37	38	39	40
41	42	43	44	45
46	47	48	49	50
Date begun:	Date finished:	Special Goal:	Reward:	

#6   NAME: _____

1	2	3	4	5	6	7	8	9	10
11	12	13	14	15	16	17	18	19	20
21	22	23	24	25	26	27	28	29	30
31	32	33	34	35	36	37	38	39	40
41	42	43	44	45	46	47	48	49	50
51	52	53	54	55	56	57	58	59	60
61	62	63	64	65	66	67	68	69	70
71	72	73	74	75	76	77	78	79	80
81	92	83	84	85	86	87	88	89	90
91	92	93	94	95	96	97	98	99	100
Date begun:	Date finished:		Special Goal:		Reward:				

adapting a worksheet for distractible students

Descriptors: Decreasing Stimuli
Attending to Task
Completing Work

Grade Levels: 1–6

Rationale: It pays big dividends to spend a little extra time creating ways to keep your students "on task" and continually learning, rather than nagging at them to finish. Furthermore, other students who are able to finish their papers quickly will be able to go on to other tasks. The following ideas are designed for the slow-moving youngsters with poor work habits.

Objective: To adapt a worksheet of thirty math problems to keep a distractible student "on task." The student is required to complete the same number of problems as other students without an overload of stimuli for that particular student.

Materials: Number problem worksheet
Blank cover sheet
Scissors
Marking pen
Exacto knife

Procedure: 1. Construct a fold-up window cover sheet with a window shade covering each problem. As the student completes one problem and is ready for the next, the student lifts the shade to reveal the next problem. Succeeding worksheets should follow the same format in order to reuse the cover sheet with fold-up windows.

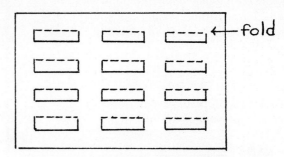

2. Use a simple outline or shape for the worksheet as a change of pace. Cut the shape into pieces of a puzzle, depending on the number of problems. Write one problem on each puzzle piece. The student draws one piece from an envelope and completes the problem. When all the problems are completed, the student may put the puzzle together as a reward for finishing the problems.

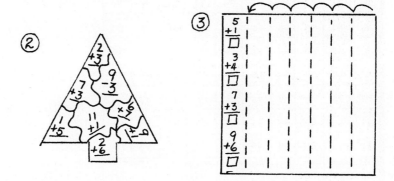

3. Put problems in rows horizontally and vertically. Then fold the page vertically so that only one row of problems is exposed at a time. As the student completes that row, s/he unfolds the page one time and begins on the next row. The page may also be folded from the left after the row has been completed to cover completed problems.

4. Cut a page of thirty problems in thirds. Staple them together one on top of the other so the child is visually stimulated by only ten problems at a time. A large circle may be drawn in the upper left corner. As each third is completed, the teacher or aid places an eye or a mouth to make a happy face.

5. Leave the page of thirty problems intact. Make a window oversheet of tagboard to clip to the math page. The window must be large enough to see ten problems. When those are completed, the window oversheet is reversed so problems at the bottom of the page are exposed. When those are completed, the window oversheet is removed and the child works the problems remaining in the middle of the page.

    The window can be made long and narrow to reveal one row of numbers. The child will manipulate and clip so only one row is seen; when that row is complete, s/he moves it to the next.

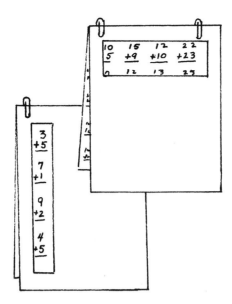

Additional Suggestions: Present a worksheet of problems with a choice of three answers next to the problem. The student must solve the problem and circle the correct answer.

assignment checklist to establish independent work habits

Descriptors: Structure
Study Skills Organization
Visual Motivation

Grade Levels: 1–6

Rationale: Many students who do not complete work in school lack organizational skills. Such students are often described by their classroom teachers as being unable to work independently, possessing a poor (or short) attention span, or as "hyperactive." Combining a visual motivation sheet (see *Visual Motivation* activity) with a check sheet of assignments helps to structure tasks for the youngster who finds it hard to finish schoolwork or who wastes time changing from one activity to another. For students who have little reading ability, rebus pictures may be used instead of written words. Many students like to monitor their own progress and readily accept the responsibility when the visual motivation sheet is adjacent to the check-off sheet.

Objective: To provide a structured format for required assignments, which a student may check off as completed, thus helping to remain "on task" until all the assignments have been completed.

Materials: Manila tagboard folder
Ditto master
Duplicating paper
Staples (or paper clips)
Pencil

Procedure:
1. The teacher designs daily or weekly assignment sheets that may be duplicated and filled in with assignments appropriate for each student's skill level.
2. A visual motivation sheet (teacher-made or commercial[4]) is stapled to the left side of manila tagboard folders—one for each student.

---

[4]Visual Motivation, Inc., Box 792, Olathe, Kansas 66061 (for commercial illustrations).

3. The students' individual assignment worksheet is stapled to the right side of his/her folder.
4. Students keep their individual assignment folders in their desks. The folders are only removed when an activity is checked off.
5. The student is instructed to complete the first assignment of the checklist, check if off, and then add to a cumulative visual motivation sheet (see *Visual Motivation* activity). The number added to the visual motivation sheet for each completed assignment is agreed on by both the teacher and the student before beginning the worksheet. Example: Color in one footprint (see illustration) for each completed assignment. Extra footprints may be awarded for more difficult requirements.

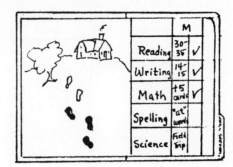

6. The student continues in this manner until the visual motivation sheet is completed. (Note: This may take several days or one to two weeks depending on the motivational level and age of the student. Some students need a new worksheet stapled over the old one each day, whereas older students may be able to use a weekly assignment sheet. However, it is important to keep in mind that too much stimulation of visual work requirements is overpowering to many youngsters and may cause them to become discouraged and, consequently, not finish any assignments. Obviously, this would defeat the purpose of the checklist. If a weekly assignment sheet is chosen, it is recommended that assignments are written down for one day at a time.)

7. When the visual motivation sheet is completed, a previously agreed on reward is awarded to the student (see *Visual Motivation* activity).
(Note: Because the students are responsible for completing their assignments without direct supervision, a visual checkmark record becomes reinforcing to otherwise nonstructured students. In order for this procedure to be successful, it is vital that the assignments be on the student's current skill level and that the student understands exactly how to follow the assignment check-off sheet.)

Additional Suggestions:

1. Worksheets without a visual motivation sheet may be used. The checkmarks alone may provide the needed reinforcement for disorganized students.
2. Beginning readers may need to use rebus pictures to know the assignment for each subject.

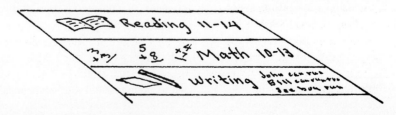

Pair each rebus picture with the correct word in order to help teach the student new sight vocabulary.

3. Parts of pictures may also be used for young students to describe the reward earned for completing each task. For example, if a large rag doll was drawn on the visual motivation sheet and the student was to color in parts for completing each assignment, the worksheet might look like the following:

Job	Finished	Color Part
Reading 📖	✓	hair
Time 🕐	✓	bow and heart
Writing ✏	✓	apron
Math 1-2-3	✓	dress
Money 💵	✓	candy cane
Other	✓	shoes, socks, eyes

When the rag doll is completed, a small reward is earned (extra free time, choosing a recess game, teacher's helper, small toy).

box "offices" to reduce distractions

Descriptors: Reducing Stimuli
Independent Work

Grade Levels: 1–6

Rationale: Many students with learning problems work better in isolation, for example, in a study carrel, away from visual distractions. Such work space may be provided within a classroom; however, it is vitally important that all students have a chance to use the space to prevent it from being considered a punishment technique used only for "poor" students.

Objective: To provide a special work space, within a classroom setting, which is free from visual distractions for students who appear to need such structure in order to complete their assignments.

Materials: Large cardboard boxes (from refrigerator or TV)
12″ × 20″ heavy construction paper or tagboard sheets
Scissors
Desks or tables
Optional: Commercial wooden or cardboard study carrels
(See school supply catalogues)

Procedure:
1. Ask the students whether they are interested in designing special areas within the classroom to be used as private offices where they can go to work quietly without distractions.
2. Choose desks and tables in specific parts of the classroom that would be appropriate for office areas.
3. Discuss with the students ways of constructing private screens (see illustrations) and assign small groups of students to the different areas to help with the construction (unless study carrels are purchased commercially).
4. Ensure that all students receive an opportunity to use an office being particularly careful to assign the most distractible students at times that appear to be most advantageous for them, for example, during academic seatwork assignments.
5. A class time schedule for student use of the "private offices" may be designed and posted.
(Note: It is important to note students who are *auditorially* distracted. The box offices are most appropriate for reducing visual stimuli, but are rather ineffective for screening out classroom noises for students who attend to such stimuli. For such students, taped seatwork and earphones are more appropriate.)

SUGGESTED BOX OFFICES

1. A folding cardboard screen with a desk well inside is one simple design.
2. A refrigerator box with one side plus the top and bottom removed help to isolate the student by providing cardboard "blinders."
3. A table-top type of carrel may be constructed from cardboard or fiber board strips to fit the length and width of the table. Cut slits two-thirds of the width of the slits and fit them together.

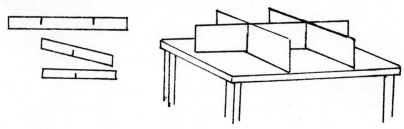

4. Cut the top and bottom off a square cardboard box. Divide the box into two sections by cutting through two opposite corners. This will yield two simple study carrels.

5. A wide accordion-type pleated screen made from folded construction paper is quickly made but not very durable.

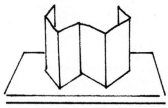

Additional Suggestions:

1. Put a typewriter in one of the "box offices" for quiet use by remedial students.
2. You may want to send a note home to parents explaining the implementation of the office space center in the classroom to ensure that parents understand that students who use the space are not being punished, similar to having to "stand in the corner."

_____ **reinforcement menu** _____

Descriptors: Behavior Management   **Grade Levels:** 1–6
Reward System
Motivation
Token System

Rationale: Students need to be recognized for good behavior and academic success. It is motivating to accumulate points for such behavior to be traded in later for classroom rewards. Reinforcement is very important for all students and, particularly, slower students who need to see their successes accumulate.

Objective: To reinforce desired academic and social behaviors and to discourage negative behaviors when necessary.

Materials:
Ditto master
Duplicating paper
Colored marking pens
12″ × 20″ tagboard charts
5″ × 7″ blank index cards

Procedure:
1. Students are given a blank index card daily on which points earned for specific behaviors are tallied.

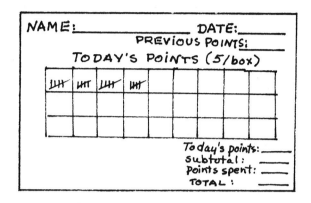

2. A Reinforcement Menu and behaviors that earn a certain number of points are written on 12″ × 20″ tagboard charts, which are placed in a prominent position in the classroom.
3. Extreme behaviors that cannot be ignored are reprimanded by taking away points as listed on the charts.
4. The teacher or aide marks points for appropriate behavior with a colored felt tip pen; students are responsible for their own point cards. Math skills are developed by allowing capable children to add and subtract their own points.
5. At the end of the day the points are exchanged for reinforcers.
6. If students do not spend all their points one day, these may be carried over to the next day.

REINFORCEMENT MENU 😊

Reward	Points
Write on chalkboard	50
Use felt pens	60
Water plants	75
Use Etch-a-Sketch	80
Use microscope	85
Teacher's helper at end of day	95
Listen to music with headphones	100
Use typewriter	100
Small-scale construction with models	150
Buy free time for one fifteen-minute work period tomorrow	200
Mini-tutoring sessions	200

THESE BEHAVIORS EARN POINTS!! 😊

Behavior	Points
Coming to activity within thirty seconds	2
Assignment started	2
Assignment finished within class period	2
0 to 25% of assignment correct	1
26% to 50% of assignment correct	3
51% to 75% of assignment correct	5
76% to 100% of assignment correct	10
Assignment done independently	5
Directions followed	3

THESE BEHAVIORS LOSE POINTS!! 🙁	
Behavior	**Points**
Hitting another person	25
Taking something that belongs to someone else	15
Swearing or screaming	10
Damage to school property	5

Additional Suggestions

When independent work is completed early and correctly, students should be able to use a recreation area consisting of art materials or games, including, clay, paper, yarn, glue, scissors, old cartons, wood scraps, sandpaper, glue, cards, table games, puppets, magazines and catalogues, cloth scraps, needle, and thread.

taking baseline data

Descriptors:
Evaluation
Behavior Management

Grade Levels: 1–6

Rationale: Baseline data are important by enabling the teacher to notice changes in student behavior very quickly. If the change is positive, the teacher will want to encourage further growth. If the change is negative, the teacher needs to take action before bad habits are formed. Baseline serves as an accurate standard against which to measure change.

Objective: To present ways of taking baseline data and translating the results into percentage charts.

Materials: Paper (plain and graph)
Marking pen
Wrist counter (optional)

Procedure: Taking baseline data is quite easy. Three simple, yet important, steps are involved.
1. *Decide which behavior is to be measured.* The behavior should be specific and easily observed (such as hitting other students, out-of-seat, excess requests for help).
2. *Carefully define the behavior to be measured.* This prevents problems in classifying "borderline" behavior (Example: out-of-seat: no physical contact with chair or desk; working: sitting in seat, feet on floor, eyes directed toward book, silent). Only actions included in the definition may be counted.
3. *Use consistent measurement.* Measurement should be made daily under the same conditions because student behavior often differs according to activity engaged in, time of day, and class conditions. Consistency is the key (measurement must take place at the same time each day, such as during individual seatwork, one hour before lunch, or while part of the class is engaged in group work). Make measurement as easy as possible, but be consistent.
4. One way to measure the occurrence of certain behavior is to use check marks or, a wrist counter, or by making small tears in a piece of paper (one tear per occurrence).

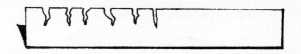

5. A second and probably more useful form of measurement is to divide the total observation time into smaller segments (Example: five minutes = 20 fifteen-second segments). If the target behavior occurs any time during the segment a check is made on the record form. At the end of the observation period, any segment with a check mark is interpreted as having been totally occupied by the target behavior. Total the time engaged in the target behavior and divide by the total observation time. The result will be the percent of class time during which the student engaged in the behavior of concern.

15 minutes observation
15 × 60 = 900 seconds
18 checks × 15 seconds each = 270 seconds

$$900 \overline{)270.00}^{.30} \quad \text{or 30 percent off-task behavior Monday}$$

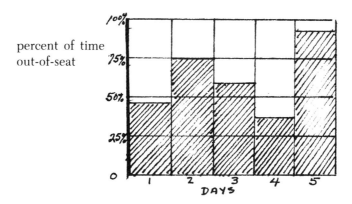

6. Measurement should be made over several days and entered on a chart or graph as baseline data.
7. Average the baseline data for a percent of time out-of-seat, for example, if you desire a weekly average. If not, stay with a daily percent.

8. Implement a change in the student's environment. Once baseline data has been obtained, performance changes can often be obtained by manipulating three variables:

   a. Task demand—give short, frequently changed tasks; make reinforcement contingent on a set number of responses; demand increased percentages of correct responses.
   b. Time dimensions—allow more time for task completion or less time for task completion or provide for set rest periods after specified work times.
   c. Physical environment—place student in a study carrel; remove distractions in the environment, move student next to a supportive and helpful peer.

Any time measurement is made in the same way and, under the same classroom and time conditions, accurate comparison to baseline can be made. Behavior changes will be reflected visually by charting them and comparing the results to the baseline data.

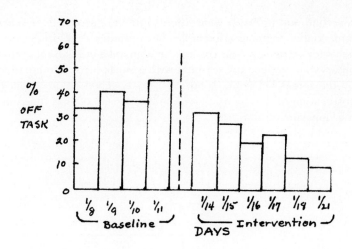

Additional Suggestions:

1. Students should be unaware that the baseline is being taken.
2. Individual measurements may vary greatly. Watch for trends over time.
3. See *Behavior Reinforcement Schedules* activity.

_____structuring the disorganized student_____

Descriptors: Structure   **Grade Levels:**   3–6
Self-Organization

Rationale: Many intermediate-level students appear to be disorganized and confused about assignments and other school activities. Such students often do not finish their work on time or hurry to complete it in a haphazard manner. Unless provided with structured strategies, these students will not learn to function well independently. This activity presents such organizational strategies.

Objective: To teach a student to complete classwork assignments independently by presenting several organizational strategies.

Materials: Masking tape
Cardboard school box
Folders (commercial or student-constructed)
Pocket calendar
Pencil and paper

Procedure:
1. Before deciding which areas need to be addressed, the teacher determines the type of problems the student is experiencing (Example: losing assignment sheets before working them, never having a pencil available, finishing work but not handing it in, consistently forgetting to bring homework assignments to school, never finishing assignments).
2. Plan specific strategies with the student to remediate the particular problem.
3. Evaluate the effect of the new program by keeping pre- and post data (Example: percent of daily papers completed—before and after new intervention, visually checking desk organization, percent correct on daily papers as shown in the grade book).
   To eliminate failure and frustration stemming from inappropriate requirements and expectations, it is assumed that all assignments are at the student's present skill level.

Problem 1: Misplaced Pens, Pencils and Erasers

Such items are usually misplaced because of the absence of a convenient, specified place for storing them. One solution is to use a cardboard school box (cigar box) for storing pens, pencils, and so on. If one pencil is used regularly, it may be taped to the desk with masking tape. The student is told that, when not in use, these items must always be returned to their place for easy retrieval when needed. Hold a weekly teacher-supervised desk-cleaning session until the students become used to desk organization. Request that two or three new pencils (sharpened) are included. If crayons are considered part of the needed supplies, these must not be bits and pieces, and all colors must be represented.

Problem 2: Does Not Complete Assignments

Often students do not complete assignments because of insufficient structure. To provide structure and to help the student remember which assignments need to be completed, have the student design a daily assignment checklist. The checklist is taped to the student's desk so that it is in front of the student at all times. Each new assignment is added to the list, and as each assignment is handed in, it is checked off. Homework assignments may also be added to the list, which is then taken home.

Assignments Harry Jacobs	Completed
Math problems p. 21	✔
Reading p. 8 to 12	
Music at 10:00	✔
Geography questions	

When long-range assignments are given, a list containing the assignments and the due dates can be taped to the inside of the desk.

Language Assignments	Due	Completed
Book Report	Wednesday, 3/21	✔
Science Project	Friday, 3/23	✔
Science Project	Monday, 4/2	

If available, a small pocket calendar with a square for each date may serve the same purpose. These are often distributed free of charge in retail stationery stores.

Problem 3: Forgetting Homework Assignments

The problem of leaving homework assignments at school can easily be solved by blocking off an area on the daily assignment checklist for homework assignments. The checklist can then be taken home with the homework. (If the checklist is taken home, the checklist may also serve as a daily report card.)

Assignments	Completed	Grade
Math problems, p. 21	✔	11/12 Good!
Music at 10:00	✔	
(Homework) Reading p. 8 to 12 Geography questions		

The problem of leaving homework at home may be alleviated by having parents pin a reminder to the student's shirt or coat to be worn the next day or by placing the homework with the coat or clothes to be worn or in a special box by the front door. The parents need to adapt such strategies to their home organization. One way to ensure the completion and return of homework is to reinforce behavior with 5 to 10 minutes of free time during the first period in the morning.

Problem 4: Messy Desk and Lost Assignments

Frequently, assignments are not turned in because they are misplaced in a messy desk full of loose papers. One way to help organize a student's desk is by having the student keep all papers in folders. The student may need separate folders for daily assignments to be completed, long-range assignments to be completed, and work that has already been graded and returned. The folders should be closed on three sides (to prevent papers from falling out), labeled, and possibly color-coded. Types of folders include large brown manila envelopes. file folders closed on three sides, or teacher- or student-constructed folders made from heavy paper and fastened with a stapler.

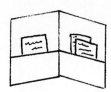 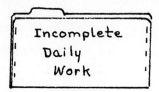

All folders should be kept together in a shirt box, filing cabinet, or tied together with string.

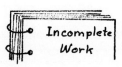 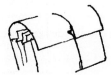

If small enough, the folders may be kept in the student's desk. If not, a place on a shelf or in a cabinet should be specially designated for this purpose.

Additional Suggestions:

1. Hold parent/student/teacher conferences to plan organizational strategies that all parties are willing to implement.
2. Periodically announce surprise rewards "No homework assignments for two days because all students have completed the requirements from yesterday!" That is, reinforce good behavior.

daily point system

Descriptors: Behavior Management
Self-Concept

Grade Levels: 4–6

Rationale: To change a student's classroom behavior may prove difficult because the student may have several teachers in the course of a day often resulting in a lack of consistency in terms of teacher expectations and management skills. The card system suggested in this teaching idea makes teachers define their expectations for a student and, in turn, advises the student of exactly what is expected of him/her.

Objective: To present an objective point system providing students with tangible evidence of their behavior as well as positive reinforcement for appropriate classroom behavior.

Materials: Blank index cards
Black marking pen

Positive Behavior	Negative Behavior	Chores	Privileges

Procedure:

1. Meet with the student exhibiting behavior problems and the teachers who have the student in activities and classes.

2. Discuss with the student a system whereby the student earns points for good school behavior. Tell the student that this system will let him/her know exactly what behaviors are expected from all the teachers.

3. Tell the student that earned points will buy certain privileges in the classroom. Ask the student to determine what privileges would be reinforcing and list them on a card. You may want to consider having some of the rewards for earned points given by the parents. If so, the student's parents need to be included in this meeting.

4. Inform that student that if s/he exhibits inappropriate behavior (as defined on a written list), points will be lost. As a result, there may not be enough points, some day, to buy recess time or the use of the volleyball. Be sure the student understands that the points are used to buy time in the library, time working on a special project, or use of certain toys in class or on the playground (or gym) as defined on a list.

5. During your meeting, have the student and the involved teachers collaborate on lists of behaviors for which the student will either earn, lose, or spend points. The student and all involved teachers will each have a copy of the lists for the sake of consistency.

Example:

Earn Points

	Pts
Completes Assignment	5
90% correct	5
Staying at desk	5

Lose

	Pts
Talking Out	3
late to class	5
Out of seat	5

Spend

	PTS
15 min. free time	25
tutor	35
Library - 10 min. extra	15

6. The student carries a new card each day with columns for listing the specified behaviors, points earned or lost, and the initials of the person awarding or taking away the points.

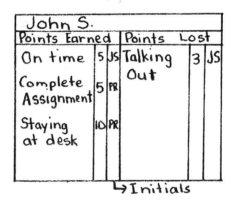

John S.					
Points Earned			**Points Lost**		
On time	5	JS	Talking Out	3	JS
Complete Assignment	5	PR			
Staying at desk	10	PR			

↳ Initials

7. The points are tallied at the end of the day and the student may choose an earned privilege or save the points for future exchange.

8. After the first week a meeting will be held between the student and the teachers involved in the point system. Point values will be reviewed and, if necessary, changed. New behaviors, purchased items, and chores will be added to the list. (Note: Values and behaviors may only be adjusted at a joint meeting of all persons participating in the system.)

9. The school counselor, principal, or psychologist may meet with the people involved in the point system to decide whether or not the student's behavior is improving as a result of the system. At this time a joint decision can be made about how and when the student will discontinue being on the point system.

Additional Suggestions:

1. Plan some privileges that are more costly but highly desirable to the student, thereby encouraging him/her to delay reinforcement.
2. Emphasize the positive aspects (points earned) rather than points lost. The initial card may only include earned points for students whose behavior is not very deviant.

sources of volunteer help in the classroom

Descriptors: One-to-one Tutoring   **Grade Levels:**   1–6
                    Shared Responsibility

Rationale: Many teachers need extra tutorial help in their classrooms for students who are having difficulty with the curriculum. Although some teachers are lucky enough to have an aide provided by the school system, others may not have such assistance. Rather than taking a fatalistic attitude, classroom teachers need to become resourceful and find their own sources of volunteer assistance.

Objective: To provide the teacher with alternative strategies for obtaining volunteers to help in the classroom.

Materials: Directory of community resources

Procedure: 1. After consulting with the school officials and obtaining their approval, the teacher should try to obtain volunteer help for the classroom by contacting the following:

    a. PTA
    b. Foster grandparents
    c. Senior citizen groups
    d. Church organizations
    e. Local college students, especially education majors
    f. Local high-school students
    g. Peer tutors
    h. Community organizations (such as Junior League or Young Matrons)
    i. Girl Scouts, Boy Scouts, Campfire Girls, Four H groups

(Note: It will probably be necessary for the teacher to appear at the local meeting of some of the above groups to explain exactly what type of help is needed, how often, and specifically what the volunteer would be doing. It is important to establish that consistent, weekly help is needed and that sporadic help would be of little value except for special field trips.)

2. Before beginning the tutoring sessions meet with the volunteers to set up a weekly schedule agreed on by all participants. It may be helpful to ditto calendars marked with each tutor's schedule (both time and date) in order that each participant understands exactly what is expected.

Jane Brink 9:00–11:00 Tues.		October				
S	M	T	W	Th	F	S
	1	Jane 2	3	4	5	6
7	8	Jane 9	10	11	12	13
14	15	Jane 16	17	18	19	20
21	22	Jane 23	24	25	26	27
28	29	Jane 30	31			

3. The teacher must take the responsibility for planning some introductory meetings with the tutors to explain instructional philosophy, curriculum, and actual class schedule. This is also the time to teach the volunteers some behavior management principles such as reinforcement, structure, and extinction, and to show the volunteers how to practice specific skills in phonics, reading, math, or writing. Any educational games in the room should be demonstrated to the volunteers.

4. The teacher should assign specific students to each volunteer and meet individually with that volunteer to discuss the strengths and weaknesses of each student and exactly which area(s) of the student's educational program the tutor will be responsible for. A schedule of tutor/student assignments should be designated at this time. The schedules should be placed in the student's individual folder to be used in all tutoring sessions. The tutor records progress notes on the right of each schedule sheet.

Example:

John Smith		Tutor Jane Ray	Notes
10/2	Math ×7	Flash Cards Game ×7 only	✓ 100%
	Writing H-h	writing paper Chalkboard	✓
10/9	Spelling - 10 words	Typewriter wkbk 33-34	
	Math ×8 (Review ×7)	Chalkboard Flash Cards Ditto paper	

5. The teacher introduces the tutor to the class and to the specific student. It is important for the teacher to supervise the first two tutorial sessions. Later the teacher and tutor should meet periodically to discuss the tutoring sessions. The teacher may offer suggestions at such times and the tutor can evaluate and discuss the progress of each of his/her students.

6. The teacher should plan some type of reception at the end of the class year to recognize the contribution of the valuable tutors. The students may write thank-you letters to them and perhaps design a certificate of appreciation.

Additional Suggestions: It may be necessary to help plan transportation for some senior citizens (or others who may not drive). (Note: The extra time required for attending community meetings to ask for help plus the time spent on planning and coordination of the tutoring sessions pay big dividends later by providing valuable help for both students and the teacher.)

developing self-concept

Descriptors: Positive Self-Image
Communication
Understanding Others

Grade Levels: K–6

Rationale: It is important for everybody to develop a positive self-concept and a respect for the uniqueness of self and others. Mainstreaming a handicapped youngster into the regular classroom provides the teacher an opportunity to introduce activities designed to develop self-awareness and promote an understanding of likenesses and differences of all students. The regular-class students must realize that the exceptional student is a person who also happens to have a handicap rather than merely being a "handicapped person."

Objective: To provide the teacher with a variety of activities designed to develop positive self-concepts in the students.

Materials: Drawing paper
Pencils
Stapler, Crayons
Photograph of each student (or Polaroid camera)

12″ × 20″ tagboard
Bowl
10″ × 12″ manila envelope

Procedure:
1. Choose an activity that is appropriate for the students' grade level and interests.
2. You must realize that

   a. Teacher attitudes and actions will play an important role in the chosen activity.
   b. The teacher must be a good listener—not only to the students' academic concerns, but also to their feelings.
   c. The teacher must not *judge* what the students say, but may let a student know if s/he disagrees. Negative judgment and disagreement are two different things.

3. Implement one of the following activities. Evaluate its effectiveness by holding a class discussion about the similarities and differences between individuals at the end of each activity.

Activity 1: Student of the Week

This activity may be initiated at the beginning of the school term and continued throughout the year. In this way, each student has several opportunities to be "Student of the Week."
1. Write the students' names on slips of paper and place them in a bowl.
2. Ask a student volunteer to draw one name out of the bowl each Friday. The student whose name is drawn is designated "Student of the Week" beginning the following Monday.
3. Send a note home to parents asking them to provide a photograph of the student the following Monday. Option: Take an instant picture of the student with a Polaroid camera.
4. Interview the student and write pertinent information on a blank newsprint flip chart. Attach the photograph to the top of the page. Record information such as student's name, age, likes, favorite food, hobby, color, sport, and music. Allow the student to decorate the chart to be displayed to the rest of the class. Give the students an oral quiz later in the week to see how much they remember about the special "Student of the Week."

5. Attach a manila envelope to the bulletin board. Encourage the rest of the class to write letters to the "Student of the Week." The messages should be about something another student especially liked about the "Student of the Week."

(Note: When it is time for a student to become "Student of the Week" again, make another chart and include new information such as height, birthday, address, telephone number, middle name, and big wish.)

Activity 2: The Monthly Calendar

Duplicate copies of a monthly calendar and give one to each student. Make a large tagboard calendar for the class bulletin board. All special dates such as holidays, birthdays, "Student of the Week," and special events are written in and illustrated. This is a good community project as well as being an activity that helps each student realize his/her importance within a week or a month.

NOVEMBER

☀ Sunday	☾ Monday	Tuesday	Wednesday	Thursday	Friday	Saturday
1	SAM 2 student of the week	🎂 3 Mellody's BD	4	5	🎂 6 Jean's BD	7
8	AMY 9 student of the week	10	🦁 11 TRIP TO ZOO	12	13	14
15	LORI 16 student of the week	17	🎂 18 Tom's BD	19	20	21
22	CARY 23 student of the week	🎂 24 Jon's BD	25	Thanksgiving 🦃	27 vacation	28
29	JEFF 30 student of the week					

Activity 3: "This Is My Life" Book

Ask each student to create a "This is My Life" book which can be shared with the rest of the class. Commercial scrapbooks may be used or staple, punch, and tie ten pieces of writing paper together. The students introduce themselves through magazine pictures, self-drawn pictures, or photographs accompanied by handwritten captions or stories. Design question outlines for the students to use as a guideline. The students share their completed books with other class members. All books are put on a special shelf to be used by other students as supplemental reading.

Activity 4: Hobby Day

Encourage students to develop a hobby. Provide time in the classroom for the students to work on their hobbies. This may be a once-a-year, monthly, or weekly event. Have students bring in their hobbies such as model planes, needlepoint, checkers, or stamps. Students who do not have a hobby are asked to work with a student who does. Hopefully, an interest will be developed in this manner. The students can make posters advertising their hobbies or plan a hobby show and invite other classes to attend.

Activity 5: <u>Introductions</u>

(To be used at the beginning of the school year.) Students' names written on slips of paper are placed in a bowl. Ask a student to draw two names of students who become partners for the introduction activity. Allow the students fifteen to twenty minutes to exchange information about themselves. Each student expresses what s/he has learned about the partner by giving a talk, writing a story, creating a book, making a collage, or recording a tape. This is a good activity for use with mainstreamed students as some mention may be made of the fact that "John uses a wheelchair. He can go almost as fast as I can without one." The introduction should focus on John as a *person*—likes, dislikes, family members, pets—instead of his handicap. You may need to supervise the first few introductions to help the students get started.

Additional Suggestions: See Chapter 1.

teacher comments on student papers

Descriptors: Positive Reinforcement
Communication
Self-Image

Grade Levels: 1–6

Rationale: Teachers often get tired of repeatedly using the same reinforcing and corrective comments on student papers. Stickers and happy/sad faces are successfully used in the lower grades; as students learn to read, teachers have an opportunity to be more creative in their comments when grading student papers.

Objective: To present alternative expressions for teachers to use when grading student papers.

Materials: Colored marking pens
Student worksheets

Procedure: Use one of the following comments when checking student papers. Writing in colorful marking pens draws attention to the message.

Good			Incorrect / Needs Improvement
% correct	Fine	I love this!	
☺ ☆	Nice	You're the best!	☹
	Very Nice	You're a champion!	
Holiday Sign	Cool	You've got it!	See Me
Stamp	Great	You made it!	Oops
Sticker	Grrreat	You should be happy!	O-Oh
OK	Super	What a winner!	Sorry
A-OK	Perfect	The Model Paper!	Good Try
	Perrfect	Pat yourself on	Messy
Wow		the back!	Messy, but good
1st	🐱	Have a Nice Day,	Almost
Speedy		You Deserve It	Not Quite
Neat	Marvelous	Go to the Head of	Just About
Pretty	Outstanding	the Class	You Slipped
Beautiful	Fantastic	Terrific	What Happened?
First Place	Lucky You	Good Job	You can do better
Good	Award Winner	Way to Go!	Better Luck Next Time
Very Good	Blue Ribbon	Good Work	

Descriptors: Self-Concept
Teaching Affect

Grade Levels: 3–6

Rationale: So often emotionally disturbed students have difficulty in expressing how they feel about themselves—what their likes and dislikes are. Such students might see themselves as being "bad," "different," or "weird." Through the following activities the teacher can help children build confidence.

Objective: To help handicapped and nonhandicapped students develop positive self-concepts through affective teaching activities.

Activity 1: "This Is Your Life"

Materials: Bulletin board
Assortment of colored construction paper
Scissors
Yarn
Set of 1-inch alphabet letters
Crayons or magic markers
Old magazines

Procedure: 1. The teacher explains how to design a "This Is Your Life" bulletin board. Each student is responsible for the bulletin board display one week during the school year.
2. Students create a display that tells their fellow classmates about their life. The following ideas may be incorporated in such a display.

Ideas for use on the bulletin board:

name of student
birthday
zodiac sign
birthstone
favorite flower
favorite free-time activity
three wishes

pets
name of hometown
sports or hobbies
favorite pet
favorite food
least favorite food
favorite holiday
brothers and sisters

3. The display stays up on the bulletin board for a week.
4. At the end of the week, after the bulletin board has been taken down, the teacher may wish to give the class an oral or written quiz to see how much they remember about the particular person. This idea may be varied according to teacher preference. This illustration provides an example of a bulletin board display.

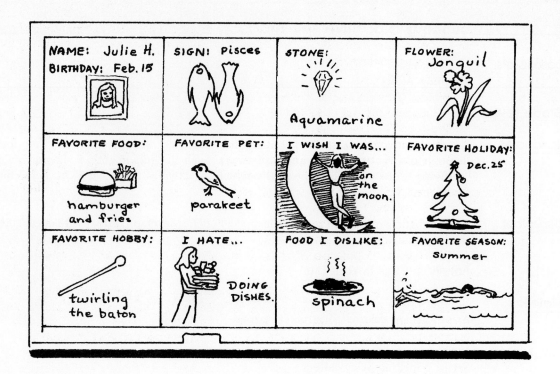

Activity 2: Me-Mobile

Materials:

Coat hanger
6 pieces of string (different lengths)
Construction paper
Magazine pictures
Scissors
Stapler (optional)
Glue

Procedure:

1. The students decide on things they like, things they dislike, favorite movie stars, favorite car model, famous people they would like to be, places they would like to go, and so on.
2. The pieces of string are tied to a hanger to make a mobile.
3. Students draw, cut out, and paste pictures on pieces of colored construction paper.
4. The papers are attached to the various strings by stapling or by tying knots through holes punched in the paper.
5. The teacher hangs the mobiles from the ceiling in the classroom.
6. Before the mobiles are hung, the teacher may want each student to share his/her mobile with the rest of the class so that each can have the experience of sharing with classmates.

Activity 3: Inside Story Collage

Materials:

Pencil
Scissors
Magazines
Glue
5-foot piece of white wrapping paper
Colored magic markers

Procedure:

1. The students work in pairs. One person lies down flat on her/his back on a large piece of paper; arms and legs are extended out from the body.
2. The second person traces around the person lying down.
3. When the outline is completed, the person lying down gets up and cuts it out.

4. The outline is then cut into large pieces making them look like puzzle pieces.
5. On each piece of puzzle the student writes, draws, or glues a magazine picture that completes the following statements:

When I grow up I want to be . . . .
My favorite subject in school is . . . .
The subject I dislike the most is . . . .
On a rainy day, when I can't go outside, I . . . .
If I could do anything I wanted, I would . . . .
If I could be anyone I wanted, I would be . . . .
If I could go anywhere I wanted, I would go . . . .
When I'm sad I . . . .
I feel good about myself when . . . .
I feel bad about myself when I . . . .
Three words to describe what I look like are . . . .

(Note: The teacher may vary these questions to best meet the students' needs.)
6. Each student shares his/her puzzle with the rest of the class by describing each piece (and the statement it answers) as the puzzle is completed on the floor.
7. The students are allowed free time to put other students' puzzles together.

Activity 4: "I Am..."

Materials: Piece of ruled paper
Pencil

Procedure:
1. The students write their first names vertically on the left side of the paper.
2. They write a poem using the letters of their first name to begin the first word of each line.
3. When the activity is completed, the students draw illustrations of their poems and share with the class.
4. All poems are displayed on the bulletin board.

E—Ellen is a happy child,
L—Loves her family, friends, and flowers,
L—Likes the weather best when mild,
E—Every day has many happy hours,
N—Never gets very wild.

_____who I am_____

Descriptors: Mainstreaming
Self-Concept
Language

Grade Levels: 3–6

Rationale: Students with a positive self-concept learn new skills more quickly. This activity is designed to help students with a low self-concept to begin to recognize what they can do well and to start working on those skills with which they are having problems.

Objective: To build a positive self-image through an art and language arts project.

Materials:

Library book about handicapped people	Crayons
White wrapping paper	Paper and pencil
Colored marking pens	Ditto master
Scissors	Duplicating paper

Procedure:

1. Read an autobiography of a handicapped person to your students. The story of Helen Keller as found in so many basal reading materials is excellent.
2. List words used to describe the person. More importantly, list the feelings expressed.
3. Introduce an art project. Provide large sheets of white wrapping paper. Students work in pairs and one of them traces an outline of the other on the wrapping paper. This becomes a life-sized portrait of each student.
4. Give each student a dittoed list of topics. Discuss how the students might describe themselves:

My physical appearance   Things I'd rather not do
Things I like or dislike   My hobbies
My strengths   My weaknesses
What makes me happy   What makes me sad
Things I don't like to do because I can't   My family
Places I've lived   My pets
People I like to be with   Places I've visited

   Ask each student to write down answers to the topics.
5. Continue with the art project. Each student fills in characteristics on the traced figure using colored pens and crayons.
6. Ask the students to write their autobiographies to be attached to the shirt, hat, or jeans of the finished art project.
7. Seat the figures in the students' desk on the evening of PTA Open House, or hang them along the chalkboard.
8. Students should begin to see that all of them are more alike than different.

Additional Suggestions:

Read each student's answers to the dittoed topics but do not give the name of the student who wrote a particular answer. Ask the students if they can guess who wrote it.

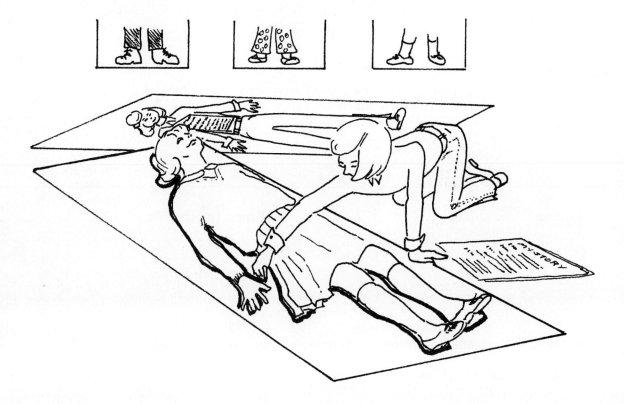

Index